one
simple
idea

one simple idea

HOW **POSITIVE** THINKING
RESHAPED MODERN LIFE

MITCH HOROWITZ

CROWN PUBLISHERS
NEW YORK

Copyright © 2014 by Mitch Horowitz

All rights reserved.
Published in the United States by Crown Publishers, an imprint of
the Crown Publishing Group, a division of Random House LLC, a
Penguin Random House Company, New York.
www.crownpublishing.com

CROWN and the Crown colophon are registered trademarks of
Random House LLC.

Library of Congress Cataloging-in-Publication Data
Horowitz, Mitch.
One simple idea : how positive thinking reshaped modern life /
Mitch Horowitz.—First Edition.
Includes bibliographical references and index.
1. Positive psychology. I. Title.
BF204.6.H67 2014
150.19'88—dc23
2013037024

ISBN 978-0-307-98649-8
eBook ISBN 978-0-307-98650-4

Printed in the United States of America

Book design by Maria Elias
Jacket design by Ben Wiseman

10   9   8   7   6   5   4   3   2   1

First Edition

To Caleb and Tobias

"The time for thinkers has come; and the time for revolutions, ecclesiastic and social, must come."
—Mary Baker Eddy, 1875

"There is a chance here in America for the creation of a new idea of God; a God reflected in the brave creations of self-reliant social pioneers; a religion based not upon surrender or submission, but on a new birth of confidence in life and in the God of life."
—Rabbi Joshua Loth Liebman, 1946

Contents

to wish upon a star

Hardly one in ten thousand will have the
strength of mind to ask himself seriously
and earnestly—is that true?

—Arthur Schopenhauer, "Religion: A Dialogue"

I have never thought positively by nature. Growing up in the 1970s, I used to suffer bouts of stomach cramps on Sunday nights in anticipation of school the next day. Hostile teachers, threatening classmates, botched assignments: my mind saw phantoms everywhere.

In hope of guidance, I sometimes gazed up at an inspirational poem on a blacklight poster hanging in my big sister's bedroom. The words, etched in velour, glowed three-dimensionally under the luminescence of a colored bulb (and sometimes with the aid of pot smoke). I memorized each one:

> *Forget Yesterday.*
> *I am where I am.*
> *I know where I could have been,*
> *had I done what I did not do.*
> *Tell me, Friend, what can I do Today,*
> *to be where I want to be*
> *Tomorrow?*

I could never track down the poet, identified only by the tagline "Sigrad." The furthest I got was determining that the Nordic-sounding name was, ironically, an Icelandic word for *defeated*.

The poem couldn't prepare me for what was immediately ahead. In the late 1970s, my family made an ill-fated move from our bungalow-sized home in Queens to a bigger house on Long Island. It was a place we could never quite afford. After moving in, my father lost his job and we took to warming the house with kerosene heaters and wearing secondhand clothing. One night I overheard my mother saying that we might qualify for food stamps. When the financial strains drove my parents to divorce, we were in danger of losing our home. Walking back from a friend's house at night, I used to wish upon stars, just like in the nursery rhyme. Since any disaster seemed possible, any solution seemed plausible.

Seeking a deeper form of guidance, I expanded my adolescent reading tastes from head-shop posters to Ralph Waldo Emerson and the Talmud. Each seemed to affirm that our outlook counted for something. "Nerve us with incessant affirmatives," Emerson wrote. "Be of good countenance," the great rabbis intoned. I clung to the hope that one's internal attitude and perspective *mattered*; that holding the mental ideal of a better reality could help make it so.

I prayed, visualized better tomorrows, and became a determined self-improver. I threw myself into attempts to earn money delivering newspapers and hauling junk to a local recycling plant. I divided my time between high school in the morning and drama classes in the afternoon. I handwrote college applications and sent letters to financial aid officers. We managed to piece together our finances and keep our home.

Positive thinking did not miraculously solve all of our problems. Decisive help, which I'll never forget, came from my mother's labor union, the 1199 hospital workers, which provided medical benefits that kept our family from disaster. But, still, I emerged from the period believing that a set of interior guideposts and principles had contributed to the solution. If my thoughts didn't change reality, they helped navigate it. And maybe something more.

Later on in life, I grew intrigued by the example of my mother-in-law, Theresa Orr. At times she seemed to gain an additional, almost magical-seeming fortitude from affirmative-thinking philosophies. The daughter of an Italian-immigrant barber, Terri received a scholarship in 1959 to Brandeis University, becoming the first woman in her family to earn a college degree. In the years ahead, she became an associate dean at Harvard Medical School. While pursuing her academic career, she raised two daughters as a divorced and single parent, cared for an elderly mother, and sponsored members of a twelve-step recovery program, all from under the roof of a two-family home in Waltham, Massachusetts.

Terri devoured works of positive thinking, from the Serenity Prayer ("God, grant me the serenity to accept the things I cannot change . . .") to affirmations from the channeled text *A Course in Miracles* to pointers in positivity from *Guideposts* magazine. She papered the surfaces of her home—literally, from the refrigerator to the medicine chest—with business-sized cards on which she penned aphorisms such as "I can choose to be right or to be happy"; "My helping hand is needed. I will do something today to *encourage* another person"; and (my personal favorite) "When am I going to stop going to the hardware store for milk?" When it came to positivity, Terri could make Anthony Robbins look like a goth kid. There was no question in her mind, or in my own, that injunctions to sinewy thoughts had made a difference in her life.

From my late twenties through midforties, my personal search took me down many spiritual paths, and into serious esoteric teachings and traditions. But positive thinking always reasserted its pull on me. The principle of positive thinking is simplicity itself. Picture an outcome, dwell on it in your thoughts and feelings, and unseen agencies—whether metaphysical or psychological—will supposedly come to your aid. Seen in this way, the mind is a causative force.

As I began my adult explorations into the roots and methods of positive thinking—many of which are considered in these pages—I experienced some kind of difference in my life as Terri had experienced in hers. Was I imagining things? The practice of determined thought could seem so naive and simplistic. Most serious people regard positive thinking as a cotton-candy theology or a philosophy for dummies.

But I like "rejected stones"—they often hold neglected truths. Some of the leading voices in positive thinking, especially in its formative days in the late nineteenth and early twentieth centuries, had, like me, pursued many avenues of thought and religion but returned to the concept that the greatest truths can sometimes be found in practices and ideas that are very simple, often so much so that they are easy to dismiss. I do not believe in the ultimate power of any single principle. But if the premise of positive thinking is defensible, something that I consider in these pages, it seems to rest upon, and be measurable through, the degree of an individual's hunger for self-change.

Positive thinking, more properly known as New Thought, is the most enduring effort in modern history to forge a truly practical metaphysical approach to the needs and urgencies of daily life. Millions use its methods. Yet as a philosophy, positive thinking is also woefully underdeveloped and incomplete. It is shot through with ethical shortcomings and internal contradictions. For this thought system to reach its maturity, its followers and critics must take fuller stock of its flaws and possibilities, its deficiencies and avenues for growth. This requires understanding the positive-thinking movement's unseen history, unfinished promise, and extraordinary potential.

Mind Pioneers

Countless people hope, as my adolescent self did, that our thoughts possess some kind of power, both on ourselves and on events around us. They tell themselves that life is not just a merciless roulette wheel or the result of impossibly large forces or happenstance; but, rather, that the content of our thoughts influences the nature of our experience, in concrete terms.

For generations, people have wanted to believe that a good attitude not only makes us better people but makes better things happen to us. In the cold light of day, this seems an impossible dream.

But is it?

Beginning in the mid-nineteenth century, a determinedly modern group of American men and women decided to find out. Immersed in new ideas in religion and psychology, a loosely knit band of psychical researchers and religious philosophers, mental-healers and hypnotists, Mesmerists and Spiritualists, Unitarians and Transcendentalists, suffragists and free-love advocates, black liberationists and Christian socialists, animal-rights activists and Biblical communists, occultists and Freemasons, artists and freethinkers, embarked upon a grand and sprawling project to investigate the parameters of the human mind. These experimenters, sometimes working together and other times in private, resolved to determine whether some mental force—divine, psychological, or otherwise—exerts an invisible pull on a person's daily life. Was there, they wondered, a "mind-power" that could be harnessed to manifest outcomes?

For them, like many Americans, the latter half of the nineteenth century was a time when hidden forces seemed to abound in daily life. From telegraph signals and electrical currents, to stories of spirit raps and

Mesmerism, the power of the unseen seemed to beckon everywhere. For a time, mainstream science and avant-garde spirituality could appear united in a search to unveil the mysteries of life. Indeed, people with mystical beliefs often considered themselves in league with social reform and the march of progress. They felt that their theories and ideas, such as the mind's influence over health, produced observable results and could help lift spirituality to a new perch of rationalism.

At the start of the twentieth century, philosopher William James believed that the thought system that emerged from these experiments, which he called "the religion of healthy-mindedness," held such promise, and hovered so mightily over modern religious life, that it amounted to the equivalent of a Reformation on the American spiritual scene. As James saw it, the positive-thinking movements,* variously known to him as New Thought, Christian Science, or Metaphysical Healing, held the potential to morph into a liberal, universal faith, one that simultaneously confirmed the deepest yearnings of mysticism and the rationalist rigor of pragmatism. "It is quite obvious," James wrote in 1907, "that a wave of religious activity, analogous in some respects to the spread of early Christianity, Buddhism, and Mohammedanism, is passing over our American world."

Predicting the destiny of religious movements is a tricky business. Thomas Jefferson wrote that every young man alive during his lifetime would likely "die an Unitarian." In the early twentieth century Mark Twain envisaged a future America dominated by Christian Science. Yet James's predictions struck closer to the mark. If the philosopher's foresights were exaggerated, it had to do only with the kind of institutional structure that this healthy-minded religion would take. No high church

---

* When referencing the overall mind-power culture, I often employ the term *positive-thinking movement* (in which I do not include Christian Science, which, as will be seen, branched into a specific denomination of its own). At various points I use terms such as *mind-cure* and *mental healing* to connote the early days of the movement. Historically, these terms—*mind-cure, mental healing,* and *positive thinking*—have taken on connotations, sometimes pleasing and sometimes displeasing, to those inside the various movements to which they refer. I use them only as historical appellations; they indicate no judgment toward one school or another.

of positive thought extends across the American scene today. But the influence of positive thinking is greater than that of any one established religion.

In my previous book, *Occult America*, I considered the history of mystical movements in the United States, including the careers of some of the early positive thinkers. I came to realize, however, that those positive-thinking pioneers—and their many counterparts who populate these pages—could not be understood merely through their *influence* on American religion. Rather, positive thinking entered the groundwater of American life. It became the unifying element of all aspects of the American search for meaning. The shapers of positive thinking fundamentally altered how we see ourselves today—psychologically, religiously, commercially, and politically. Their story is the backstory of modern America.

Peer into any corner of current American life, and you'll find the positive-thinking outlook. From the mass-media ministries of evangelists such as Joel Osteen, Creflo Dollar, and T.D. Jakes to the millions-strong audiences of Oprah, Dr. Phil, and Mehmet Oz, from the motivational bestsellers and seminars of the self-help movement to myriad twelve-step programs and support groups, from the rise of positive psychology, mind-body therapies, and stress-reduction programs to the self-affirmative posters and pamphlets found on walls and racks in churches, human-resources offices, medical suites, and corporate corridors, this one idea—*to think positively*—is metaphysics morphed into mass belief. It is the ever-present, every-man-and-woman wisdom of our time. It forms the foundation of business motivation, self-help, and therapeutic spirituality, including within the world of evangelism. Its influence has remade American religion from being a salvational force to also being a healing one.

Positive thinking is an indelible part of our political climate, as well. When Ronald Reagan used to routinely announce in his speeches that "nothing is impossible," his listeners were able to make sense of his sentiments due to decades of motivational psychology. Reagan's *America-*

can-do anything philosophy, for good or ill, reshaped the nation's political landscape (and, not incidentally, sounded a lot like the mail-order self-improvement courses to which the president's father subscribed during the Great Depression). Reagan's oratory compelled every president who came after him, whether Republican or Democrat, to sing praises to the limitless potential of the American public. In this sense, positive thinking is our national creed.

"It's All Such Bullshit!"

Most sensitive, educated people are taught to believe that positive thinking is a foolish quirk of modern culture. Barbara Ehrenreich has chronicled the dreary, dystopian experience of being told to think sunny thoughts as a cancer patient. The social critic Richard Hofstadter observed in the early 1960s that hearty thinking was a pitiable substitute for a careful understanding of the social forces that weigh on people's economic lives. The punk band X, my high-school heroes, agreed with Ehrenreich and Hofstadter when they sang sardonically: "I MUST NOT THINK BAD THOUGHTS . . ."

I once found myself explaining to a media executive the manner in which evangelist Pat Robertson had reworked the so-called Law of Attraction into his more acceptable-sounding Law of Reciprocity—but before I could continue, I was cut off. "It's all such bullshit!" my host exclaimed, pointing out how such a system was, in effect, used to blame the poor or ill for their plights. "I hope I haven't insulted your belief system," she said. No, I told her, she hadn't. The fact is, she was right. But, like most critics, only partly so. And only about those people who see such metaphysical "laws" as an overarching, cause-and-effect rule of life. Or those who believe in the popular New Age precept "there are no accidents"—a bromide that forms the Achilles' heel of the positive-thinking philosophy and has kept it from attaining greater moral seriousness, a topic I will consider.

Other critics have rightly observed how prohibitions against "negative thinking" can amount to blaming a patient or injured person, or to setting up the expectation that the absence of recovery will be the patient's fault. Being told how to think is the kind of wearying and dubious advice that no sick person should ever have to endure. Indeed, the human proclivity for dispensing advice (rather than concrete assistance, in time or money) is rarely anything more than the vanity of cheap talk, and often causes more anxiety than relief. Once in a maternity ward I overheard the distraught mother of an ill newborn being urged by a relative to "think positive." It is difficult to imagine crueler or more impotent words at such a moment.

Over the past two decades, I have seen some of the best people in the positive-thinking movement—that is, members of metaphysical churches or positivity-based support groups—depart or distance themselves from such organizations after experiencing the contradictions that an ill-conceived program of affirmative thought can visit upon a suffering person. A support-group leader for female survivors of sexual abuse—someone who had spent many years within a positive-thinking metaphysical church—wrote to me in 2012. She said that she had experienced both sides of the positive-thinking equation, witnessing how survivors could ably use a program of mental therapeutics to rebuild their sense of self, but also observing the kind of mindless victim-blaming that affirmative-thinking nostrums could visit upon those recovering from trauma. She continued:

> My husband, who experienced a massive stroke at the age of
> 22 while in "perfect" health and working as a farm hand, has
> also felt an ambivalence toward the positive-thinking teach-
> ings. Such an emphasis gets placed on physical healing as a
> manifestation of right thought that it can alienate those peo-
> ple living with disabilities whose healings have manifested
> in other, possibly non-physical, ways.

In conclusion, she wondered: "Is there room for a positive-thinking model that doesn't include blame and single-model definitions of success?"

This book takes the attitude that such a model can exist. But to reach that point requires not only understanding the background, breadth, and flaws of this movement, but also realizing that it is often the most sensitive people within a movement who are its clearest critics, and not necessarily those onlookers who believe that positivity-based philosophy deserves little more than a disdainful eye roll or a withering exposé. Spiritual and social movements that do not write their own history get it written for them, often by historians who are indifferent toward, or derisive of, a movement's aims and ideals, and are thus unable to see the possibilities and values that emanate from it.

Hence, it is from the inside that I approach this book—as someone who has worked with positive-thinking ideas not only in my personal life but for much of my professional life, as well. As I write this, I am vice-president and editor-in-chief at a publishing house that specializes in self-help, New Age, and positive thinking. The positive-thinking movement is one that I love—for its sense of possibilities, its challenge to religious conformity, and its practical ideas; yet it is also a movement that I sometimes disdain—for its lack of moral rigor, its inconsistencies, and its intellectual laxity.

Perspective on the Positive

"The term 'positive thinking,'" wrote historian Gary Ward Materra, "has permeated American culture to such an extent that it is difficult to overestimate its influence." Yet the positive-thinking paradigm, for all the vastness of its reach and the importance of the questions it raises about the mind, has not been understood—historically, theologically, or practically. The outlook of this book is that positive thinking is less than its most enthusiastic exponents believe—it is not a psycho-spiritual magic wand or an all-encompassing, result-making law of life. But it is also a great deal more than what its critics see it as, namely a fool-baiting philosophy of refrigerator magnets and page-a-day calendars.

Rather, positive thinking is an approach to life that stems from the late Enlightenment era's boldest attempts at self-understanding, starting with a ferment of ideas at the close of the eighteenth century from which emerged independent spiritual innovators who struggled to assemble a psychological view of life, and to devise practical applications of old and new religious concepts. For all its shortcomings, positive thinking has stood up with surprising muscularity in the present era of placebo studies, mind-body therapies, brain-biology research, and, most controversial, the findings of quantum physics experiments. When reported without sensationalism or half-baked understanding, the data emerging from the quantum physics field suggests some vital, not-yet-understood verity about how the mind interplays with the surrounding world. The questions that quantum physics raises about the nature of the mind may challenge how we come to view ourselves in the twenty-first century, at least as much as Darwinism challenged man's self-perception in the Victorian age.

But in dealing with any practical philosophy, one must finally leave behind the various and disputatious claims about quantum-this and placebo-that. Any defender or detractor of positive thinking must weigh his perspective against one simple, ultimate question: *Does it work?* To find out, we will consider where this radical idea arose from; how it grew beneath our culture like a vast root system, touching nearly every aspect of life; the persistence of its ethical problems (and possible paths out of them); and, finally, what positive thinking says about our existence and what it offers people today.

chapter two

positive nation

Be All You Can Be

—U.S. Army recruiting slogan, 1980–2001

Twenty-first-century Americans are shaped by the imperative to think positively. Whether someone displays a "positive attitude" is considered a mark of ambition or apathy, effectiveness or ineptness, success or failure.

The song of the affirmative emanates from wildly disparate sources. Kansas physician George Tiller, murdered in 2009 by an anti-abortion vigilante, was known for wearing a lapel button reading "Attitude Is Everything." At the start of the 2008 recession, media minister Joel Osteen counseled his television viewers on three rules to avoid being laid off:

improvement of job skills; expansion of responsibilities; and a positive attitude. Longevity studies frequently cite five correlates to a longer life: low or no alcohol, no smoking, low caloric intake, exercise, and a positive outlook.

In consumer culture, the language of self-affirmation has shaped some of advertising's most memorable campaigns, such as the recruitment slogan of the U.S. Army, "Be All You Can Be"; Nike's "Just Do It"; MasterCard's "Master the Possibilities"; and Merrill Lynch's "To Know No Boundaries."

Positive thinking forms the keynote of modern life. Like all widely extolled principles, from healthy eating to thrifty spending, aspiration toward positivity seems like it has always been with us. But the concept is newer than we think.

A century and a half ago, if you told someone that "thinking positively" could bring solutions, you would have been looked at in puzzlement. Not that America lacked a literature of character development. Such works extend back to Puritan writings of the seventeenth century and Benjamin Franklin's colonial-era guide to conduct, *Poor Richard's Almanack*.* But the pamphlets, sermons, and chapbooks of early America focused mostly on injunctions to piety, frugality, hard work, reliability, early rising, and good neighborliness—not to the workings of inner will or the psychological or spiritual dimensions of an attitude. Where did such notions come from?

A Brief History of the Mind

Seen from a certain perspective, every idea that's ever been thought has always been with us. The general concept of the mind as an *influencing agency*, whether psychological or metaphysical, has ancient roots.

Shortly before the dissipation of the ancient world, and the

---

* There were subtle but important differences between Franklin's ethical literature and that of the Puritans. While the Puritans believed that man's improvement was a matter of salvation and service to God, Franklin encouraged material success and the advancement up society's ladder.

widespread embrace of Christianity, a branch of Greek-Egyptian philosophy arose called Hermeticism. It grew from a body of wisdom attributed to Hermes Trismegistus, or "Thrice-Greatest Hermes," a mythical Greco-Egyptian sage who was seen as an incarnation of Thoth, Egypt's god of writing. Hermeticists reasoned that man had access to *nous*, or a universal over-mind—and that with the proper preparation of prayer, ritual, and meditation, an individual could be permeated by the universal mind, and would thus receive temporary powers of prophecy and higher realization. This Hermetic concept got preserved within a small cluster of Arabic, Greek, and Latin manuscripts. These writings reemerged during the Renaissance, when European scholars grew fascinated with the occult philosophies of antiquity.

In the early eighteenth century, the Irish bishop George Berkeley sounded a transformative note in Western philosophy when he argued that material reality had no existence outside of man's mental-sensory perceptions. What appears in our world is a result of our observation, Berkeley reasoned. Without a sensate observer, phenomena have nothing in which to be grounded. Berkeley's insights gave rise to the thought school later called Idealism. Yet the Anglo-Irish philosopher stopped short of anointing man as the inventor of reality: there also exists, he insisted, a *rerum natura*, or fixed nature of things, of which the sole author is God.

The next generation of Idealist philosophers, most significantly Immanuel Kant and G. W. F. Hegel, also saw reality as a product of man's perceptive faculties—but our senses, they argued, were limited in their ability to perceive the true nature of things. The mind was finally experiencing itself, Kant and Hegel reasoned, and not ultimate reality. Like Berkeley, Kant and Hegel also believed, more or less, in a fixed nature or set of universal laws, within which an awakened person could serve as an extraordinary actor but not as an agent of creation.

Some mid- to late-nineteenth-century modernists, such as Arthur Schopenhauer and Friedrich Nietzsche, extolled the powers of human will and spoke of an inner-self that formed an invisible seat of power.

But, again, such views did not elevate the mind as the author of reality. Indeed, all of the major Idealist philosophers and their offspring, from Kant to Emerson to Nietzsche, held that natural man could ally himself with universal forces, and thus attain a kind of greatness or at least a right way of living, but none broke with Berkeley's assertion that the shapes and shades of reality "are not creatures of my will."

A countercurrent of sorts emerged in the eighteenth-century writings of Swedish scientist and mystic Emanuel Swedenborg. Swedenborg's vast and challenging cosmic philosophy depicted the presence of God as a "Divine influx"—an animating body of energies and ideas—that permeated all of nature, including the mind. Swedenborg's "Divine influx" echoed aspects of ancient Hermetic thought. In turn, the American philosopher and essayist Ralph Waldo Emerson took partial influence from Swedenborg's ideas. In a vastly more engaging manner than the Swedish mystic, Emerson, starting in the 1830s, depicted the mind as a capillary of divine influence, and he described human thought as a kind of concentrically expanding awareness, ultimately capable of godlike perception. Emerson extolled the power of ideas to shape a person's life, noting in his 1841 essay "Spiritual Laws" that "the ancestor of every action is a thought." Emerson saw the touch of divine power in an active, sensitive human mind.

All of these ideas presented tantalizing possibilities to liberal religious thinkers. Yet even by the mid-nineteenth century, the notion of an empirically empowering mysticism, one that could create and shape circumstance, was unheard-of within either reformist or mainstream congregations—and certainly not within Calvinist Protestantism and Catholicism. The modern West possessed no concept that our thoughts, much less a healthful sense of self-worth, could influence or reorder outer events.

It was only deep within subcultures of religious experimentation that the positive-thinking ideal actually began to take shape—and in settings far removed from universities, seminaries, or philosophical societies.

In the 1830s, a handful of New Englanders, some raised in America and others transplanted from England and France, started to probe the inner workings of the mind. The New England experimenters, in a period before modern psychological language, gave birth to a set of hypotheses about the effects of thoughts and emotions on health, and about the power of a deeply held idea to alter behavior or outer events.

"I Gave Up to Die"

A dramatic turn in how the Western world came to view the mind played out in Maine in 1833. This development hinged upon the experience of a simple and extremely influential man: a New England clockmaker named Phineas P. Quimby. That year, quietly and with little forethought, Quimby embarked on a psychological experiment that formed the germination of the positive-thinking outlook.

A man in his early thirties, Quimby was suffering from tuberculosis. Under doctor's orders he had been ingesting calomel, a popular though disastrous therapy in the first half of the nineteenth century. It was a mercury-based toxin that induced massive salivating and foaming of the mouth. Calomel was a common treatment among physicians who practiced "heroic medicine." The theoretical framework behind heroic medicine was that the draining of bodily fluids could rid a patient of disease and serve as an overall tonic to health. The champion of this approach was physician Benjamin Rush, a friend of Thomas Jefferson's and a signer of the Declaration of Independence. Rush was broadminded in matters of religion. He was among the few friends in whom Jefferson confided his own heterodox religious views, including his disbelief in Biblical miracles. But Rush's medical ideas, which dominated the American scene for generations, were medieval.

Along with calomel ingestion, Rush prescribed bleeding or bloodletting, a protocol embraced by other American doctors, who added a variety of measures to drain bodily fluids, such as open or "weeping" wounds, the ingestion of toxins and narcotics to produce profuse sweating, and—almost unbelievable in the modern era—the application of bloodsucking leeches. Rush viewed illness not as something to be healed but to be combated. "Always treat nature in a sick room as you would a noisy dog or cat," he told students, "drive her out at the door and lock it upon her." This was the reality facing Quimby and most American patients in the first half of the nineteenth century.

By the early 1830s, the ingestion of calomel was causing Quimby to suffer from mercury poisoning. The side effects were disfiguring. "I had taken so much calomel," he later wrote in his journals, "that my system was said to be poisoned with it; I lost many of my teeth from that effect." He continued, "In this state I was compelled to abandon my business and, losing all hope, I gave up to die." At this time Quimby and his wife, Susannah, had two sons and an infant daughter. How they managed to support a family during Quimby's illness is a trial of which he makes no mention.

With little left to lose, Quimby turned to a therapeutic procedure recommended by a friend: horseback riding. "Having an acquaintance who cured himself by riding horseback," he recalled, "I thought I would try riding in a carriage as I was too weak to ride horseback." In actuality, Quimby was reprising a treatment known to the ancient Greeks, who used vigorous horseback riding as a tonic. One day Quimby set off in his carriage in the countryside outside Belfast, Maine. He had a "contrary" horse, which kept stopping and finally would not budge unless the clockmaker ran beside him. Exhausted from running the horse up a hill, Quimby collapsed into the carriage and sat stranded two miles from home. He managed to call to a man plowing a nearby field and asked him to come and start the horse. "He did so," Quimby continued,

> and at the time I was so weak I could scarcely lift my whip.
> But excitement took possession of my senses, and I drove the
> horse as fast as he could go, up hill and down, till I reached

home and, when I got into the stable, I felt as strong as I ever did. From that time I continued to improve, not knowing, however, that the excitement was the cause . . .

Quimby grew intrigued at how the frenetic carriage ride seemed to lift his symptoms of tuberculosis. As his spirits rose, he noticed, so did his bodily vigor. The carriage ride formed Quimby's earliest notions that the mind had an effect on the body. But it would take the experience of an occult philosophy called Mesmerism, which was then reaching America from Paris, to make Quimby ponder the full possibilities. Mesmerism, the work of self-styled eighteenth-century Viennese healer Franz Anton Mesmer, ignited a new range of hypotheses about the human mind.

Mesmer's Revolution

Born in 1734, Franz Anton Mesmer was a German-speaking physician of the late Enlightenment era. In the 1770s, Mesmer theorized that all of life was shot through with an invisible ethereal fluid, which he called *animal magnetism*. If this vital fluid was out of alignment, Mesmer reasoned, illness resulted. He claimed to correct the flow of animal magnetism by placing a patient into a trance state, or a *magnetized* condition. Mesmer induced trances by making a series of hand and eye gestures, or "passes," around a subject's face and head. Once a subject was entranced, his vital energies, Mesmer believed, could be realigned. Most notably, Mesmer also discovered that trance subjects were receptive and malleable to his commands.

This is the practice that was redubbed "hypnotism" in the early 1840s by Scottish physician James Braid. Braid considered it a mental process and not an occult manipulation of unseen energies. Indeed, Mesmer himself did not perceive his method as an occult healing, but as a practice in league with Enlightenment-age principles.

Mesmer attained his greatest public acclaim, and notoriety, in 1778 after moving to Paris, a place already roiling with intrigues and tensions in the years preceding the French Revolution. Mesmer conducted public *séances,* or sittings, where he would attempt to heal patients in a dramatic group atmosphere. During Mesmer's séances, people suffering from maladies ranging from consumption to joint pain to melancholia were seated, hands linked, around a wooden tub, or *baquet,* containing iron rods and fillings, which had been specially "magnetized" to realign a subject's vital energies. During séances, patients were expected to experience convulsions and fainting—which Mesmer dubbed "crises"—as a signal that their bodily magnetism was responding to treatment.

While Mesmer acknowledged that his treatments depended upon sympathies between the patient and Mesmerist (someone who practiced his art), he rarely probed the matter further. "There is only one illness and one healing," Mesmer wrote, steadfastly insisting on the existence of an invisible fluidic flow. The eighteenth-century healer possessed neither a vocabulary nor the background to pursue questions about mind-body healing and subliminal states. The question of mental suggestion went unasked.

Many advocates of social reform in France took a deep interest in Mesmerism. To these enthusiasts, the susceptibility of all people, from peasants to noblemen, to enter a Mesmeric trance validated the ideal of an innate equality within human beings. Indeed, in France of the late eighteenth century, every advance in science or industry took on political overtones. To Mesmer's supporters, efforts to discredit Mesmerism amounted to the ploy of entrenched aristocratic interests, such as the French Academy of Sciences, to suppress a medical practice that was outside their purview and that could be used to aid common people.

Benjamin Franklin, who was then serving as America's ambassador to France, considered Mesmer a dangerous fraud and questioned whether sexual liberties were taken while subjects were entranced. In March 1784, King Louis XVI asked Franklin to chair a royal committee to investigate Mesmer's methods. The Franklin commission, composed of members of the French Academy of Sciences and the Paris Faculty of Medicine, conducted a series of trials to test the healer's theories.

Franklin's shaky health kept the elder statesman from witnessing most of the trials firsthand. And Mesmer himself had departed Paris in the lead-up to the investigation. One of Mesmer's students, the physician Charles d'Eslon, consented to work with the commission, though somewhat contentiously. The Franklin committee encompassed luminaries, such as chemist Antoine Lavoisier, astronomer Jean Bailly, and physician Joseph-Ignace Guillotin (whose name was later applied to the most dreaded device of the French Revolution). In trials, the investigators discovered that magnetic treatments could move patients to convulsions, or Mesmer's "crises," and other kinds of violent bodily effects, from coughing blood, to temporarily losing the power of speech, to sensations of heat or cold, and, in a few limited cases, to claims of comfort or cure.

The panelists noted that many patients, when blindfolded, could be induced to convulsions if they merely thought they were being subjected to Mesmeric methods. Hence, the royal panelists concluded in August 1784 that Mesmer's "cures" were all in the imagination, induced either by the charisma of the healer or by the copycat effect of convulsions that occurred en masse in séances. In their report to the king, the Franklin commission members wrote that their "decisive experiments" had proved "that the imagination alone produces all the effects attributed to magnetism; & when the imagination does not act, there are no more effects."

Left unaddressed by commission members was the question of why the subject's imagination should produce any results at all. Content to dispel notions of etheric magnetism, commission members left dangling what may have been their most significant observation. Regardless, the panel's conclusions irreversibly sullied Mesmer's reputation. He never again resided in Paris. Mesmer eventually returned to the German-speaking Swiss region where he was born and lived out a mostly quiet existence, corresponding with supporters and seeing patients until his death in 1815.

Until the end of his life, Mesmer stood by his theories of etheric fluid. Yet the healer's protégés edged away from questions of animal magnetism. They adopted a more psychological language. One of the most gifted of them, the Marquis de Puységur, undertook experiments in late 1784 and early 1785 that persuaded him that the suggestive powers of the Mesmerist, and his "rapport" with the patient, was the agency behind the reported cures.

"Animal magnetism," Puységur wrote, "lies not in the action of one body upon another, but in the action of thought upon the vital principle of the body." In terms Mesmer would not use, the student made the connection between mind and body.

Puységur fashioned a terminology that was remarkably anticipatory of the tone found in later generations of motivational psychology. When Puységur was dispatched to take command of a French artillery regiment in Strasbourg in August 1785, he began teaching classes in Mesmerism to a local Freemasonic lodge. At the end of the course, the Mesmerist gave his students an affirmation that extolled the forces of the mind:

> I believe in the existence within myself of a power.
> From this belief derives my will to exert it.
> The entire doctrine of Animal Magnetism is contained in two
>   words: *Believe and want.*
> I *believe* that I have the power to set into action the vital
>   principle of my fellow-men; I *want* to make use of it;
>   this is all my science and all my means.
> *Believe and want,* Sirs, and you will do as much as I.

Mesmerism Comes to Maine

For all the enthusiasm of Mesmer's followers, the practice of Mesmerism faded in France. The revolution in 1789 sent some of Mesmer's aristocratic students fleeing, and others to the guillotine (a fate met, too, by some of the members of the Franklin commission, including Bailly and

Lavoisier). Puységur spent two years in prison, after which he was able
to recover his property and begin some of his research anew. But Mesmerism slipped from the public memory. Séances and magnetic trances
were supplanted by political tracts and revolutionary intrigues.

While the influence of Mesmerism dimmed in Europe, the healer's philosophy—or rather the version reinterpreted by his followers—
began crossing the Atlantic. In America, a new generation of Mesmerists
migrating from France and England discovered a public hungry for innovation.

In August 1836, Quimby encountered a traveling Mesmerist lecturer
in Bangor. A French expatriate named Charles Poyen visited the Maine
city on a lecture tour. Poyen himself was a product of the marriage between Mesmerism and French social reform. His dedication to Mesmerism was jointly forged in his opposition to slavery—and his experience
of a strange medical episode.

While studying medicine in Paris in 1832, Poyen suffered a digestive
disorder and "nervous disease." After eight months of fruitless treatment
the medical student sought out a Mesmerist. His Mesmerist employed an
innovative twist on the practice. He placed an assistant, a "Madame V,"
into a state of "magnetic sleep" from which the medium astonished
Poyen by seeming to clairvoyantly diagnose his illness. "That lady had
never seen me before, and very probably did not know even my name,"
Poyen wrote. "How much surprised was I, when, after communication
had been established between us, I heard her giving a correct and minute description of the symptoms of my disease, as though she experienced it herself . . ."

Acting on the medium's advice, Poyen sought to rest his nerves with
an extended visit to his family's sugarcane plantations in the French West
Indies. What he witnessed on the islands of Martinique and Guadeloupe
transformed his view of life. Some of the island's slaveholding planta-
tion owners were themselves skilled in Mesmerism, which they demonstrated on their field hands. Poyen was deeply moved to discover that
African slaves and French slaveholders both entered trance states and

experienced the same effects. For Poyen, this suggested the basic same-
ness of human beings. It moved him to revile slavery.

"Those cases were altogether remarkable," he recalled, "and they en-
abled me, more than any thing else, to form the opinion that the human
soul was gifted with the same primitive and essential faculties, under
every climate, among every nation, and under whatever skin, black, red,
or white, it may be concealed."

After Poyen's fourteen-month stay in the islands, however, his digestive condition was no better. In a somewhat strange choice, he decided
to see if the cold winds of New England would prove a better tonic than
the tropics. Poyen arrived in Portland, Maine, in late 1834 and in the
following year settled in Lowell, Massachusetts. It proved a good match
for the young Frenchman. The town was a center of abolitionism and
frequently hosted antislavery speakers. Poyen struck up a friendship with
Lowell's mayor, a Brown-educated physician who was intrigued by what
Poyen told him about Mesmerism. With the mayor's encouragement,
Poyen embarked on lecture tours to Boston and other parts of New England in 1836 to speak on magnetism's benefits.

Public speaking did not come easily to Poyen. With a halting command of English, he struggled before audiences. In another difficulty, his
face was almost half-covered by a dark red birthmark (leading at least
one observer to surmise that the Frenchman was himself a former Afro-
Caribbean slave). Poyen contemplated returning to a more "comfortable
existence" in the West Indies but found the islands' slave-based society
"repugnant to my sympathies." He also felt that abandoning his speaking
tour would mean allowing Mesmerism to die in America.

Poyen decided to add some drama to his presentations through
live demonstrations in which he would place volunteers into trances.
This was his practice when he attracted the attention of Quimby during
his visit to Bangor in November 1836. Though intrigued, Quimby was
hardly overwhelmed. Poyen, Quimby recalled in his notes, "did not appear to be highly blest with the power of magnetising to the satisfaction
of his audience."

Never fully breaking through in America, Poyen resumed his medical studies in Paris in 1841. He planned to make a new tour of the United States in 1844, but he died of unknown causes at Bordeaux just as he was embarking on his return journey.

While Poyen's reach was limited, he did stimulate Quimby's interest. And in a few years the clockmaker encountered the work of a more impressive Mesmerist. In fall 1841, a British physician and magnetic healer named Robert H. Collyer made his way to Belfast, Maine. A skilled and persuasive speaker, Collyer attracted large audiences with a style that was far more polished than Poyen's. The October 1, 1841, *Republican Journal* of Belfast reported on Collyer's method:

> The Doctor carries a subject with him, a youngster some 18 years old. They both took chairs upon a table, so as to be in full view. The Doctor then took the boy's knees between his, and both the boy's hands. They then commenced looking each other in the eyes; the Doctor making a very slight movement of the head, neck, and stomach. In this way they remained, say ten minutes, when the boy gradually closed his eyes and fell asleep, leaning very much over on one side. . . . He was stiff as though frozen in position.—When one sleeps they are perfectly limber. The boy was stiff.

Collyer used on his assistant the same trance method that had been practiced by Mesmer himself. As Quimby witnessed Collyer's ability to affect the bodily state and sensations of his assistant, he grew more interested in what he felt Mesmerism uncovered: a link between the state of the mind and the experience of the body. The existence of a mind-body connection confirmed the relief he felt during his carriage rides. Quimby began to ponder ways of further testing and using this connection. If the mind impacted the body, he wondered, what other powers might it contain?

The Cure Is in the Confidence

Quimby was not a philosopher or a pedant but an experimenter. Although he possessed an extraordinarily sharp mind and a keen grasp of mechanical details, he was unable to write much beyond the level of a schoolhouse boy, a fact that embarrassed him. Quimby did maintain voluminous notebooks, into which he sometimes dictated his ideas with the assistance of others or, more commonly, arranged for friends and helpmates to rewrite his notes. But Quimby's aims were beyond the printed page. He was in search of a usable, practical method: Quimby wanted to rework the revelations of Mesmerism, in combination with his own personal experiments, and devise a protocol to treat the sick.

Shortly after attending Robert H. Collyer's 1841 Mesmerist demonstrations in Belfast, Maine, Quimby found a practical way of acting on his ideas. He met a seventeen-year-old boy who, similar to the medium once visited by Charles Poyen, could diagnose diseases from a trance state. Quimby believed that the local boy, Lucius Burkmar, was capable of clairvoyantly peering into the mind and body of subjects.

In fall 1843, Quimby and Lucius were traveling as a team throughout Maine and nearby New Brunswick, Canada, treating the sick, often in the presence of a local physician. Their method was to sit facing each other, knee to knee, while the older man gazed into Lucius's eyes and gently waved his hands around Lucius's face, placing him into a clairvoyant trance. This was an almost exact echo of the practice that Quimby had witnessed in Collyer and his young assistant.

From his magnetized state, Lucius attempted to mentally scan the diseased organs of patients and prescribed them folk remedies such as herbal teas. The local physician would often prepare and administer the tea. Other times, Quimby would assist area surgeons by inducing a patient into a state of "mesmeric anesthesia." Lucius and Quimby's activities attracted a great deal of attention among New Englanders, and many swore that the pair had relieved their ailments, from migraines to tuberculosis.

But Quimby grew unsatisfied. He found that Lucius's "cures" were

often no different from those that had been administered previously, and unsuccessfully, by a physician. The only difference seemed to be that the patient was aroused to an experience of relief by the presumed authority of the medium. Quimby grew convinced that it was neither the boy's clairvoyance, nor his herbal remedies, that were curing people. Rather, it was his ability to awaken hope: "The patient's disease is in his belief," Quimby wrote in his notes. And "the cure," he continued in a letter to the *Portland Daily Advertiser*, "is not in the medicine, but in the confidence of the doctor or medium."

Quimby had the same insight as Mesmer's best students, who theorized that the effects of the mind, rather than magnetic fluid, were helping patients. While no communication existed between Quimby and Mesmer's protégés, each inched toward similar conclusions.

Armed with this insight, Quimby stopped working with the clairvoyant around 1847. He began treating people on his own. Quimby's method was to sympathetically sit face-to-face with a patient, never denying that the subject was sick but rather encouraging him to "understand how disease originates in the mind and [to] fully believe it." If the patient's confidence in this idea was complete, Quimby would then urge the patient to ask: "Why cannot I cure myself?"

Quimby had devised some of the earliest methods of suggestibility. But he didn't see his work in those terms. Quimby's vocabulary was grounded not in psychology but in New England religious experimentalism. While Quimby disliked institutional religion (like a true New England freethinker), and would, by turns, speak of "matter"—both ethereal and physical—as an impersonal, mechanistic force, he ultimately came to view the mind and body as subject to scientific spiritual laws. "All science is a part of God," he wrote in an unpublished manuscript called "Questions and Answers."

Quimby also believed that all intelligence emanates from a universal source, and forms a continuum of spirit, mind, and matter. Since this inflowing force is perfect, he reasoned, it follows that "false beliefs"—or ignorance of universal goodness—cause disease or strife. He developed the idea that all of man's experience is determined by his perceptions. "Our happiness and misery are what follow our belief," he wrote in his notes.

On rare occasions Quimby referred to man possessing "an unconscious power that is not admitted," or a "wisdom that is invisible and unconscious," enunciating a remarkably early psychological insight. Quimby could sound like a medieval alchemist in one breath and a proto-modern psychologist in another; in actuality, he was a bridge between the two.

It is not always easy to understand how Quimby affected his patients. Edwin Reed, who had been the mayor of Bath, Maine, claimed that Quimby had cured him of complete blindness. A young woman who had been unable to speak for four years told the *Portland Daily Advertiser* on April 29, 1862, that Quimby had cured her after two months of treatment. News of Quimby's mental cure spread so widely that between the mid-1840s and his death in early 1866, he treated about three hundred people a year—amassing literally thousands of followers, many of whom deeply believed in his honesty and decency. "His patients come from the four winds of heaven," wrote an admirer in the *Portland Daily Advertiser* on February 5, 1862.

Late in his career Quimby was charging five dollars for mental treatments. But records show him accepting considerably less, and sometimes returning the money until a cure manifested. A boyhood neighbor who knew him in Belfast recalled a certain mystique about the man: "He had keen, restless, fascinating black eyes, with which he would look intently at those who sought him for treatment. . . . He was known widely in the community and was highly regarded and respected. He was known by all to possess peculiar powers and he practiced and exhibited these powers for many years."

Others were less impressed. Recalling her treatment years earlier, a former patient wrote in 1907:

One treatment was by wetting his hands in water and passing over the temples and forehead, which produced as bad a headache as I ever had. He would not locate disease. I was not benefitted in the least by his treatment. He said I did not have faith enough, yet I tried the exercise all that was necessary.

The Mystical Minister

Quimby's following was among farmers, housewives, and ordinary people. But his ideas attracted the attention of formidable religious thinkers. One of the most significant was Warren Felt Evans, a New England Methodist minister who left his pulpit in early 1864 to dedicate himself to the ideas of Emanuel Swedenborg.

The previous summer, while struggling to combine his Methodist beliefs with Swedenborgian mysticism and his own experiments into mental healing, Evans had sought out Quimby. He was stimulated by the mind-healer's theories. Followers of Swedenborg often took naturally to Quimby's methods, which seemed to suggest that the mind was a tool that could channel and direct the cosmic laws Swedenborg had written about. Evans went on to write about mental healing in six books, and he proved an enormous force in shaping the positive-thinking culture.

Open nearly any history of alternative religions or the mental-healing movement and you will encounter the following scenario: Persuaded by Quimby's approach, and, by some counts, healed through it, the erudite Evans became a disciple of the mind-healer and went on to become Quimby's chief chronicler and popularizer. This scenario got launched, as will be seen, in a debate over the origins of mental and spiritual healing, waged in the years just before and after Evans's death in 1889, when the minister was unable to point out the obvious: that Evans regarded Quimby not as a mentor but as a colleague with whom to discuss mutual findings. Indeed, Evans had already worked through his own outlook on mental healing by the time he met Quimby.

Starting in early 1859, Evans had struggled with a breakdown in his health that seems to have involved a painful bowel disorder. "My health so completely failed me last April that I could not preach," he wrote in his journal on September 19, 1859. "I have not preached for more than six months." In what must have been a particular sorrow for the learned minister, "There was a time when I could not so much as read."

In the grip of his illness, Evans looked for answers in both religion and the reaches of his own mind. By the following spring he was convalescing, and recording some of his earliest connections between disease and mental state. He wrote in his journals on April 12, 1860:

> My health is not yet adequate to the full work of ministry. I long for strength to employ it in the work so dear to my heart . . . I have hope of regaining my former power. The Lord is my strength. "He is the health of my countenance and my God." I will find in Christ all that I need. He can cure every form of mental disease, and thus restore the body, for disease originates generally, if not always, in the mind.

Like Quimby, Evans was perched between religious and psychological language—imploring God to cure his "mental disease." By the time Evans wrote those words, he was already a renegade in the Methodist ministry for his interest in Swedenborg. He had begun exploring Swedenborg's theology around 1858, and for several years he attempted to combine his Methodist beliefs with Swedenborg's outlook. Evans's efforts at marrying the two thought streams began breaking down, however, in 1862 when he aroused church ire with his publication of *The Celestial Dawn*, a short book that explored Swedenborgian mysticism (though without naming the Swedish seer as its source of insights).

Evans's discovery of Swedenborg not only marked his drift away from Methodism, but brought him to the threshold of a mental-healing methodology. He was thrilled by statements that he found in Swedenborg, like this one from the seer's final 1771 book: "There is not anything in the mind, to which something in the body does not correspond; and this which corresponds may be called the embodying of that."

Evans did not always capture such statements in full context, as will later be explored. But within the folds of Swedenborg he discovered justification for his developing outlook that disease and suffering "is only an appearance" based in the images of the mind. "All disease," Evans later wrote, "so far as it has a material or bodily expression, must have had a preexistence in us as a fixed mode of thought, that is, as an idea."

By April 1863—shortly before Evans met Quimby—the minister recorded in his diaries an insight that he somewhat struggled to articulate. It contains the keynote of the next century's positive mental therapeutics: "I see how it is that by believing I have the thing for which I am praying causes me to have it."

Faith, Evans continued, "proceeds from God" and "if my belief of it is a truth received from God, or if my faith is the faith of God, it becomes a substantial reality."

At this crucial point Evans arrived at his insight that *faith is a force*, which manifests "an actual realization of what I am praying for." While framing this principle in Christian terms, Evans is saying that *mental certitude and visualization, backed by faith, is the engine of creation*. If Evans had put down his pen at that moment, and written no more, he could be credited with the founding premise of positive thinking.

In Evans's later books, the qualities of faith and right-thinking became increasingly interchangeable. "If thought and existence are identical," he wrote in 1885 in *The Primitive Mind-Cure*, "then it follows to think rightly is to be well and happy." It was a simpler—and more radical—sounding of the insight Evans first recorded in his journals in 1863.

Hence, Evans, by the time he met Quimby, had already developed significant portions of his mind-based metaphysics. Evans left no record of how he initially learned about Quimby's mental healing, or precisely what he hoped to gain from him. His personal attitude toward Quimby was perhaps most clearly voiced in a little-known interview Evans gave toward the end of his life. In early 1888 a Chicago writer and editor, A. J.

Swarts, himself a former Methodist minister, ex–Christian Scientist, and devotee of mind-cure philosophy, interviewed Evans at his Massachusetts home. In the March 1888 issue of his *Mental Science Magazine*, Swarts recalled meeting the movement's elder statesman:

> I visited Dr. W. F. Evans at Salisbury, Massachusetts. He is the most erudite author in the principles of Mental, Christian or Spiritual Science. My visit with the noble veteran and man of God was satisfactory and profitable to me. . . . The Doctor intends to live and work for humanity many years yet. It is thought by some that he formerly worked with Dr. P. P. Quimby; this is a mistake. He called twice briefly on Dr. Q. in Portland nearly twenty-five years ago, and his interviews satisfied him that his own methods of cure were like those which Dr. Q. employed. He speaks well of him, and of all the workers, simply desiring all to be honest and to "give credit where credit is due."

In the same interview Evans told Swarts that in summer of 1863 he "was passing through Portland"—not that he ventured there in search of a personal cure—and "that he called upon Dr. Quimby . . . to ascertain his methods of treatment, and that he found them to be like those he had employed for several years."

Julius Dresser, a friend of Evans's who had also worked with Quimby, recorded Evans saying in 1876 that he had been something of an eager student to Quimby, and that their time together was brief only because Evans's grasp of the master's methods was quick and sure, and his teacher gave him the nod to begin healing patients on his own. It is possible that this depiction of Evans's mentorship was accurate, and that Evans, as an older man speaking to Swarts, was minimizing Quimby's contribution. But whatever foreknowledge Evans brought to Quimby's door, and precisely what he experienced there, Evans's body of work leaves no question that he developed the earliest and clearest public articulation of the philosophy of mental manifestation and affirmative thought.

Because Quimby published almost nothing during his life—his edited notebooks did not begin to see publication until 1921—it is the records and writings of Evans, rather than the methods of Quimby himself, that impacted the first generations of the positive-thinking movement. Early mental healers and students of positive-mind philosophy may have believed that they were imbibing the thought of Quimby in Evans's books, when, in fact, they were receiving Evans's own independently worked-through insights.

This misperception—which persists today in metaphysical classes and New Thought seminaries—was due to polemical lines that were drawn in a debate involving another, far better known, spiritual thinker who passed through Quimby's world.

Wounded Healer

Starting in October 1862, Quimby began treating a New Hampshire woman named Mary Glover Patterson. In later years remarriage would change her name to how it is remembered in religious history: Mary Baker Eddy.

In the 1870s, Eddy went on to found one of the nation's most significant new religions, Christian Science. Rather than extol of the powers of the mind, Eddy's Christian Science saw the human mind as the seat of all illness, violence, and illusion—conditions that were to be overcome by the realization of the one true reality: the divine, all-permeating Intelligence of God. The human mind and earthly matter, Eddy reasoned, possess no ultimate reality; rather, all things are grounded in the true Mind of God, who wishes only good for his creation. Where prejudice, sickness, and sorrow appear, they are merely the false perceptions of man and the illusory world of shadows in which he lives.

Christian Science sought to resurrect the healing ministry of Christ through a rediscovery of spiritual scientific laws of healing and a radical metaphysic that rejected that existence of earthly matter. It became a movement of tremendous growth and influence in the late nineteenth and early twentieth centuries. By the time Eddy met Quimby, however, she had not yet embarked on her theology. Whether, and to what extent, she adapted that theology from Quimby became the subject of a fiery and long-standing debate.

When Eddy reached Quimby's door in fall 1862, she had already contended with years of hardship. Her rural childhood played out under the rule of a taciturn and sometimes eccentric father. "My father was taught to believe that my brain was too large for my body and so kept me much out of school," she recalled. Not infrequently confined to her household, the young Eddy attained a remarkable self-education with the help of siblings who shared their classroom lessons, giving her a working knowledge of Biblical and classical languages.

By the age of twenty-three in 1844 Eddy was widowed while carrying an unborn son in her womb. In frail health, Eddy was eventually unable to care for her child, and she watched helplessly as her boy, George Glover (named for his deceased father), was adopted at age six by the Eddy family's former domestic servant and her husband. The adoptive parents lived a carriage ride away in New Hampshire so Eddy was able to see the boy from time to time. When George turned eleven, however, his guardians moved away with him to Minnesota. To avoid any struggle by George to stay near his mother, his adoptive family told the boy that she was dead. The mother and son did not see each other again until George was in his thirties.

In 1853, Eddy was remarried, this time to a philandering dentist, Daniel Patterson, who off-and-on vanished from Mary's life, and was finally taken prisoner by the Confederate Army during the Civil War. The man wasn't a Union soldier but was foolish enough to go sightseeing on an active battlefield at Bull Run.

Alone, confused, and suffering from a chronic and undiagnosed spinal disorder, Eddy sought out Quimby's "mind-cure" in fall 1862. Under Quimby's care she began to feel her strength return. She visited again in the summer of 1863 and several times after until the spring of 1865.

Eddy grew absorbed with Quimby, talking privately with him, taking notes, occasionally writing local articles and delivering talks about his work. But her time with Quimby was also fated to be relatively brief. The man she called her "doctor" died in January 1866, less than four years after they met. Eddy's own father had died three months earlier. And her second husband, after escaping his imprisonment, was largely absent and unfaithful. Further still, soon after Quimby's death Eddy suffered a fall on an icy sidewalk in Lynn, Massachusetts, in February 1866, which left her bedridden and frayed her nerves.

It was a time of psychological extremes for Eddy. Yet at such moments she could display steely determination, vowing to walk again and poring over Scripture for succor and insight. She later called it a period of great spiritual discovery. Yet she also, and inevitably, felt the agony of the near-simultaneous losses of a father, a spiritual healer, and a husband, all of it compounded by her poor health.

In her distress, Eddy looked for a new mentor. She wrote to another of Quimby's former students, Julius Dresser, the acquaintance of Warren Felt Evans. Writing on February 15, 1866, Eddy implored Dresser, who was working as a journalist in Yarmouth, Maine, to take up the helm of Quimby's work.

"I am constantly wishing that you would step forward," Eddy wrote. ". . . I believe you would do a vast amount of good and are more capable of occupying his place than any other I know." Eddy struck a tone of desperation: "Now can't you help me? . . . Please write at once."

Dresser took almost three weeks to reply on March 2. It was a busy time for the Dresser family, as Julius's wife, Annetta, had given birth weeks earlier to the couple's first child, Horatio, who arrived the day before Quimby's death. Horatio would later gain note on his own as a historian and philosopher. While Julius felt deep affection for Quimby, and sincerely believed that he and his wife owed Quimby their health, he had no intention of revisiting the past. He refused Eddy's plea. "As to turning Dr. myself . . . it is not to be thought of for a minute," Julius replied. "Can an infant do a strong man's work? Nor would I if I could."

By now an established newspaperman, Julius regarded Quimby as a failure of sorts for having spent so much time tending to patients and so little time formalizing his methods. "Dr. Q's work killed him," Dresser wrote, "whereas if he had spared himself from his curing, and given himself partly . . . to getting out his theory, he would have, at least, come nearer to success in his great aim than he did."

Somewhat oddly, Dresser compared Quimby's failure to that of the original spiritual healer, Jesus Christ: "So with Jesus. He had an effect which was lasting and still exists. But his great aim was a failure. He did not succeed, nor has Dr. Q succeeded in establishing the Science he aimed to do." His reply closed the door on any relationship with Eddy.

Isolated and uncertain, Eddy devised a way to answer her own calling for spiritual guidance. Reflecting on her experiences of Quimby's healing methods, and embarking on her own intrepid reading of Scripture, she began to lay the groundwork for her theology of Christian Science. Eddy's revelation, however, differed in both subtle and significant ways from Quimby's teachings. While the clockmaker saw the human mind as a vessel of divine power, Eddy saw it as an instrument of illusion. The "mortal mind," she reasoned, must be eradicated so that the Mind of God could be revealed as the one absolute reality.

Eddy insisted that evil and sickness were unreal. They are products of the corrupt and illusory man-mind. The only true reality is the Intelligence of God, in which man is an image. Did Eddy literally mean that evil was unreal? When asked if Christian Scientists believe that evil exists, Eddy responded: "Yes, inasmuch as we do know that evil, as a false claim, false entity, and utter falsity, does exist in thought; and No, as something that enjoys, suffers, or is real." The subtlety of her rejection of the ultimate reality of evil could easily lend itself to misunderstanding, especially among people or movements that wanted to embrace Eddy's ideas about the unreality of evil but found it difficult to make the leap to her denial of the actual existence of matter, which included the uses of "material medicines."

By about 1872, Eddy seemed to have left behind any earlier sense of mentorship by Quimby. Although she had once eulogized him as a man "who healed with the truth that Christ taught," she began working on the text of her own testament and vision, the book that would become known as *Science and Health*. The book laid out Eddy's philosophy that the healings of Christ were not a onetime miracle but an "everoperative divine Principle" available to modern people. Quimby, to her mind, was, at most, a way station in her journey of discovery, but he was not a teacher. Although Eddy later wrote that she "loved . . . his high and noble character," she found that the philosophy she called *Quimbyism* "was too short, and would not answer the cry of the human heart for succor, for real aid"; hence, "I went, being driven there by my extremity, to the Bible, and there I discovered Christian Science."

In the years ahead, Eddy saw herself—and her followers saw her—as an inspired religious leader. As such, she wanted no association with what she saw as the Mesmeric-influenced outlook of "Quimbyism." Nor did she want any part of the "New Age" movement anticipated by Evans,* with its affirmations, inducements to right-thinking, and openness to a plethora of spiritual influences. In a letter to a friend on July 11, 1871, Eddy dismissed Evans, whom she seemed to know only in passing from her Quimby years, as a "half scientist." This marked a decisive split between Christian Science and the developing movements of alternative spirituality.

Family Feud

Following the publication of *Science and Health* in 1875, Eddy's ideas quickly gained popularity. Her prayer therapy treatments, which she taught in

---

* Evans coined the term *New Age*, in its modern spiritual-therapeutic sense, in his 1864 work *The New Age and Its Messenger*. The "Messenger," in this case, was Swedenborg.

classes and wrote about in pamphlets and articles, had deep appeal to a nation suffering under the lingering grotesqueries of "heroic medicine." Yet Eddy's success as a new religious voice, and her decisive break with the memory of Quimby, attracted an unwanted figure from the past: a man with an impassioned and newfound sense of ire toward Eddy.

In May 1882, former Quimby patient Julius Dresser, who had expressed little interest in Quimby's ideas in 1866, and showed less still in Eddy, reemerged on the Boston scene. It is difficult to understand precisely why Dresser left his newspaper job in Oakland, California, and uprooted his wife, Annetta, and family, now grown to three sons, to reappear in the New England mind-cure milieu that year. According to Dresser's supporters, Julius arrived to stand up for Quimby's reputation; he believed that Eddy was now passing off the doctor's ideas as her own, giving her former mentor no credit. Eddy partisans have a different account, which places Dresser back in the Boston area to assume his place, financially and otherwise, in the prospering cultures of Christian Science and mind-cure, which had grown in tandem since the appearance of Eddy's *Science and Health*. Indeed, Dresser's motives may have been an amalgam of idealism and self-interest. Whatever the case, it was not until Eddy began to gain national attention that Dresser reawakened to his interest in Quimby.

Resituated in Boston, Dresser partnered with a disputatious ex-student of Christian Science, Edward J. Arens, who had pirated some of Eddy's writings in his own booklets. Arens gave Dresser some old letters and articles of Eddy's, in which she pledged fealty to Quimby, and which would later serve as a source of embarrassment to her. Dresser, by his turn, provided Arens with a potted (and ultimately unsuccessful) legal defense for his pilfering of Eddy's writings, which sought to identify the deceased Quimby, and not Eddy, as the source of the innovative healing ideas.

The Dresser-Eddy feud went public in early 1883. In the *Boston Post*, Julius Dresser and Mary Baker Eddy, each former patients of Quimby, commenced a series of dueling letters in which they first circled one another like sharks, each subtly, even inscrutably, feinting rushes at the other before charging into an all-out attack.

Their correspondence began in February under assumed initials—Dresser was "A.O." and Eddy was "E.G." Dresser threw the first stone, intimating in a letter of February 8, 1883, that it had reached his attention that "some parties healing through a mental method"—he meant Eddy—"did, in reality, obtain their first thoughts of this truth from Dr. Quimby."

Eddy attempted to respond to his stone with a boulder, writing on February 19—under the initials "E.G."—that Quimby had been little more than a stage performer, with no clearly enunciated method; his writings mere "scribblings," she wrote, and Quimby had only a slap-dash, Mesmeric method of healing the sick. In the next letter, of February 24, Dresser, now using his real name, played his hand. In a move that must have made Eddy seethe, Dresser aired her private letter to him of winter 1866, in which she had begged Dresser to step forward as her new healer after Quimby's death. Dresser quoted Eddy, writing at what had probably been the most vulnerable moment of her life, saying that she was frightened and now "find myself the helpless cripple I was before I saw Dr. Quimby." For a woman now at the helm of a growing religious movement it was a humiliating revelation.

Using her real name, Eddy replied on March 9 in a letter that assumed a more officious and careful tone. Of Quimby's memory, she wrote: "He was a humanitarian, but a very unlearned man; he never published a work in his life, was not a lecturer or teacher. He was somewhat of a remarkable healer, and at the time we knew him he was known as a mesmerist. . . . We have no doubt that Dr. Q's motives were good, for we understood him to be a moral man." Of greater concern to Eddy was the airing of the "private letter which the gentleman"—after which she added "(?)"—"Mr. Dresser, has on exhibition."

The chill between the two former Quimby patients was permanently set.

By early 1887, Dresser opened a second front. In February, he issued his most effective polemic against Eddy in a popular Boston lecture, which was quickly issued as a pamphlet called *The True History of Mental Science*. Dresser's contentions came to shape how the history of positive thinking has been written and understood, including to the present day. The skillful broadside argued that Eddy had lifted her ideas from Quimby during the time she had his confidence as a patient, and that she was now passing them off as her own without crediting the Maine healer. Dresser singled out Warren Felt Evans for high praise, holding him up as an example of a man who, unlike Eddy, knew how to give proper credit to his old mentor.

Yet Evans himself had actually made no mention of Quimby in his groundbreaking 1869 book, *The Mental Cure*.[*] Over the course of Evans's six works on mental therapeutics, written between 1869 and 1886, he made just one reference to Quimby, in his second book on the topic, *Mental Medicine*, in 1872.

No sooner did Dresser's pamphlet conclude its praise of Evans than it intoned more darkly: "Amongst those who were friends as well as patients of Quimby during the years from 1860 to 1865, and who paid high tributes to his discoveries of truth, and the consequent good to many people and to the world, was one who, for some strange reason, afterwards changed and followed a different course." Juxtaposing the good son, Evans, to the thankless offspring, Eddy, Dresser thus began his critique of the Christian Science founder, airing her past statements of praise for Quimby, noting her time spent with him, and finally concluding: "It is now easy to see just when and just where she 'discovered Christian science.'"

Arguments tend to coarsen rather than lighten over time. And the

---

* The book's references to a "positive mental force" gave the movement some of its hallmark language. References to a "Positive Mind" had also appeared earlier in the work of a medium and spiritual writer from New York's Hudson Valley, Andrew Jackson Davis, known as the "Poughkeepsie Seer." In 1847, Davis described the universe as the product of the "active energies of the Divine Positive Mind."

argument that Dresser embarked upon later solidified into a conviction about Eddy, one that got repeated to me this way by a librarian at a metaphysical center in 2012: "She stole all her ideas from Quimby!"

That, in lesser or greater terms, is the judgment many historical writers settled on in the Eddy-Quimby affair, with Evans often cast in a role that he never conceived for himself: the loyal scribe who owned up to his debt to Quimby, versus the less-forthcoming Eddy. In the heat of responding to the charges, Eddy worsened matters by dismissing Quimby's writing as "scribblings" and calling him "illiterate" in the *Christian Science Journal* in June 1887. In a term that would assume a life of its own, Eddy described Quimby in a letter in 1886 as an "ignorant Mesmerist."

Yet Eddy's attitude could also markedly soften. In the late 1880s, Eddy issued a series of autobiographical pamphlets on the development of Christian Science. With each successive revision, between 1885 and 1890, she grew fonder in her tone toward Quimby. In 1885, Eddy called her former teacher a "distinguished mesmerist" and a "sensible old gentleman with some advanced views on healing." By 1890, Eddy was referring to Quimby as "a humane, honest, and distinguished mesmerist. . . . He helped many sick people who returned home in apparently good health."

For Quimby's partisans, those branches were considered too small in spirit, and the continued reference to Quimby as a "mesmerist" was considered a tendentious and inaccurate characterization. After Julius Dresser died in 1893, his eldest son, Horatio, became a brilliant and prolific critic and historian of the New Thought movement. In 1902 Horatio began graduate studies at Harvard and became something of a protégé to William James, under whose tutelage he earned a Ph.D. in philosophy. Horatio also took up his father's crusade against Eddy. In a series of handwritten letters, the budding philosopher issued a challenge to Eddy. In a departure from the measured and erudite tone of most of Horatio's published works, his letters, at times, assumed an almost menacing quality. In 1900—with the Quimby controversy still boiling—Horatio, in elegant handwriting on the stationery of his family's metaphysical magazine, *The Higher Law*, addressed Eddy on February 3:

My dear Madame,

You may be surprised to hear from me, but I write to tell you that if you choose you can forestall a great downfall. If you come out frankly and acknowledge that the truth in your "revelation," the method of healing, etc., came from Dr. Quimby, (as your letters show that you know) the world will respect you and you will go down to history with a reputation. But if it all comes from outsiders, and after your death that which many are now withholding, it will be a very bleak record which will throw you into utter discredit.

I know those who have hunted up the whole history. . . . I know too of those who are preparing the evidence in regard to your indebtedness to Dr. Quimby, and I know what will come out, little by little, and that nothing can stop it *for the people demand it. It is utterly useless to try to head it off*, or to reiterate the old statements.

And so I advise you to make a clean breast of it.

If you do, these darker things may not be published.

I make this appeal both for your own sake, and because *every day that you delay you are permitting people to believe and to convince others of a falsehood.*

Around the same time that Horatio wrote to Eddy, he dispatched two letters, on January 15 and on February 3, to Judge Hanna, a high-ranking figure in the Christian Science church. "Books are being prepared," he warned Hanna in January, "which will inform people, and the Quimby Mss. are being held in reserve as the climax." The actual contents of the Quimby manuscripts remained a mystery. Quimby's son George refused to release his father's manuscripts. Acting for sometimes inscrutable reasons of his own, George had guarded the manuscripts from view during Eddy's lifetime, keeping them inside an iron safe, and at one point even shipping them to relatives in Scotland to avoid the possibility of their being subpoenaed. It was not until years later—after the death of George Quimby loosened his grip on his father's writings—that the climax Horatio foretold finally arrived.

With the cooperation of George's widow, Horatio succeeded in 1921 in publishing *The Quimby Manuscripts,* an edited compendium, in which the historian argued—to a good deal of influence—that Quimby alone was the forefather of the mental-healing movement, and the forerunner of Eddy's ideas. Yet the book settled no controversies. Because Quimby's manuscripts had been under lock and key for so many years, and given that the collection was composed of edited selections of a vast array of writings, the portions that Dresser published didn't decisively move the margins of the debate in one direction or another. In some sense the Quimby selections functioned more like a mirror in which either side saw the validation of its own long-held positions.

The book did, however, represent an important piece of scholarship, since prior to it Quimby's writings were virtually unavailable in any form. With legal wrangling never far away in the Quimby-Eddy debate, Horatio had to revise the book later that year after the Christian Science church objected to his use of some of Eddy's correspondence to Quimby.

As seen from his handwritten letters, Horatio sometimes seemed to relish playing the part of intellectual cop. Yet Horatio simultaneously wrote with depth and sincerity of feeling, as though he rued the whole mess. Writing to Hanna of his admiration for the mental-healing philosophy and fires of controversy surrounding it, Dresser offered on January 15: "I regret too more than I can say that the movement should have been so hampered. For I love its truth."

Eddy, too, could blunt the sharpness of her pen and express affection for Quimby in her historical pamphlets. All of the parties seem to have gotten caught up in a debate whose fires raged and engulfed them in ways they had never foreseen.

A Bridge Not Too Far

From the early 1880s to the early 1920s, the Quimby-Eddy debate produced literally hundreds of articles, books, pamphlets, and lectures, and it remains a touchstone in the history of mental healing. Yet the closer one gets to its flames the lesser the differences seem. If either side had moved an inch toward the other—Eddy acknowledging Quimby's role in preparing her for her later discoveries and the Dressers conceding the distinctiveness of Eddy's metaphysic—most of the larger points of contention could have been resolved. No really serious observer ever concluded that Eddy plagiarized Quimby, whose writings were sprawling, vast, and unfocused. Nor could any thoughtful person deny that Quimby was anything less than a profound early influence on the one-time anxious and sickly young Eddy, who sought him out at a period of broken marriage, parental death, and a shattered relationship with her only child.

Indeed, in the fall of 1862 in Quimby's household in Portland, Maine, Eddy seemed to embark on the mission of her life. But the manner in which Eddy carried out that mission, shaping its theology and structure, was largely—and brilliantly—her own. In the years following Quimby's death in early 1866, Eddy arduously, and with vision and intellect, codified Christian Science theology into her *Science and Health*. Followers considered it a revelatory work. Some observers, including Mark Twain, remarked on what they considered suspicious embellishments as the book passed through a series of revisions until its final edition in 1907. To critics, such changes suggested that the supposedly inspired text benefited from the hands of unseen writers and editors. But this kind of argument showed rigidity on the part of detractors more than it revealed concealed footsteps by Eddy, who was forthright about embarking on a continued refinement of her vision.*

Is there evidence that Eddy devised portions of *Science and Health* from

---

* Contemporary readers who approach *Science and Health* will find, contrary to commonly held views, not a turgid, difficult-to-get-through tome but, rather, a book of surprisingly sprightly passages that often anticipate present-day concepts in the uses of prayer and meditation for health.

Quimby's unpublished notes, to which she would have been privy as a student? As foreshadowed in Horatio Dresser's 1900 letters, a source no less august than the *New York Times* seemed to believe so. Six years before Eddy's death, in a withering, unsigned two-page spread published in July 1904, the *Times* depicted Mrs. Eddy as an ambitious student who picked over Quimby's writings. The article included side-by-side columns of text that appeared to reveal an echo of Quimby's notebook writings in the work of Eddy.

For her part, Eddy stuck to a version of events that depicted her not as a protégé but as a burgeoning teacher, even while under Quimby's care. "I re-arranged a few of his short essays," Eddy had written in 1888, "and gave him also some of my own writings which remained among his papers, and have been spoken of by persons unfamiliar with the facts as his own." Eddy's claim that some of her writings got integrated with Quimby's evoked indignation among partisans. Yet a review of Quimby papers shows that Eddy's claim that her writing, and that of others, got sorted in with Quimby's may have merit.

Quimby's son and executor, George—no friend to Eddy's memory— acknowledged that Eddy had spent personal time with Quimby, "sitting in his room, talking with him, reading his Mss., and copying some of them, writing some herself and reading them to him for criticism." A review of transcribed Quimby manuscripts shows that in 1868 Eddy had added a preface to the Quimby manuscript called "Questions and Answers," which she and a few other students circulated among themselves. The *New York Times*, in its two-column comparison of similarities between the Quimby and Eddy writings, erroneously included this Eddy passage in the Quimby column, crediting it to him and further muddying the waters about who wrote what. In the experimental atmosphere of Quimby's Portland circle, his unpublished manuscripts were copied and passed around, discussed and amended, dictated, revised, and recirculated. While the vast preponderance of Quimby's material is original to him, a portion grew out of collaborative efforts at clarification and refinement, with the occasional commingling of notes.

Eddy was a woman of literary skill and verve, a force of thought and originality whose publishing, theological, and educational institutions were already carefully formulated by the early twentieth century. Quimby, for all his prescience and originality, produced many pages of sometimes ponderous concepts, which were amassed into folios that remained unread decades after his death, and even in their edited versions are rarely penetrated today.

Quimby was a great Yankee mystic and foresightful healer—a thinker who set the stage for New England's mid-nineteenth-century renaissance of mental experimentation. He possessed a seminal, early understanding of the subconscious mind, which he fitfully sought to articulate. But Quimby was not the covert founder of Christian Science, nor was he the sole progenitor of mental healing. He was, rather, an instigator, a heroic experimenter, and a figure capable of inspiring intellects more disciplined than his own, among them Mary Baker Eddy, Warren Felt Evans, and Horatio Dresser.

From the ferment of these relationships emerged the philosophy of positive thinking. Swelling beyond the borders of the New England mental-healing scene, positive thinking would soon take on new names, such as New Thought and Unity, under which it entered American households. As its influence grew, however, the philosophy sometimes conflicted with the aims of the pioneers themselves.

chapter three

"to redeem defeat by new thought"

The day is plastic to you.

—Emma Curtis Hopkins, 1888

I n 1884, a Manchester, New Hampshire, housewife in her early thirties left behind her husband and young son to move to Boston to devote herself to Mrs. Eddy, as followers called the Christian Science founder.

The housewife's motives were at once evident and inscrutable. She had heard Eddy speak at a neighbor's home in October 1883 and was enthralled with her Christian Science philosophy. The younger woman's religious and intellectual interest intensified later that year when she traveled to Boston to take a class with Eddy. By August 1884, she resolved to leave her husband and nine-year-old son in order to join Eddy and the Christian Science fold in Boston. Though she hinted at abuse in her debt-ridden marriage to a high-school English teacher, all she wrote to Eddy was, "I am happily married to a young man . . . and have one sweet little son." Whatever the true nature of her home life, her passion was for Christian Science alone.

This was Emma Curtis Hopkins. A mystic, a suffragist, and a brilliant student of Christian Science, she seemed fated to become one of Eddy's most trusted companions. Instead, she became a source of Eddy's ire—and later her competitor and scourge. The split between the Christian Science founder and her onetime student formed the opening of a chrysalis from which emerged a new and greatly popular strain of mind-power philosophy that went under the name New Thought.

From Apostle to Apostate

Emma Curtis Hopkins first encountered Mrs. Eddy in the fall of 1883 when the healer was visiting Manchester and staying at the home of one of her local students. Eddy's hostess prevailed upon her to deliver a short discourse on Christian Science to a group of visiting neighbors. Emma was among them. For her, hearing Eddy was like an intellectual parting of the Red Sea.

She was enthralled with Eddy's idea of a Divine Mind infusing all of life. By December, Hopkins wrote to Eddy saying that the same neighbor who had hosted her had cured Hopkins of "a late serious illness" using Christian Science methods. Hopkins told the Christian Science founder that she wanted to dedicate herself to her efforts. "I lay my whole life and all my talents, little or great, to this work," she wrote Eddy on January 14, 1884.

Before Hopkins left her home to join Eddy in the late summer of 1884, Eddy granted the erudite younger woman the visible and valued position of editor of the church's house organ, the *Journal of Christian Science* (renamed the *Christian Science Journal* in April 1885). Hopkins became the first person other than Eddy to hold that title. She was also given a place to live in the women's dormitory of Eddy's Massachusetts Metaphysical College in Boston. Hopkins asked only that Eddy not reveal that her job as the *Journal*'s editor paid no salary, so that her family wouldn't have further cause to question her judgment in uprooting herself. "I must go to Boston without letting anybody (my relatives, I mean) know that I go as editor of a paper without salary," she wrote to Eddy on August 16, 1884. For Hopkins the move meant a chance to study at the feet of the master, and that was everything she wanted.

She assumed editorship in September 1884, but by October 1885, little more than a year later and without any obvious warning, Hopkins found herself dismissed from the *Journal* and expelled from her room at the Metaphysical College's women's dormitory. All support was pulled out from under her—without even a clear explanation as to why. In an undated letter to Eddy, Hopkins complained: "I received a peremptory message from Dr. Frye [Eddy's secretary] to vacate my room at the college, accompanied by a notification from Mrs. Crosse that my services were no longer necessary on the *Journal* in view of the lack of funds."

The attractive and intelligent Hopkins came to believe that she had crossed Eddy's unwritten rule: never to make references to having your own communication with the Divine. This was something that Hopkins had fleetingly done in a September 1885 *Christian Science Journal* editorial, which otherwise defended Eddy from critics. In the offending piece, "Teachers of Metaphysics," Hopkins wrote: "I was made to know Him face to face of whom I had heard by the hearing of the ear as a name only." It was the kind of reference, however oblique, that could make Eddy uneasy.

"You remember that it was said the article *Teachers of Metaphysics* would get me in trouble," Hopkins wrote her friend Julia Bartlett on November 4, 1885. She went on to describe a chilling atmosphere:

> Everything I said and did after that was watched and exaggerated and reported. I really was under heavy fire mentally.

> If I were to report what the students said to me I could get them into trouble, but I never did, for deep under all sudden resentments, I heard the sweet chord strike in every student—worshipful, reverent love for their teacher. But they could not understand my complex way of expressing myself, nor know that I was digging for facts.

By "digging for facts," Hopkins was apparently referring to the Eddy-Quimby controversy. And in that matter she came down squarely on Eddy's side. "I saw all the letters said to be written by Mrs. E. to Dresser and Quimby and *not one of them* could be held as argument against her supreme originality," Hopkins wrote Bartlett. Yet a subtler conflict simmered below her inquiries.

The Freethinker

Hopkins was digging not only for facts but for ideas. She was apparently reading broadly in metaphysics, Eastern religions, and the occult. This, possibly more than her editorial, cut against the culture Eddy was establishing within the church. Perhaps wary of the slapdash manner in which Quimby's manuscripts had been handled, and the confusions and controversies that later resulted, Eddy strove for order and discipline within her fold.

By the 1880s, Christian Science had become a strict church, with a liturgy composed of prayers and readings dedicated to revealing the healing power of Christ. Eddy decreed that the church's core texts and practices would be subject to no adjustments, innovations, or outside influences. In the months following Hopkins's arrival, Eddy made it clear that students were not to go sampling the varieties of metaphysical literature that were abounding on the New England scene, from Theosophy to mind-cure.

Yet even before Hopkins was made editor of the *Christian Science Journal*, she had been forthright about her eclectic spiritual interests—and in the

Journal's pages, no less. In a short article Hopkins wrote for the *Journal* in April 1884, "God's Omnipresence," she stated: "There is Truth in every religious system of the world, else it would find no followers." Diffuse faiths, Hopkins argued, are "blessed evidence of the universal goodness and impartiality of God, that to every people and nation of the earth He has manifested Himself as Life, Truth, Holiness—and Health." To drive home her point, she hailed the common truths expressed through "the Buddhist Nirvana," "Algazel [or Al-Ghazali], a Mohammedan philosopher of the twelfth century," Spinoza, Confucius, the Zend-Avesta of Zoroastrianism, the Chandogya Upanishad, Hebrew and pagan traditions, and the Desatir, a collection of ancient Persian sacred writings that had been popularized by late-nineteenth-century Theosophists.

At an early stage Hopkins was openly, even insistently, eclectic. This adds another layer of perplexity to her expulsion. Eddy was obviously aware of the breadth of Hopkins's outlook—indeed, it could be argued to Eddy's credit that Hopkins's article proved no barrier to her being named editor. Why then the split? It may have arisen from Eddy's growing concern to curb some of the larger personalities in the movement. These included women such as Ursula Gestefeld, an energetic student of Eddy's and contemporary of Hopkins, who in 1888 published her own interpretation of Christian Science. Eddy deeply disapproved of the move, which led to Gestefeld's public feud and split with the founder. Eddy would tolerate no unorthodox interpretations of Christian Science, and especially not from students setting up independent followings or experiments of their own. On this count, Eddy was unyielding. Shaped by the brunt of court battles, and by the widespread pilfering of her vocabulary, Eddy eventually copyrighted the term *Christian Science* and by the mid-1880s effectively expelled any follower—no matter how gifted—who hinted at independent directions or committed the heresy of studying work from figures in the Quimby circle, especially Warren Felt Evans.

For violating these parameters, many of her most intrepid students were frozen out. Indeed, by the late 1880s disputes and faction splits cost

Eddy an estimated one-third of her movement. It may be difficult for spiritual seekers today, who select freely among a vast array of offerings and ideas, to see why dedicated and growing numbers of people would have flocked into such a conservative, if not stringent, atmosphere. For all Eddy's rigidity, her ideas could also reflect great humanity and compassion. The bedside prayer treatments she devised and taught to Christian Science practitioners were vastly gentler than the often-harmful practices of late-nineteenth-century medicine. Christian Science practitioners did something that would remain almost unheard-of in medicine through much of the early twentieth century: When sitting and praying at the bedside of patients, they paid attention to the moods, fears, and emotional needs of the individual. For suffering people, it was a radically new experience. In a sense, Eddy's theology formed an unrecognized influence on the growth of humanistic medicine in the late twentieth century.

Moreover, American medicine in the nineteenth century had no standard licensing procedures, and late into the century backwoods physicians persisted in the "heroic" remedies of bloodletting, narcotics, alcohol, weeping wounds, and mercury ingestion, methods that were used even on children. The routines of heroic medicine were especially dangerous for women. In Victorian-age America the diagnosis of hysteria, or neurasthenia, was frequently applied to women and implicitly cemented the idea of female health as inherently fragile. Physicians sometimes regarded the uterus as the seat of the symptoms of depression or hysteria, and they subjected female patients to almost inconceivably grim protocols. In such cases, noted historian Gary Ward Materra, "treatments might include leeching, injections, ovariotomies, and/or cauterization of the clitoris. Leeches were placed on the vulva or on the neck of the uterus, and sometimes the leeches progressed into the uterus itself, causing acute pain. Cauterization was accomplished by chemicals such as nitrate of silver or hydrate of potassa, or by a white-hot iron, and cauterization treatments were performed several times at intervals of a few days."

Eddy sought to keep women out of what may have been the least healthy place for them in the Victorian age: the examination room. While Christian Science was never a politicized movement, Eddy presented an impressive, even extraordinary, figure as the first female leader, both intellectually and spiritually, of a major American faith.

Women, in particular, flocked into Eddy's movement.* Often they were deeply intelligent, independent, and driven by the liberating atmosphere of a female-led church. Those who remained within the Eddy fold, either long or short term, often experienced a sense of personal agency. Anyone who found relief through Christian Science treatments could, in turn, train to become a practitioner. This summoned up feelings of equality not only in matters of health but often in religious and social matters, as well.

Ironically, when Eddy shunned those followers who were deemed overly ambitious or unorthodox, she unintentionally created a cohort of ardently curious, dedicated—and churchless—experimenters, many of whom had come to believe that divine laws could be experienced, and wielded, in modern life. Set loose from a congregational setting, this brigade of spiritual freethinkers included a large number of women who had once been drawn to Eddy as a model of female leadership.

This was the backdrop for the arrival, and sudden departure, of Emma Curtis Hopkins, at one time among the most promising and magnetic of Eddy's converts. If Hopkins had come and gone quickly, she just as swiftly developed into an independent and popular teacher on her own terms. Indeed, Hopkins's post–Christian Science career formed a wave of influence that is still being felt on the spiritual scene today.

---

* The predominance of female Christian Scientists was striking. In 1900, for example, of 2,564 Christian Science practitioners, or trained healers, 79 percent were women; ten years later, of 4,350 practitioners, 89 percent were women.

The Metaphysical Midwest

Forced onto her own resources in 1885, Hopkins ventured to Chicago, where she established herself as an independent teacher of metaphysical healing. Chicago was an exciting and natural destination for maverick spiritual seekers in the late nineteenth century.

When Hopkins settled there, the midwestern city already hosted large circles devoted to mind-cure and Christian Science, stocked with followers and ex-followers of Eddy's. Chicago also had thriving subcultures in Theosophy, occultism, and metaphysical publishing. The city was home to A. J. Swarts's *Mental Science Magazine*, the journal that had featured the final interview with Warren Felt Evans. Ironically, Hopkins had criticized Swarts from the pages of the *Christian Science Journal* in July 1885 for synthesizing sundry metaphysical methods into Christian Science, the very thing that she was later suspected of. Hopkins was quick to patch things up with Swarts, and the two ex–Christian Scientists were co-editing his magazine by March 1886.

Chicago offered one more attractive feature—it took Hopkins far away from her New England roots, where there would be no explaining to do over departing her family, only to see her relations with Eddy wither. While Hopkins visited her siblings at High Watch Farm in Kent, Connecticut, she never again settled in New England.*

For the next ten years the enterprising seeker threw herself into Chicago life. By Hopkins's side was another freshly minted apostate of Christian Science, former Eddy student Mary H. Plunkett. Plunkett was a fiercely independent figure whose multiple marriages, children outside of wedlock, and advocacy of free love made her an anomaly in the buttoned-up Eddy world. An outspoken spiritual experimenter, Plunkett was fated to last no longer than Hopkins within Eddy's circle.

---

* Hopkins continued a relationship of sorts with her husband, George. The two did not divorce until 1900 (after which he remarried), and George visited her at least twice in Chicago. Less clear are Hopkins's relations with her son, John. He was apparently left in the care of relatives back in New England. John died in 1905 at age thirty, probably of influenza. At the time he was living near his father in Manchester, New Hampshire.

Historian Stephen Gottschalk reckons that Plunkett, who had be-friended Hopkins while she was editing the *Journal*, encouraged the new convert in expanding her spiritual horizons. The women's friendship may have deepened Eddy's suspicion. In any case, Plunkett served as a source of encouragement to Hopkins after they relocated to Chicago. The two women collaborated in independent Christian Science classes and healing sessions, and in 1887 they launched a journal, *Truth: A Magazine of Christian Science*. Hopkins, like other ex-students, continued to use the term *Christian Science*, to Eddy's deep chagrin.

But Hopkins and Plunkett drifted apart within three years of land-ing in Chicago. Plunkett traveled to New York, where she frenetically embarked on new metaphysical ventures and schools. After a botched effort to patch things up with Eddy in 1889, and a new marriage to a younger man (who turned out to be a bigamist and embezzler), Plunkett departed America for New Zealand. Following further marital breakups, and factional splits within the metaphysical movements she had started, Plunkett took her own life there in 1901 at age fifty-three.

Hopkins remained rooted in Chicago, where she built a growing and respected reputation as a teacher. In classes, lectures, and mental-visualization sessions, she instructed seekers, first from the Midwest and soon from many other parts of the nation, on how to use the divine power of thought. She fostered an atmosphere of encouragement, open-ness, and possibility. Hopkins's theology edged away from Eddy's focus on health and illness, and she began to expound her own variant of "Christian Science"—remaking the philosophy as an overall metaphysi-cal approach to happiness.

In a manner inconceivable to Eddy, though foreseen in Hopkins's earliest articles, the ex-disciple employed ideas from Kabbalah, Bud-dhism, and Hinduism, as well as occult teachings from Theosophy. Theosophy was an esoteric spiritual movement cofounded in 1875 by the widely traveled Russian noblewoman Madame H. P. Blavatsky, who claimed tutelage under hidden spiritual masters, and spoke compellingly of an occult philosophy that formed the basis for the world's faiths. This ideal seems to have struck a chord with Hopkins. The Chicago teacher at times seemed to struggle in her class notes to make reference to every esoteric or Eastern tradition one could possibly cite. At one point she validated the insights of mental science through "the written statement of Eadras," "the oral teachings of the Hebrew lawgiver Moses," "the Christian Bible and Hindu Sacred Books, Egyptian Ancient Teachers, Persian Bibles, Chinese Great Learning, Oriental Zohar, Saga, and many others." The many others included "Hermetic philosophy, Chaldean inner laws, the Vedanta, Brahmin tenets, and Pythagorean conclusions." Given that these references appeared in 1888—three years after Hopkins left the Eddy fold—it is not always clear how deeply read she really was in such material.

While Eddy would not have recognized the Hopkins philosophy, the former student still venerated Eddy and echoed key concepts of her work, such as the illusory nature of evil, illness, and the material world. "*There is no matter*," Hopkins told students, in the classic Eddy vein, and continued: "*There is no sensation in matter.* . . . *There is no sin, sickness, or death.*" All that we perceive as matter or reality, she insisted, is permeable to the ever-flowing power of thought, which Hopkins saw as a divine instrument belonging to mortal men and women—a fissure with the Eddy approach, which held that God alone was reality and man was an illusion.

Nonetheless, Hopkins continued to apply the term *Christian Science* to her classes and publications, and for years continued to see Eddy as her inspiration, if not her teacher. If Hopkins had hoped for reconciliation, though, it never came. "Oh, if you could only have been mental enough to see what I might be and do," she wrote Eddy, for the last time, on Christmas Day of 1886, "and given me time to work past and out of the era through which I was passing when Mrs. Crosse suddenly ordered me to leave." There was no reply.

But Eddy had her ear to the ground about Hopkins and her ventures. She wrote in the *Christian Science Journal* in April 1887: "If one half of what I heard of Mrs. Hopkins teaching on the subject of Christian Science is correct she is deluding the minds she claims to instruct."

In what may have been a reaction to the Hopkins episode, Eddy that same year amended the constitution of her Christian Scientist Association to stipulate that no one could be a member "who does not use for his textbooks The Bible and *Science and Health*, or who uses any other textbooks in this cause." The following year Eddy published in the *Journal* a set of rules that prohibited teachers or students from studying books on mind-healing other than Eddy's own.

"These teachers shall supply themselves and their students with no literature, on Christian Science Mind-healing," Eddy wrote in April 1888, "except such as is used by my College, and shall require their students to abide by this condition."

Hopkins's departures, meanwhile, grew increasingly radical. She encouraged the use of affirmations for personal happiness, which had been pioneered by Warren Felt Evans. She gamely expanded upon Evans's idea that the mind is an engine of well-being. "The day is plastic to you," she told students. "Write on its still walls your decree that the good and true are victorious already. Be explicit. Name the special good you would see through to pass. Declare that it is brought to pass already." (While Hopkins's phraseology could sound surprisingly contemporary, it partly echoed earlier works by Ralph Waldo Emerson, who in his 1836 essay "Nature" wrote of "the plastic power of the human eye.")

In addition to vesting powers of manifestation to the individual, Hopkins extolled Evans's concept that within man dwells an Inner God, an extension of the Divine. In terms that would have repulsed Eddy— and that became familiar lexicon of the New Age movement in future years—Hopkins spoke freely of a "God-Self" within. "When the judgment faculty awakens," Hopkins wrote, "then the divine Self of you shines and puts all the dark pictures, which the senses make, quite away."

Eddy again made her displeasure known in the pages of the *Christian Science Journal* in March 1888 where she assailed the "dishonesty—yea, fraud" in the "verbose lectures of Mrs. Emma Curtis Hopkins. She adopts my ethics, or talks them freely, while departing from them."

By the time Eddy made those statements Hopkins's following had grown beyond Chicago. She had taught classes across the West, from Kansas City to San Francisco, and had also made tours of Milwaukee and New York City. In 1888, alumni of Hopkins's classes could be found in seventeen branches of the Hopkins Metaphysical Association, from Maine to California. Hopkins not only offered a looser atmosphere than the Eddy classes, but evinced an ability to remake mystical ideas as tools for personal fulfillment and problem solving. She seemed to provide immediate solutions, without Eddy's demanding and radical metaphysic of viewing all of material life as illusory.

"Her instruction not only gives understanding to the student by which he can cure the ills of himself and others," wrote one early follower, "but in many instances those who enter her classes confirmed invalids come out at the end of the course perfectly well. She dwells so continually in the spirit that her very presence heals and those who listen to her are filled with new life."

Many of Hopkins's students noted the encouragement and possibility they experienced in her presence. Wrote another: "Her brilliance of mind and spirit was so marked that the very few could follow in her metaphysical flights, yet she had marked power in quickening spirituality in her students."

In a further counterpoint to Eddy, Hopkins urged followers to write, teach, and freely spread the word. In this way, her students became the driving figures of the New Thought movement in the next generation. They included Charles and Myrtle Fillmore, founders of Unity, a widespread Kansas City–based healing ministry of magazines, books, and classes; Ernest Holmes, the founder of Science of Mind, an influential twentieth-century mind-power philosophy; Malinda Cramer, who spearheaded the Divine Science movement, which gained popularity in San Francisco and Denver;* the widely read prosperity author and

---

* Cramer is often cited as taking a class with Hopkins in 1887 in San Francisco—though this is sometimes disputed.

suffragist Helen Wilmans; writer William Walker Atkinson, who built
a robust metaphysical publishing business in Chicago; Annie Rix Mil-
itz, who founded Homes of Truth spiritual centers throughout the West
Coast; Frances Lord, an energetic British student who devised some of the
earliest mental wealth-building methods in the late 1880s; Alice Bunker
Stockham, one of the nation's first female physicians and a widely read
feminist who advocated a new model of sexual parity in Victorian-era
marriages; and the inspirational poet Ella Wheeler Wilcox, who penned
the world-famous lines: "Laugh, and the world laughs with you; Weep,
and you weep alone."

These were the foundational figures of mind-power spirituality—
what would later be known as New Thought.

"Woman's Hour Has Come"

Hopkins and her many female students inherited from Eddy a sense of
feminine social mobility as much as a spiritual philosophy. "It is not an
exaggeration," wrote feminist scholar Margery Fox, "to describe Christian Science in the early years as largely a religion in which women
helped other women overcome suffering." As such, Christian Science
and the early mind-power movement provided some of the nation's earliest and most visible forms of independent female leadership.

The Christian Science church had a pronounced awareness of having
a woman at its helm, and of the maternal qualities of God. The main
sanctuary in Boston was termed the Mother Church. Eddy spoke of a
"Father-Mother God." The cover of each issue of Eddy's *Christian Science
Sentinel* featured two classically robed female figures bearing lamps and
gazing at one another from the margins of the page. Beneath each figure
were two lines by Henry Wadsworth Longfellow:

A lady with a lamp shall stand
In the great history of the land,

A noble type of good,
Heroic womanhood.

Nor was Eddy indifferent to the social dimensions of her work. "Civil law," she wrote in *Science and Health*, "establishes very unfair differences between the rights of the two sexes" but "Christian Science furnishes no precedent for such injustice."

"Eddy's very life," wrote religion scholar Gage William Chapel, "stood as an example of the emancipated woman." Yet, for all of the church's feminine imagery, it would be a mistake to conclude that Eddy's congregation directly espoused an emancipatory or suffragist outlook. Eddy viewed social equality as a just value but not as a parallel cause or campaign. "Christian Science promoted the exclusive authority of one woman," noted historian Ann Braude, "rather than promoting women's leadership as a principle."

Hopkins, however, was more explicit in devising her movement as an emancipatory vehicle. Still relying upon Eddy's vernacular, Hopkins in 1888 founded her Chicago-based Christian Science Theological Seminary. When Hopkins's first class of seminarians graduated on January 10, 1889, the class comprised twenty-two students—of whom twenty were women. To some early feminists, it was a signature moment.

Louisa Southworth, a literary collaborator to Elizabeth Cady Stanton, spoke at the graduation ceremony on Chicago's South Side. Southworth proclaimed the day "the Ceremony of the New Era, the ordaining of women by a woman, and the sending forth to do both moral and physical healing by the power of the Spirit."

The graduation ceremony's main speaker was Elizabeth Boynton Harbert, a suffragist and the women's editor of the *Chicago Daily Inter-Ocean*. Harbert declared it previously unimaginable to stand before a class of female seminarians. Before that day, Harbert said, "it seemed impossible that our desire to preach (or secure for women the recognized right to tell the unhappy and ignorant of the wonderful love of the Creator) could ever be fulfilled"—but now "woman goes forth to proclaim the radiant realities of the Good."

The most stirring oratory belonged to Hopkins—a woman who little more than three years earlier was without home, family, or resources. Hopkins described the students assembled before her in terms she might have once used for herself:

> Their hearts being moved with compassion, have strength-ened their judgment till they cry out with one voice against the old dispensation and with one voice declare for a new and a true, where the poor may be taught and befriended, women walk fearless and glad, and childhood be safe and free.

The same month, Hopkins wrote in her magazine *Christian Science* (again, taking her title from Eddy) that a new era of spirit was dawning—a time when "woman's hour has come," and all would "see how woman, the silent sufferer and meek yoke-bearer of the world is stepping quite out of her old character or role, and with a startling rebound from her long passivity is hurling herself against the age with such force and bold decision as to make even her friends stand aghast!"

Hopkins allied her movement with political causes. The previous fall she placed her student association in coalition with the Women's Federal Labor Union to campaign for improved labor conditions for Chicago's maids and working girls. Several of Hopkins's female students—who had a strong knowledge of the Bible and a passion for social equity—became editorial collaborators to Elizabeth Cady Stanton on *The Women's Bible*, the feminist pioneer's massive revision of Scripture. (I consider Stanton's forays into mind-power in the next chapter.)

But Hopkins chiefly focused her energies on producing new gradu-ates from her seminary. In so doing, she laid tracks that went beyond establishing a congregation or a new breed of spiritual practitioners. Rather, Hopkins's students began to transform the makeup of the American ministry. Historian J. Gordon Melton estimates that "approximately 90 percent of Hopkins's students were women who left her classes to assume roles as professionals in the religious community. She actually ordained over 100 ministers who moved on to create centers and mobilize a mass following (and in the process became the first female in modern history to assume the office of bishop and ordain other females to the ministry)."

The students that Hopkins ordained in 1889 and in the years ahead, as well as the pupils whom the Hopkins graduates in turn tutored, formed a cohort of women's religious leadership from Massachusetts to the Pacific Coast. This body of workers established ministries, publishing houses, spiritual learning centers, journals, and metaphysical churches. Their efforts made female religious leadership into a gradually accepted fact of American life. By the time the dramatic and nationally known Protestant evangelist Aimee Semple McPherson began her rise to fame with tent revivals in 1915, female graduates of the Hopkins seminary had already been on the American spiritual scene for more than twenty-five years.

The Dawn of New Thought

As the influence of Hopkins and other mind-power practitioners grew in the early 1890s, Mrs. Eddy tightened control on the term Christian Science. She wanted it forever out of the hands of apostates, and sometimes sued people who used it without her permission.

The Hopkins brand of mind-power philosophy started to be called by different names. Inventive and original labels popped up, usually from her students: Divine Science, Mental Science, Science of Right Thinking, Christian Healing, Christian Theosophy, Faith-Cure, Truth-Cure, and Thought-Cure.

Yet a phrase used by Ralph Waldo Emerson seemed to capture the movement's broadest ideals: New Thought. In December 1858, Emerson began delivering a lecture called "Success," which he published as an essay in 1870. In it he wrote: "To redeem defeat by new thought, by firm action, that is not easy, that is the work of divine men."

Emerson had loosely used "new thought" earlier. "There are new lands, new men, new thoughts," he wrote in "Nature" in 1836. But it was in the context of "Success," and the broader exposure it received in 1870, that the phrase seemed to stick. *To redeem defeat by new thought.* The precept seemed not only to define the goals of the burgeoning movement but also the life path of Hopkins and its progenitors.

By the mid-1880s the term "new thought" began circulating in mental-healing books and journals. Eddy's ex-student Edward J. Arens used it several times in his 1884 book *Old Theology in Its Application to the Healing of the Sick*, writing, "we live the new thought, and it becomes attached to us as a part of us" and "we enter into a new thought,—a spiritual thought of things that are real and eternal."

A key reference to "new thought" appeared in 1887 in *Condensed Thoughts About Christian Science*, a pamphlet by a Chicago homeopathic physician and Swedenborgian named William Henry Holcombe. Holcombe, who had studied with Hopkins's student Frances Lord, wrote: "New thought always excites combat in the mind with old thought, which refuses to retire."*

In 1892, journalist Prentice Mulford fatefully and prominently featured the term in his essay "The Accession of New Thought," in which he described the new metaphysical perspective. In 1894, *New Thought* became the title of a Massachusetts mental-science journal. The following year, a prominent group of mental-science thinkers began using the term in their Boston Metaphysical Club. (This circle, which included Horatio Dresser and writer Henry Wood, should not be confused with an earlier Metaphysical Club, a philosophy group formed by William James and

---

* Horatio Dresser, in his 1919 *A History of the New Thought Movement*, said Holcombe "was the first writer in the mental-science period to employ the term 'New Thought,' capitalized, to designate the new teaching in the sense in which the term is now used." While this reference is widely repeated, the Holcombe pamphlet, in fact, does not show that capitalization. Nonetheless, Holcombe's buoyant and accessible work did call out the phrase.

Oliver Wendell Holmes Jr. in 1872 in Cambridge, Massachusetts.) And, finally, in February 1899, a "New Thought Convention" convened in Hartford, Connecticut; a larger follow-up was held in October in Boston.

The movement had found its name. The term *New Thought* encompassed the mind-power culture's highest aims: The ascension of man through his thoughts. And it suggested none of the old ties to Mrs. Eddy.

The name New Thought did not please everyone. One of Hopkins's most influential students, Charles Fillmore, founder of the Unity School of Christianity in Kansas City, was an early dissenter. In the published proceedings of the 1899 New Thought Convention at Boston, Fillmore is listed as an officer—but with an asterisk beside his name, denoting that by the time the convention program was at the printer's the Missourian had resigned. Fillmore wanted no association between his sizable Unity ministry and the movement grouped under New Thought.

"New Thought," Fillmore wrote in 1905, "is the common denominator of a complex and often contradictory mass of metaphysical doctrines which have sprung up in the past few years." Nor did he like what he detected about the movement's focus on acquisitiveness. "What may be termed the Mental Science School," Fillmore continued, "holds that God is not a being of Love and Wisdom, but a force of attraction." By contrast, Fillmore saw his Unity movement in more traditionally Christian terms, and wanted his healing philosophy called "Practical Christianity."

To drive home the point, Fillmore twice separated his large ministry from the International New Thought Alliance, or I.N.T.A., the umbrella organization that grew from the 1899 conventions. The first Fillmore split occurred in 1906, when he complained again about the diffuse qualities of New Thought after attending that year's I.N.T.A. convention in Chicago. "I asked several people to give me a definition of New Thought," he wrote, "and they differed greatly in their concepts. It dawned on me that the name 'New Thought' had been appropriated by so many cults that . . . it had ceased to express what I conceived to be absolute Truth."

Fillmore returned to the I.N.T.A. in 1919, however, and even invited the organization to hold its next annual meeting in his hometown of Kansas City. It did so in 1920, and Fillmore seemed mollified. He attended the following year's convention in Denver. Yet just months after expressing his public satisfaction with the relationship, Fillmore once more, and with finality, broke away in March 1922. Many New-Thoughters were dismayed at the reversal—as were a number of Fillmore's own students, who demanded an explanation.

"We have proclaimed Jesus Christ as the head of our work," Fillmore wrote that year. "This the I.N.T.A. has refused to do, although it claims to carry out Christian principles. When we advocated a change of name to include the word 'Christian' the proposal was quickly hushed up in the executive board meeting. The argument was that, although I.N.T.A. was a Christian movement, it should not put anything in its name to antagonize non-Christians who might otherwise be induced to join."

Fillmore had been working behind the scenes on this measure and several other doctrinal demands, to which the determinedly loose New Thought alliance would not bend. He cut all ties.

Fillmore's misgivings aside, most of Hopkins's students embraced the term New Thought, or proved adaptable to it. Many students and practitioners liked the elasticity and looseness of the term, the very things that gave Fillmore an allergy. What's more, the name New Thought finally gave the mental-science culture a clear future outside of Eddy's shadow—with Hopkins celebrated as the young movement's "teacher of teachers."

Yet even as all tributaries seemed to be flowing to her, Hopkins grew weary of being the figurehead of a spiritual movement. As seen by the Fillmore kerfuffle, even movements as liberal and porous as New Thought were prone to internal squabbles, doctrinal disputes, and splits. After ten years of playing a public role, Hopkins yearned to spend time alone.

In 1895, the teacher departed Chicago for New York and eventually took up residence in a two-room suite at the Iroquois Hotel on West Forty-Fourth Street in Manhattan. She lived there for much of the remaining three decades of her life, receiving guests and students, though rarely leaving her quarters or venturing beyond the midtown block. (Her taste for solitude may have factored into her decision years earlier to leave her New Hampshire family.) Hopkins continued seeing students in her reception room, but she wanted few worldly attachments. "I do not want to *own furniture*," she wrote a friend on September 16, 1919.

The Prosperity Gospel

Even during the Chicago years when Hopkins inaugurated her free-wheeling mental-science philosophy, New Thought did not yet look and sound the way it would to Americans of later generations. Its basic language and methods were in place, but one familiar emphasis was missing: money.

The movement's dominant aim was thinking one's way to *health and happiness*—not to riches. Hopkins remained within the gravity of Eddy's teachings about the corruption of the material world. In 1888 she cautioned students against the "vainglory" of "the riches, profits, and advantages of material transactions." It was a perspective from which she never wavered. "Life," Hopkins wrote a friend on November 20, 1919, "is not made up of bric a brac."

While America had long possessed a literature that celebrated the pursuit of success—from the bootstraps principles of Benjamin Franklin's *The Way to Wealth* to the rags-to-riches tales of Horatio Alger—money-getting was not a primary theme or even an accepted idea among most inspirational thinkers of the nineteenth century.

The New Thought poet Ella Wheeler Wilcox conceded in 1902 that the teachings of mind-power could be used for wealth. "But woe unto him who cultivates his mental and spiritual powers only for this purpose," she wrote, adding: "The clear thinker and careful observer must realize there is one and only one main object in life—*the building of character*."

Wilcox and New Thought's other leading lights taught in the vein of William Wordsworth's poem "Character of the Happy Warrior," which depicted the soulful warrior as one who "makes his moral being his prime care." Such a tone prevailed in England, as well, where nineteenth-century writers adapted some of the motivational themes heard in America.

The prosperity gospel that most people associate with New Thought did not take shape until the 1890s—and even then it grew slowly and fitfully. Two causes contributed to its growth.

First, the American public in the late nineteenth century experienced a flurry of economic changes, both promising and disconcerting. For the first time, a wave of mass-produced consumer goods, from glassware to furniture, appeared on store shelves, in shop windows, and in catalogues. As these items proliferated, the economy itself was shifting from its agricultural foundation to a more urban-centered, manufacturing base. Money and markets were spreading, as were the cravings and anxieties of consumerism.

Second, in addition to economic changes, the late nineteenth century saw medical advances that brought overdue improvements into the examination room, easing the desperation of patients and, for the first time, creating reliable medical protocols. "Heroic" medicine vanished, and mainstream procedures grew safer and more effective. In response to calls from allopathic physicians, state legislatures also began to regulate and license medical professionals, with an eye toward restricting or eliminating the activities of mind-power practitioners and other "irregular" healers, such as homeopaths and botanists.

These shifts in economics and medicine changed the needs of the American public, and the face of New Thought.

chapter four

from poverty
to power

The working class may become the
master class whenever they will
begin to do things in a Certain Way . . .

—Wallace D. Wattles, *The Science of Getting Rich,* 1910

The 1890s was an age of medical progress. Ads for patent medicines, from digestive syrups to baldness-curing creams, could still be found in most magazines, but medicine, like other fields of study, became more scientific and systematized. Colleges began graduate programs in the sciences and psychology. Physicians and researchers made dramatic advances in treating and preventing microbial diseases. The American public for the first time began to view doctors as figures to be trusted rather than feared. State legislatures and courts, meanwhile, started to stringently scrutinize the mental-healing philosophies.

In several well-publicized cases, patients had died after receiving Christian Science treatments rather than normative medical care. No prosecutions resulted, as the courts were unable to demonstrate that conventional treatment would have resulted in different outcomes. In the wake of the controversy, the state of Massachusetts began to pass licensing laws designed to prevent religious healers from calling themselves medical practitioners. Other states had been tightening medical laws for several years: as early as 1880 the New York state legislature barred magnetic, or Mesmerist, healers from practicing medicine.

In Boston, Harvard philosopher William James grew alarmed that such moves would dampen the country's mood of inquiry and experiment. In 1894 and 1898, James personally lobbied against licensing bills in Massachusetts intended to prohibit nontraditional medical practice, particularly the activities of Christian Scientists and mind-healers. Both times James won measured victories. He believed that mental healing was an unknown territory filled with possibilities, and that to place limits on it so early in its existence could stifle its potential. "I regard therapeutics as in too undeveloped a state for us to be able to afford to stamp out the contributions of all fanatics and one-sided geniuses," James told a friend in 1894.

James personally used mind-cure and Christian Science methods several times between 1887 and 1909, receiving treatment for insomnia, depression, anxiety, and angina. He found the results could be at once tantalizingly effective and frustratingly elusive—a fact over which he agonized. "I think," he wrote a friend in 1909, "there is a certain impediment in the minds of people brought up as I have been, which keeps the bolt from flying back, and letting the door of the more absolutely grounded life fly open. They can't back out of their system of finite prudences and intellectual scruples, even though in words they may admit that there are other ways of living, and more successful ones."

James's position was difficult for his narrowest critics to understand. It wasn't that he wanted to be *right* about the merits of mind-cure; rather he wanted to be *thorough*. He believed that allopathic medicine remained mired in its own brands of half-tested ideas, blind spots, and a general lack of transparency. Hence, James encouraged an open search for clinical possibilities—in both traditional and irregular fields of practice. Above all, he loathed seeing experiments in mental therapeutics stilled or stigmatized.

James brought to the mental-healing question the same passion for intellectual inquiry that fueled his interest into laboratory research of claimed psychical and paranormal phenomena. He nurtured a truly constructive skepticism—an approach that would be lost on future generations of critics, who were often unable to balance intellectual discretion with radical inquiry.

"It seems to me," James wrote to a friend in 1898, "it is not a question of fondness or non-fondness for mind-curers [heaven knows I am not fond and can't understand a word of their jargon except their precept of assuming yourself to be well and claiming health rather than sickness which I am sure is magnificent] but of the *necessity* of legislature interference with the natural play of things."

James's crusade for the open study and practice of mental healing came into public view in 1894. That year the Massachusetts state legislature was considering a bill prohibiting medical practice other than by physicians who held degrees from recognized medical colleges. In a letter of March 17, James protested the bill to the *Boston Evening Transcript*, naming three grounds for its rejection:

I.   It is too grandmotherly, and goes against the best political habits and traditions of our State.

II.   It adds but an infinitesimal degree of security to the citizens' chances of being faultlessly treated when sick.

III. It tends to obstruct the process of therapeutic knowledge.

To those reasons, James added one additional note, which drew upon the public's lingering mistrust of the mainline medical profession, even near the dawn of the twentieth century: "The *serious* therapeutic inadequacy which the population of Massachusetts, taken in bulk, is exposed to is the inadequacy of the regularly educated profession."

Within about two weeks, the legislature struck a compromise, which James supported. Mental-healers and other nontraditional practitioners could function as they wished but could not advertise themselves as doctors or M.D.s. "In principle," James wrote to the *Evening Transcript* on April 2, "such a bill seems to me excellent. The people have a right to know who is regular and who is irregular, and to follow their several affinities."

All sides seemed more or less placated with the compromise. Within four years, however, the legislature was considering a stricter amendment to the bill, one that would once more outlaw medical practice by any but regularly licensed M.D.s. This time, James personally appeared at the statehouse in Boston to oppose the move.

In a packed meeting room on March 2, before a crowd that spilled outside the doors, the Harvard philosopher spoke before the legislature's Committee on Public Health. His speech critiqued the persistence of a guild mentality among medical and research professionals. Cliquish thinking in any medical or professional culture, James said, served to elevate the opinions of those who are apprenticed within a given system, while disparaging or neglecting outsider perspectives. He asked the committee:

> How many graduates, recent or early, of the Harvard Medical School, have spent twenty-four hours of their lives in experimentally testing homeopathic remedies, or seeing them tested? Probably not ten in the whole Commonwealth. How many of my learned medical friends, who to-day are so freely denouncing mind-cure methods as an abominable superstition, have taken the pains to follow up on the cases of some mind-curer, one by one, so as to acquaint themselves

with the results? I doubt if there is a single individual. "Of such experience as that," they say, "give me ignorance rather than knowledge." And the Club-opinion of the Massachusetts Medical Society pats them on the head and backs them up. I don't blame any set of practitioners from remaining ignorant of all practice but their own. . . . But when ignorance and narrowness, instead of being humble, grow insolent and authoritative, and ask for laws whose only immediate result can be to consecrate and perpetuate them, then I think that every citizen interested in the growth of a genuinely complete medical science should rise up and protest.

In his typical style, James concluded by shaking off his scolding tone with a wry conclusion: "The death-rate is not rising, in spite of all quackery." The testimony represented James at his most skillful as a public intellectual. The committee unanimously voted down the bill. Yet it was not a complete victory for James. He was assailed in medical journals, including the *Boston Medical and Surgical Journal*, which called him "a spokesman of medievalism and an ally of quackery."

It was also clear that the licensure movement, with or without James at its back, was rapidly spreading. By the time of James's statehouse address, new licensing laws had been enacted in Ohio and New York, and were advancing elsewhere. During the 1890s, thirty-five states established some form of regulated licensure for medical graduates, and in fourteen of those states licensing was limited to graduates of board-approved schools. By the close of the decade, the Alaskan Territories alone lacked some kind of licensure laws.

Medical Progress

While James was concerned that the licensing legislation might cast a chill over experimentation and intellectual inquiry, the overall state of mainstream medicine was, in fact, dramatically and rapidly improving.

Before the 1890s, American medicine had, for generations, lagged behind the nation's progress in other areas of science. This was partly due to a lack of teaching and research facilities. At the start of the nineteenth century, only three hospitals existed throughout the country: in New York City, Boston, and Philadelphia.

Although Europe's medical science and caring institutions of the nineteenth century were not dramatically advanced over America's, Europeans benefited from a body of practical medical knowledge, from wound dressing to botanical remedies, which had gradually emerged from medieval guilds. Apprenticed apothecaries and informal healers ministered to dwellers of villages and industrial towns, while a higher class of physicians, who were trained in royal academies and universities, served the upper classes, who afforded them a good deal of respect. Europe's immigrants to America generally came out of farming and craft trades; few trained physicians (who might be able to teach others) crossed the Atlantic.

Because American towns had little means of educating physicians, people often were left at the mercy of self-taught, erratically trained doctors, who were rarely held in esteem. The situation could be particularly difficult in frontier territories. In 1850, a survey of medical practitioners in eastern Tennessee found that 201 physicians served a population of 164,000—and of those practitioners only 35 were graduates of some kind of regular school. Almost half said they had received no instruction, beyond personal reading.

The crisis in American medicine experienced a dramatic turnaround in the early 1890s. Two factors brought improvements. On the research front, the "Paris School," a late-nineteenth-century group of French biologists and physicians, developed advances in germ theory, which convinced doctors in Europe and America that many diseases arose from infections and disorders in specific organs. This finally ended the painful therapies of fluid-letting or bleeding, and introduced new protocols of sanitation and treatment of infections. Second, the Johns Hopkins Medical School opened its doors in 1893 with the express purpose of normalizing and standardizing the manner in which medical education and licensure functioned from state to state. Universities and medical schools began to model themselves on the Hopkins teaching program, which imported methods from German teaching hospitals and medical schools, including mentored residencies and research requirements. With these advances, the nation's medical profession began correcting the abusive practices that Christian Science and the mind-cure culture had arisen partly in response to.

Christian Science was not out of the picture in the new era—the church gained some flexibility from licensure regulations on grounds of religious freedom. Nor did Christian Science and the various mind therapies lose their sense of purpose. Indeed, James continued to experiment in these areas until his death in August 1910 (a year that also marked the passing of Mary Baker Eddy). But a good deal of the desperation that had once driven Americans to seek alternatives within mind-cure or Christian Science was lifting as the twentieth century opened.*

Hidden Forces

For all the medical changes of the early twentieth century, many Americans remained eager to explore—and, above all, to make practical use of—the hidden frontiers of the mind. Advances in science actually stoked rather than dampened this enthusiasm. The dawn of the century marked a rapid discovery of previously unseen forces. The physical sciences detected subatomic particles and pioneered the uses of x-rays, streaming

---

* Some newer ministries continued to emphasize healing. The early twentieth century saw the rise of the Pentecostal movement, which by the 1920s hosted its own thriving scene of tent revival meetings. These revivalist meetings often featured fervent faith-healings and medical prayers. While the healing dynamic never fully faded from Pentecostal and later Charismatic movements, two developments pushed healing to the backseat in that world, too. The first was a series of fraud allegations against faith-healers in the 1950s, and the second was a shift instigated in the late 1960s by the movement's most influential voice, Oral Roberts. In his publications and public statements, the Oklahoma-based minister and university founder began emphasizing prosperity over healing, a development that will be explored in Chapter 7. Hence, Pentecostalism traveled the same trajectory as New Thought, shifting its focus from healing to prosperity.

electricity, wireless signals, and radio waves. Physicians isolated viruses and microorganisms. Psychologists probed the unconscious roots of neurosis and trauma. On all fronts, scientific progress pointed to a world of covert influences.

Money itself could seem to emerge from out of unseen realms. The expansion of stock markets, bond trading, and share holding presented increasing numbers of people with a means of profit making no longer bound to the tangible exchange of goods and services. In turn, a thickening stream of consumer products appeared in the pages of catalogues and the windows and aisles of convenient, modern stores.

In his 1921 essay "My 'New-Thought' Boyhood," writer Charles Thomas Hallinan reflected on the changes he saw as he was growing up in Minnesota during the late nineteenth century: "A big department store—the first of its kind in the country—had sprung up in our raw, windy Western city. . . . That department store played the very devil with our peace of mind. It multiplied enormously the apparent necessities of life, and brought the luxuries just without our reach." To this material problem, many people sought a spiritual solution.

Americans began to ponder the question of how to use mental power to attract money. But this idea did not get its start in the brandy-addled minds of business barons sitting in gentlemen's clubs, or among gimlet-eyed hucksters devising get-rich-quick schemes. In actuality, the concept of a metaphysical approach to wealth was set into the public firmament by people with socially progressive and even radical instincts. As seen in the experience of the early graduates of Emma Curtis Hopkins's seminary, the New Thought movement represented a mosaic of seekers who had simultaneous impulses for avant-garde religion and radical politics.

A circle of turn-of-the century social progressives, who moved in between cultures of metaphysical experiment and political reform, saw the money-attracting powers of the mind as a path to social equity, a means of evening out and redistributing the balance of wealth. When such figures identified themselves politically, they were variously suffragists, democratic socialists, black liberationists, trade unionists, and animal-rights activists. Their values squared less with the business worldview of Gilded Age magnates than with the redistributive impulses of the "Social Gospel" and even the economic radicalism of Eugene V. Debs's Socialist Party of America. The prosperity gospel that dominates many of today's largest and most conservative evangelical churches begins with the story of these spirited radicals.

"God Is Not Poor"

An Englishwoman with a passion for suffragism helped bring the prosperity gospel to America. Her name was Frances Lord, and she journeyed to the United States as a guest of feminist leader Elizabeth Cady Stanton. Stanton sought Lord's assistance in devising *The Women's Bible*, a radical retelling of Scripture that recognized the role of women. But Stanton's helpmate quickly removed herself from this work in order to venture into metaphysical realms that developed on the edges of the women's rights movement.

Before coming to America, Frances Lord was known as an advocate of progressive education methods, as well as an early English translator of Norwegian playwright Henrik Ibsen. In 1882 Lord made the first English translation of Ibsen's *A Doll's House*. She was attracted by the radicalism of Ibsen's tale of Nora, the awakened housewife who determines to break free of her domestic role. Concerned that readers would mistake *A Doll's House* for children's literature, Lord retitled the play *Nora*.

In 1883, Elizabeth Cady Stanton and her daughter, Harriot, met Lord on a trip to England. Stanton found the English translator "a woman of rare culture." She also discovered Lord to be a woman of occult passions. Through Lord's influence, Stanton recalled, "my daughter and I had become interested in the school of Theosophy and read *Isis Unveiled* by Madame Blavatsky." Lord directed Stanton to other works that emerged from the occult revival generated by Blavatsky, including journalist A. P.

Sinnett's *The Occult World* and mystical writer Anna Kingsford's *The Perfect Way.*

"Full of these ideas," Stanton wrote, "I soon interested my cousins in the subject, and we resolved to explore, as far as possible, some of these Eastern mysteries, of which we had heard so much." Once back home in America, Stanton visited her cousin Elizabeth Smart Miller in Geneva, New York. The cousins tried to lure mystical thinker and Egyptologist Gerald Massey to travel from New York City to tutor them. But Massey was ill, and Stanton shifted her attention to other goals—specifically, a radical interpretation of Scripture intended to annotate and highlight the contributions of women in shaping the Judeo-Christian tradition. The project would consume Stanton for some nine years.

Stanton's re-visioning of Scripture grew out of a perspective she had developed during her study of philosophy in the 1860s. She grew particularly interested in the ideas of positivism—which held that the world, in all its facets, is governed by discernible laws. In the same way that nature and the cosmos function under cycles of immutable laws, Stanton reasoned, social laws would inevitably anoint women as the progenitors of a spiritual and societal revolution. But for women to commence this cycle, she believed, female intellects first needed to explore alternatives to orthodox Christianity and the limits it had placed on feminine accomplishment. This gave rise to Stanton's sympathies for Blavatsky and the female leaders of New Thought.

Stanton saw a reformulated Scripture as the ignition point of feminine awakening. Yet her closest confidant and collaborator, Susan B. Anthony, was, by the 1880s, uninterested in spiritual matters, of either the occult or traditional variety. To Anthony religion belonged to a dead past. "Barbarism does not grow out of ancient Jewish Bibles," she wrote Stanton, "but out of our own sordid meanness!!"

If Stanton was going to complete her feminist retelling of Scripture, she required new helpers. "It was perhaps this search for soul mates," wrote historian Kathi Kern, "that drew a hesitant Stanton toward the practice of Mind Cure and New Thought in the decade of the 1880s. Several new friendships beckoned her into the circles of these popular 'new religions.' "

In Stanton's eyes, Frances Lord had shown impeccable metaphysical, literary, and reformist instincts. In 1886 Stanton and Harriot appealed to Lord to travel to America and help them begin their project. Accepting the invitation, Lord reached Stanton's home in Tenafly, New Jersey, on August 4, 1886. Things started out well enough. "Miss Lord and I worked several weeks together," Stanton recalled. The younger woman "ran through the Bible in a few days, marking each chapter that in any way referred to women. We found that the work would not be so great as we imagined, as all the facts in teachings in regard to women occupied less than one-tenth of the whole Scriptures."

But Lord's interest soon wandered. She began hearing word of the mind-cure scene, and especially the classes being taught in Chicago by Emma Curtis Hopkins. Lord had complained of discomforts of the ear, eye, and leg, and she resolved to journey west to seek out mind-cure lessons. She experienced some early, encouraging improvements. Her experience in Chicago gave her the faith that mind-cure represented "a Great Social Reform" that would allow individuals—and women particularly—to assert control over their health.

Throughout 1887 and 1888, Lord was in and out of Chicago, where she took classes from Hopkins, purchased a New Thought–oriented newspaper called *The Woman's World*, and—in the mold of Hopkins's earliest student-practitioners—began teaching mind-cure methods herself.

Stanton had lost Lord's assistance, but that didn't deter her from enlisting other women in the New Thought world—including ex–Christian Scientist Ursula Gestefeld and suffragist Louisa Southworth, a speaker from the Hopkins graduation. Stanton wistfully wrote off Lord. "Miss Lord became deeply interested in psychical research," she concluded, "and I could get no more work out of her." This disappointment, however, did not mean the end of their friendship. By early 1887, Lord had persuaded Stanton and her daughter to enroll in a mind-cure class when they made a return trip to England. In the spirit of intellectual inquiry that marked Stanton's career, she agreed to take the metaphysical course, she told a friend, because "we are not fanatical on the question but searchers after truth."

Within the American New Thought scene, meanwhile, Lord had discovered her natural element. In the space of several months she became an independent teacher, a newspaper publisher, and, in fall of 1888, the author of a substantial and rigorous manual, *Christian Science Healing: Its Principles and Practice with Full Explanations for Home Students.* It was here that Lord struck the opening note of the prosperity gospel.

Lord's massive book focused chiefly on physical healing and emotional well-being, mostly by means of affirmations, prayers, and denial of the "false" conditions of illness or bodily pain. But Lord's most significant departure, toward the close of the book, was a "treatment" for overcoming poverty.

Lord provided a six-day program of affirmations and exercises to break down the mental bonds of poverty. On the first day, readers were to disabuse themselves of the idea that they were "unlucky," disadvantaged, or in any way lacking in the ability to become good earners, and declare:

> *God is my life; there is no other.*
> *God is not poor; I cannot be poor.*
> *God is my intelligence; I can see aright; I can see what is really there.*
> *God is my wisdom; I can judge rightly; I know what I ought to do.*
> *God is my will; I have no desire but to do what is right.*
> *God is my love; my path is pleasant.*

A notable element of the Lord affirmations was her emphasis on ethics. By the time the six-day program is ended, Lord reminded the reader: "As Spiritual life intensifies, the desire for mere possession of wealth always lessens." She assured that "Money will come to serve you when you are fit to rule it." She warned against the desire to " 'keep up appearances' " and to "extend the Ego artificially by having a share in all that is going on around, whether it concerns us or not."

For Lord, the extension of mind-cure methods into prosperity was entirely natural. Her aim was not self-inflation but liberation. Just as mental therapeutics could free the body from the former abuses of the medical profession, so, she believed, could the prosperity mind-set contribute to the liberation of women or working people from the strains of the Industrial Age, a goal that steadily gravitated to the center of New Thought.

Thoughts Are Things

The writer who most decisively advocated the wealth-building power of the mind is a journalist almost no one remembers: Prentice Mulford. In a sense, Mulford's work is the "missing link" in the positive-thinking movement's transition into a contemporary philosophy of personal success. Mulford's writing of the late 1880s reflects the crucial moment when the abstruse, nineteenth-century language of the movement fell away; in Mulford's work there emerged a remarkably modern and appealing vernacular, which won a vastly expanded audience for mind-power metaphysics.

In some ways, Mulford was the most important of all the early self-improvement writers. His personal life was itself an exercise in repeat transformations—and, toward its end, he struggled to live by the principles he pioneered.

Mulford was born to a wealthy Long Island family in 1834. His father's early death cut short his fortunes. At age fifteen, he was forced to leave school to support his mother and three sisters by running the family's sole remaining property: a four-story hotel in Sag Harbor, Long Island. After about four years the hotel failed. Day labor was too dull and dead-end a prospect for Mulford. The ambitious and curious young man instead went to the sea, joining the last leg of Sag Harbor's whaling industry.

By the late 1850s, with whaling in decline, Mulford found himself stranded in San Francisco. With the Gold Rush booming, he took up life as a prospector, working in mining camps among other displaced men. It was a punishing daily routine spent bending over, digging and panning. Readers were hungry for news about prospecting, which was heavily romanticized at the time. Although Mulford hadn't set his mind on becoming a writer, in late 1861 he began producing wry newspaper portraits of mining life, under the pen name "Dogberry." Unlike other writers, who made the Gold Rush seem like a great adventure, Mulford depicted its losses, hit-and-miss luck, and physical hardship. Miners saw him as a voice of their own.

By 1866, with his mining ventures stagnating and his freelance articles paying meagerly, Mulford finally got a break. He was offered an editing position at *The Golden Era*, a San Francisco literary journal whose contributors included Mark Twain and Ambrose Bierce. A friend recalled Mulford showing up in the city looking like "a weatherbeaten young man, as shy as a country boy, and with many traits that must have resembled Thoreau in his youth." Mulford recalled arriving with "an old gun, a saddle, a pair of blankets, an enfeebled suit of clothes and a trunk with abundant room for many things not in it."

Mulford's writing at *The Golden Era* contributed to a post–Gold Rush literary boom in San Francisco. Historian Franklin Walker considered Mulford one of a handful of writers whose muckraking, realistic portraiture helped birth that renaissance. Yet the former gold digger soon fell back on old business instincts (which, in actuality, were never very sharply honed). In 1872, Mulford raised five hundred dollars from local businessmen to send himself on a lecture tour of England to promote business opportunities in California, still a little-known place. Some biographers have viewed the English tour as an example of Mulford's guile, but it was a period as difficult as his gold-prospecting days. The writer-lecturer was forced to live on ten shillings a week, the equivalent of less than two dollars. The tour was more hardship than triumph.

Returning to America the next year, Mulford become a newspaper reporter in New York City. But in time he "grew thoroughly tired and sick of chronicling in short meter day after day the eternal round of murders, scandals, burglaries, fires, accidents and other events which people deem it indispensable to know and swallow after breakfast."

Bored and depressed—familiar themes in his life—and coming off a marital split, Mulford quit newspaper work and in 1883 spent fifty dollars building a cabin in the swampy woods of northern New Jersey, seventeen miles from New York City. He entered the woods to live like Thoreau, but the forest idyll became another disappointment. Lonely rainy days were difficult for him to bear. At such times, he recalled, "I raked up certain old griefs out of the ashes of the past, borrowed some new troubles out of the future and put them all under the powerful microscope of a morbid imagination, which magnifies the awful about a thousand times, and diminishes the cheerful."

Mulford experimented with using his mind to control his moods. "But I couldn't," he found. "I failed." Yet he clung to the belief that an assertive mind could bring light into the dark corners of life. "I do retain a faith in its curative properties for the blues, if long enough persisted in," he wrote in his diaries.

Mulford's struggles with depression gave him an idea for a new type of work. In 1884 he left the cabin to resume his writing, but in a fresh way that would allow him to pursue the topics of his choosing, without facing newspaper deadlines or a police blotter. That year he conceived of creating his own line of advice-oriented pamphlets. Although his mental therapeutics had failed in the woods, Mulford believed that the mind, while perhaps too weak on its own, could summon spiritual laws to its aid.

He had gotten his first inkling of this notion back in San Francisco, where he covered séances and the local Spiritualist scene for *The Golden Era*. Mulford first participated as a bemused skeptic and later as a believer, though always with a touch of sardonic remove, writing in *The Golden Era* in tones that could have been ascribed to H. L. Mencken if the famous skeptic had awakened one morning, to his dismay, to find himself a believer in talking to the dead:

> I am not particular that my readers should imagine that I am a sort of spiritual Barnum keeping a keen look-out for curiosities of this sort. Nearly all I have seen of this science has come into my path. I have been forced to see it. I have no inclination for [séance] circles. As a general rule I detest them. I rank them with wakes and revival prayer meetings. I am perfectly willing to grant that what we term wonderful things can be done through invisible agencies. . . . I am already being sought after as a sort of inspector general and ghost detective for haunted houses. I waive the honor. Catch your own ghosts and convince yourselves that it is a reality or a humbug. True, the subject is very interesting to me. But it has slums and I desire not to wade through them.

Mulford's forays into Spiritualism nonetheless convinced him of the existence of "invisible agencies" and higher laws. His hunch that these hidden forces could aid man in daily life seemed to crystallize when he visited Boston in 1884. There he came under the influence of the mind-cure culture, or as it was sometimes called, the "Boston Craze." The city was developing a reputation, parallel to Chicago's, as the northeastern capital of the mind-power scene. Mulford acknowledged this influence obliquely: "It was for some mysterious reason necessary to go to Boston to start any new idea or movement."

In May 1886, Mulford raised enough money to finance his first run of advice pamphlets, which he published under the name "The White Cross Library." He produced them steadily, seventy-four in all, until his death in 1891. First sold by mail subscription, Mulford's pamphlets were later repackaged into a six-volume book, *Your Forces, And How to Use*

Them, issued by a New York publisher beginning in 1890. This body of work arguably became Mulford's steadiest and most influential literary achievement—it was certainly his most commercially successful.

Mulford was never wholly upfront about his sources, but he seems to have drawn upon the work of Warren Felt Evans and Swedenborg. He repeatedly used the phrase *thoughts are things.* It became one of the mottos of the mind-power movement and today is a keynote of business motivation. The expression was actually tucked into the folds of Warren Felt Evans's 1876 book, *Soul and Body.* Evans had used the term in a Swedenborgian manner to describe the spiritual world in which our inner-selves dwell: "In that world thoughts are things, and ideas are the most real entities of the universe." What transpires in the spirit world, Evans believed, is mirrored in our own. Mulford had a knack for detaching such ideas and phrases from their mystical moorings. In his hands "thoughts are things" became a formula for profitable thinking.

Mulford's writing in *Your Forces, And How to Use Them* could be seen as the most successful popularization of Swedenborg. Echoing the Swedish mystic, Mulford described the world of spirit and the world of thought as extensions of the same reality. While only once naming Swedenborg, Mulford argued that every individual routinely experiences the same out-of-body journeys as the seer:

> You travel when your body is in the state called sleep. The real "you" is not your body; it is an unseen organization, your spirit. It has senses like those of the body, but far superior. It can see forms and hear voices miles away from the body. Your spirit is not in your body. It never was wholly in it; it acts on it and uses it as an instrument. It is a power which can make itself felt miles from your body.

In a tantalizing passage for mind-cure acolytes, Mulford explained his perspective on the mind's divine power: "Thought is a substance as much as air or any other unseen element of which chemistry makes us aware. It is of many and varying degrees in strength. Strong thought or mind is the same as strong will." And elsewhere: "In the chemistry of the future, thought will be recognized as substance as much as the acids, oxides, and all other chemicals of to-day." This seemed to complete the promise that "thoughts are things."

To sympathetic readers, Mulford's explanation of the powers of the mind sounded at once metaphysical and scientific. In particular, his approach combined New Thought philosophy with news of experiments that were emerging from the British Society for Psychical Research, which was founded in 1882 to test claims of after-death communication and nonlocalized mental phenomena, or ESP. In essence, Mulford's ideas conjoined the emergent field of psychical research to a contemporary-sounding iteration of Swedenborgian philosophy. Whereas the published case studies of the British psychical researchers were clinical and demanding, and Swedenborg's translations were dense, verbose, and difficult to follow, Mulford's writing was delightfully simple, exuding pithiness, practicality, and adventurousness.

Unlike Emma Curtis Hopkins and Frances Lord, for whom prosperity was one factor among many in the march of the happy warrior, Mulford addressed the wealth question head-on. One of the first chapters in *Your Forces, And How to Use Them* was an essay called "The Law of Success." The title probably came from Ralph Waldo Emerson's lecture of the same name, which Emerson adapted into his 1870 essay "Success." Emerson's essay celebrated the powers of enthusiasm, but with a tough world-weariness that denied man the ability to seize his every wish. Mulford was nowhere as discriminating as Emerson, but neither was he without accomplishment by his own lights. Mulford's 1886 "Law of Success" pretty thoroughly laid down the template for spiritual self-help. He wrote in terms that the genre has never really deviated from, or surpassed:

> Your prevailing mood, or frame of mind, has more to do than anything else with your success or failure in any undertaking. . . . The mind is a magnet. It has the power, first

of attracting thought, and next of sending that thought out again. . . . What kind of thought you most charge that magnet (your mind) with, or set it open to receive, it will attract most of that kind to you. If, then, you think, or keep most in mind, the mere thought of determination, hope, cheerfulness, strength, force, power, justice, gentleness, order, and precision, you will attract and receive more and more of such thought elements. These are among the elements of success.

In his 1888 essay "The Necessity of Riches," Mulford was blunter on material matters, sounding much like a twenty-first-century prosperity guru: "It is right and necessary that you should have the very best of all this world's goods—of clothing, food, house, surroundings, amusements, and all of which you are appreciative; and you should aspire to these things." He disputed the old-fashioned ethic of self-sacrifice: "Does 'Early to bed and early to rise make men wealthy?' Who get up the earliest, work the most hours, and go to bed earliest? Thousands on thousands of the poor . . ." Rather, Mulford saw a spiritual solution: "All material wealth is gained through following a certain spiritual law." What is this law? Only the simple dictum of Christ: "Seek ye first the kingdom of God, and all these things shall be added unto you." Once more, Mulford was bringing in his version of Swedenborg. The "kingdom of God," he argued, is a "kingdom of spiritual law" in which men's thoughts are actual creative forces. And "if you put those thoughts or forces in one direction, they will bring you health and the good of this world to use and enjoy. . . . Your every thought is a force, as real as a current of electricity is a force."

Mulford set the parameters of New Thought philosophy. In his work, physical healing was downplayed; and prosperity, business success, and power were pushed to the front.

Mulford's gifts for wrestling spiritual philosophies into glib practicalities may have irritated some, but his skills did not escape literary notice. Mulford was one of a handful of New Thought authors whom

William James mentioned by name. James, in a March 29, 1888, letter to his wife, Alice—with whom the philosopher explored mind-cure
methods—wrote: "I will send you a mind-cure theosophist book by one
Mulford. . . . Pray read it if you can and tell me what is in it when we
meet." The report must have been reasonably positive, for Mulford remained on James's mind more than a decade later when he was noted in
the philosopher's 1899 essay on mind-power therapeutics, "The Gospel
of Relaxation." James mentioned Mulford, Horatio Dresser, and Ralph
Waldo Trine as New Thought figures that moved him to conclude that
"it really looks as if a good start might be made in the direction of
changing our American mental habit into something more indifferent
and strong." (By indifferent James meant serviceable and utilitarian.)

At a time when Mulford was enjoying his largest readership, his life
slipped away. He died not only relatively young, having just passed his
fifty-seventh birthday, but also mysteriously. In late May 1891, Mulford
set out from Sheepshead Bay, Brooklyn, on his small sailboat, White Cross.
He told friends that he planned to make a leisurely trek to his childhood
home of Sag Harbor, Long Island. It was a seaborne version of his hermitage in the New Jersey woods. His boat was well stocked with food,
an oil stove, pens, ink, writing paper, art supplies, blankets, and a banjo.
Ever the inventive explorer, Mulford had fitted the boat with an awning
that could enclose, tent-style, the vessel's 16-foot frame, providing shel-
ter from the weather and snug sleeping quarters. But when onlookers
from the shore of Sheepshead Bay noticed that the covered boat had been
unattended for a few days, they went to explore. On May 30 they found
Mulford's body aboard. He had been dead for three days. There was no
sign of illness, injury, or foul play.

"How or why Mulford should have died on an open boat within
easy reach of assistance and where the sound of his voice could have
been heard ashore is the only mysterious feature that remains of this
remarkable case," the New York Times reported on June 1, 1891.

Suicide could not be ruled out. Mulford had once again been writing
of his old depression, and struggling to apply his mind-power ideas to

himself, in search of a way forward. On May 11, he wrote in his journal: "The depression you feel is the old self of six years ago. . . . You will soon throw it off and enjoy more than ever before. Exercise very gently and when your old condition comes out, complain in words, for you then materialize it—which helps to get rid of it much faster."

And on May 25, two days before his death: "Now you see your mind seizes immediately on trifles and makes mountains of them. I brought you under these conditions that I might more clearly show you this. It is the fear of these things, so bred in the mind, that does the injury; and your mind, in these periods of isolation, will be more readily cleared of these tendencies than in any other way."

In his struggle, Mulford seemed to think, finally, of the audience who took succor in his work and what he owed them: "You are now fighting for thousands, as well as for yourself and me. . . . Remember the chief end and object of the boat is to help you get into an element of thought. It is not going so far with the boat—it is going into that new element. . . . Your material part does not like to get out of the world— your spiritual part does. (The body and the soul did not fit each other.) Recognize the first feeling of gloom that comes as an evil thought. Push it off directly and it is not so apt to find lodgment."

Toward the end, the physical and spiritual worlds seemed to converge for Mulford. Friends had already expressed concerns over his renewed interest in Spiritualism, automatic writing, and reincarnation. Two old friends swore on the day of his death that they encountered Mulford's apparition vainly trying to speak to them.

Mulford's interest in the spirit world wasn't morbid so much as it was part of an inner struggle. In his personal tradition of self-sufficiency— from his whaling days through gold prospecting, from newspaper reporting to his sojourn in the woods—Mulford strove to use the agencies of his mind, coupled with the metaphysical possibilities he perceived in a spiritualized thought-world, to push back the darkness. It may not have been enough. He was buried in his hometown of Sag Harbor; his gravestone bore the sole epitaph "Thoughts Are Things."

Other writers quickly picked over Mulford's legacy. In the years following his death, his essays were, if not pilfered, liberally borrowed from. In 1910, inspirational writer Christian D. Larson used Mulford's iconic title, *Your Forces, And How to Use Them* for a book of his own. In 1928, a young Napoleon Hill called his first series of books *The Law of Success*, echoing Mulford. Mulford's insistence that "the mind is a magnet" found new expression in 1928 in a series of pamphlets called *The Life Magnet* by motivational writer Robert Collier. Mulford's ever-ready slogan "thoughts are things" became a mantra of inspirational literature, appearing in countless books and articles and eventually in Norman Vincent Peale's 1952 *The Power of Positive Thinking*. And Mulford made one of the first, fateful uses of a phrase that took flight across the nation, and which will soon be looked at more closely: "Law of Attraction."

The Conquest of Poverty

In considering the rise of Prentice Mulford, it is tempting to conclude that the mind-as-money-magnet approach took fire in an instant. Motivational thought and mental manifestation laid the basis for many popular books and articles at the turn of the twentieth century. Still, money was only occasionally emphasized.

The leading inspirational works of the period were Ralph Waldo Trine's *In Tune with the Infinite* from 1897, and Elbert Hubbard's *A Message to Garcia* from 1899. A committed New-Thoughter and self-identified socialist, Trine believed that happiness could be attained through generosity, good wishes for others, and determined optimism. Hubbard, a horseback-riding man of nature and the founder of the American wing of the arts and crafts movement, maintained that life rewarded the man who threw himself into challenging tasks, either great or small, without a whimper or a "but." Both men were advocates of New Thought, but neither made more than a passing reference to money.

Even the tantalizingly titled self-help manifesto *Acres of Diamonds* by Russell H. Conwell, which the minister and Temple University founder delivered thousands of times as a lecture before it was published in 1890, defined worldly success as the product of character and inventiveness, but with scant reference to the mind as a wealth-building tool. Likewise, the success writer Orison Swett Marden, who rose to popularity in the 1890s, extolled the development of iron character but said relatively little about the power of prosperous thoughts. In his 1894 *Pushing to the Front*, Marden wrote, "He who would grasp the key to power must be greater than his calling, and resist the vulgar prosperity that retrogrades toward barbarism . . . *character is success, and there is no other.*"

The first major work after Prentice Mulford to devise a mental approach to wealth came from a woman who was deeply rooted in the reformist instincts of the Progressive Era. She was a suffragist and labor activist named Helen Wilmans. And in 1899 she produced her manifesto, *The Conquest of Poverty*. The book was dedicated "to working men and women everywhere." Wilmans, once a farmer's wife, recounted her life story as a New Thought parable of personal liberation.

As a struggling, unhappy housewife living on a farm in Northern California in the 1870s, Wilmans was not unlike Ibsen's Nora, though with the grit of farm dirt under her fingernails. She broke from her domestic role—but with careful planning and forethought. Wilmans placed her two daughters in San Francisco schools. By 1877, after an on-and-off reconciliation, she finally left her hard-edged husband, and farm life, for good. Wilmans traveled to San Francisco with just enough money for a day's lunch and the cheapest lodging. There she began walking to the offices of every newspaper in town and finally landed a job as a journalist at a small, four-page weekly. Wilmans soon became known for her coverage of the local labor scene and as a women's rights advocate.

New journalistic offers took her to Chicago. In the early 1880s, however, Wilmans grew critical of the labor movement that she had once devotedly covered. In a *Chicago Express* article called "Willing Slaves of the Nineteenth Century," Wilmans complained that most working men lacked any sense of personal aim, self-betterment, or higher aspiration. Given the chance, they didn't want to build a new world for themselves and others, so much as to trade places with their bosses, shake down their neighbors, and keep women one rung beneath them.

The problem, she argued, stemmed less from social forces than from the mental habits of workers themselves:

> The moment one of you begins to think he ceases to belong to that class to whom this article is addressed. Are you willing to come up to the dignity of manhood by an effort to comprehend the true situation and to arouse within your brain the thought that will meet it? . . . The world calls on all men now for brain. It asks you for thought, that through thought it may develop the finer and as yet unexplored forces of nature.

Whatever the abuses of the bosses, the real problem, she told the working man, is: "You will not think."

Wilmans had not yet developed a New Thought outlook. But she was certain that human liberation could be summoned only by fresh thought patterns and personal action. People needed to realize a "sense of power in themselves."

By June of 1886, Wilmans's convictions drew her into a new circle: the Chicago mental-healing classes of Emma Curtis Hopkins. A few months after meeting Hopkins, Wilmans experienced a simultaneous social and spiritual awakening. It hit her with the force of a religious conversion.

The change occurred one day after an argument with her boss at the *Chicago Express*. Wilmans told her employer that she wanted to start her own paper and hoped to get his support. He ridiculed the idea. Dejected and disappointed, Wilmans left her desk and wandered through the Chicago streets on a darkening November afternoon. After years of planning and hard work, she realized that she was entirely alone in the world—there was no one on whom she could lean. But this realization, instead of bringing her to despair, suddenly filled her with a sense of freedom and inner strength. "I walked those icy streets like a school boy just released from restraint. My years fell from me as completely as if death turned my spirit loose in Paradise."

She felt determination well up within her. She wanted no one else's help. Wilmans charged back to her boarding house and began writing the maiden article that would eventually launch her own newspaper, *The Woman's World* (this was the paper later bought by Frances Lord). Wilmans received help from unexpected places, including her dour landlord, who became so excited over her venture that he put up money and floated her rent.

Wilmans insisted that her passage into peak productivity could be summoned by anyone—through the right mental state. "What!" she wrote in *The Conquest of Poverty*. "Can a person by holding certain thoughts create wealth? Yes, he can. A man by holding certain thoughts—if he knows the Law that relates effect and cause on the mental plane—can actually create wealth by the character of thoughts he entertains." But, she added, such thought "must be supplemented by courageous action."

Wilmans developed a more achievement-oriented outlook than her teacher Emma Curtis Hopkins. Wilmans never mentioned Hopkins by name, and she actually believed that Hopkins's version of "Christian Science" was amorphous and incomplete. Wilmans rejected the implication that "the individual is to get rid of his individuality and lose himself in nothingness." Rather, "Individuality . . . became my great theme."

Wilmans believed in muscular self-directedness and personal action. She called her outlook "realistic idealism."

After the launch of her newspaper, Wilmans quickly expanded into book and magazine publishing, lectures and classes, and a distance-prayer mail-order service (in which she would "affirm" a result for a client). She got remarried and in the early 1890s moved to Florida near the town of Seabreeze in Daytona Beach. There she began building a real-estate empire and laying plans for a New Thought–oriented "University of Psychical Research." The school was intended to teach the traditional arts and sciences while also tutoring students in the methods of applied thought and "Mental Science." Wilmans intended this well-rounded program to give people the tools for self-liberation. Her aims were announced in the title of the magazine she launched in 1893: *Freedom*.

By 1901, however, the postmaster general called Wilmans's distance-prayer treatments a scam and began an aggressive campaign against her, including a ban on her receiving mail. The following year a federal judge cleared her of fraud charges. But in 1904 Wilmans was targeted in a new mail-fraud case, which was very likely instigated by Florida real-estate magnates who disliked the encroachment of a newcomer—and a woman, no less—into their territory. A circuit-court judge threw out the case on appeal in February 1905 and scolded the government for attempting to drag Wilmans's metaphysical beliefs before the federal bench. "The court is a not a society for psychical research," he said.

Wilmans's vindication arrived too late. The mail ban, as well as the time and money consumed by the court trials, had decimated her businesses and left her despondent. In 1906, she attempted to launch a new magazine, *Men and Gods*, but once more the postmaster general—completely disregarding the circuit court's ruling of the prior year—barred her from using the mails. A further blow came in June 1907 with the death of her second husband and business partner, Charles Post, whom she had met in her early years of freedom in Chicago. The strains were too much.

"I am so tired, tired beyond description," she wrote to a friend on August 31, 1907, ". . . I am not sick, but I am tired of everything on earth. I would give anything just to lie down and go to sleep and never to awake again. I will stop. I am only hurting your gentle heart." Wilmans died five days later at age seventy-six.

Although Wilmans had reached hundreds of thousands of readers, her writings and plans for a university quickly faded after her death. Yet another social reformer and mind-power advocate arose in her wake. He was an Englishman who had once seemed destined to live out his life as a factory worker. Against all odds, however, he brought news of the powers of the mind to millions of everyday Americans. His work not only survived his death but became some of the most widely read inspirational literature of all time.

Working-Class Hero

With the exception of Mary Baker Eddy, few figures from the metaphysical culture were known by name to Americans. For all their influence, impresarios such as Emma Curtis Hopkins, Prentice Mulford, and Helen Wilmans were more often copied or co-opted by more popular writers than directly read themselves.

One of the few mind-power pioneers who did attain broad recognition was an English author who, during his brief career, introduced creative-mind principles to vast reaches of people. A social reformer and animal-rights activist, his name was James Allen. His short, meditative book, *As a Man Thinketh*, is found today in dozens of editions—and in many households where there is otherwise no direct interest in New Thought, Christian Science, or any of the metaphysical movements that shaped his worldview.

James Allen was born in 1864 in Leicester, an industrial town in central England. His father, William, was a successful knitting manufacturer who cultivated James's taste in books and philosophy. A downturn in the textile trade drove William out of business, and in 1879 he traveled to New York City to look for new work. His plan was to get settled and pay for the rest of the family to join him. But the unthinkable occurred. On the brink of the Christmas season, just after James had turned fifteen, word came back to the Allen household that its patriarch was dead. William had been found robbed and murdered two days after reaching New York. His battered body, with pockets emptied, lay in a city hospital.

James's mother, Martha, a woman who could not read or write, found herself in charge of James and his two younger brothers, with no means of support. "Young Jim" would have to leave school and find work as a factory knitter. The teenager had been his father's favorite. An avid reader, James had spent hours questioning him about life, death, religion, politics, and Shakespeare. "My boy," William told him, "I'll make a scholar of you." Those hopes were gone.

James took up employment locally as a framework knitter, a job that occupied his energies for the next nine years. He sometimes worked fifteen-hour days. But even amid the strains of factory life, he retained the refined, studious bearing that his father had cultivated. When his workmates went out drinking, or caught up on sleep, Allen studied and read two to three hours a day. Coworkers called him "the Saint" and "the Parson."

Allen read through his father's collected works of Shakespeare, as well as books of ethics and religion. He grew determined to discover the "central purpose" of life. At age twenty-four he found the book that finally seemed to reveal it to him: *The Light of Asia* by Edwin Arnold. The epic poem introduced Allen, along with a generation of Victorians, to the ideas of Buddhism. Under its influence, Allen came to believe that the true aim of all religion was self-development and inner refinement.

Shortly after discovering *The Light of Asia*, Allen experienced a turning point in his outer life, as well. Around 1889 he found new employment in London as a private secretary and stationer—markedly friendlier vocations to the bookish man than factory work. In London he met his wife and intellectual partner, Lily.

By the mid-1890s Allen had deepened his inquiry into spiritual philosophies, immersing himself in the works of John Milton, Ralph Waldo Emerson, Walt Whitman, and early translations of the Bhagavad Gita, Tao Te Ching, and the sayings of Buddha. He marveled over the commonalities in the world's religions. "The man who says, 'My religion is true, and my neighbor's is false,' has not yet discovered the truth in his own religion," he wrote, "for when a man has done that, he will see the Truth in all religions."

Allen also grew interested in the ideas of America's New Thought culture through the work of Ralph Waldo Trine, Orison Swett Marden, and, later, Christian D. Larson. His reading of New Thought literature sharpened his spiritual outlook—in particular his idea that our thoughts are causative and determine our destiny.

By 1898, Allen found an outlet for his intellectual interests. He began writing for the *Herald of the Golden Age*. In addition to metaphysical topics, the journal was an early voice for vegetarianism and humane treatment of animals, ideas that Allen had discovered in Buddhism. In 1901, he published his first book of practical philosophy, *From Poverty to Power*. The work extolled the creative agencies of the mind, placing equal emphasis on Christian ethics and New Thought metaphysics. The following year, Allen launched his own mystical magazine, the *Light of Reason*, and soon came another book, *All These Things Added*.

It was a period of tremendous productivity, capped in 1903 by Allen's third and most influential work—the short, immensely powerful meditation, *As a Man Thinketh*. The title came from Proverbs 23:7: *As he thinketh in his heart, so is he*. In Allen's eyes, that brief statement laid out his core philosophy—that a man's thought, if not the cause of his circumstances, is the cause of *himself*, and shapes the tenor of his life.

As the book's popularity rose, the phrase "as a man thinketh" became the informal motto of the New Thought movement, adopted and repeated by motivational writers throughout the century. Indeed, twentieth-century New-Thoughters frequently borrowed, cross-referenced, and repurposed one another's language—sometimes to the point where an original reference, or its meaning, got lost. This was the case with Allen's portentous title phrase. Read in context in Proverbs 23:6–7, the precept "as a man thinketh" is not a principle of cause-and-effect thinking, but rather a caution against covetousness and hypocrisy:

> Eat thou not the bread of him that hath an evil eye, neither desire thou his dainty meats:
>> For as he thinketh in his heart, so is he: Eat and drink, saith he to thee; but his heart is not with thee.

This kind of misunderstanding was common in New Thought. The early positive thinkers were passionate to describe their ideas as the fulfillment of ancient doctrines. Hence, they tended to retrofit the positivity gospel to Scripture and other antique sources, sometimes ignoring the context of favored passages.

Regardless, Allen's book was otherwise marked by memorable, aphoristic lessons, which have withstood the passage of time. *As a Man Thinketh* defined achievement in deeply personal terms: "You will become as small as your controlling desire; as great as your dominant aspiration." Toward the end of *As a Man Thinketh*, Allen wrote in a manner that amounted to autobiography:

> Here is a youth hard pressed by poverty and labor; confined long hours in an unhealthy workshop; unschooled, and lacking all the arts of refinement. But he dreams of better things: he thinks of intelligence, of refinement, of grace and beauty. He conceives of, mentally builds up, an ideal condition of life; vision of a wider liberty and a larger scope takes possession of him; unrest urges him to action, and he utilizes all his spare time and means, small though they are, to the development of his latent powers and resources. Very soon so altered has his mind become that the workshop can no longer hold him.

As a personal rule, Allen used his life experiences as the backbone of his teaching. "He never wrote *theories*," Lily noted in 1913, "or for the sake of writing; but he wrote when he had a message, and it became a message *only when he had lived it out in his own life*, and knew that it was good."

The impact of *As a Man Thinketh* was not fully felt during Allen's lifetime, but the book brought him enough of an audience (and sufficient pay) so that he was able to quit secretarial work and commit himself to writing and editing full-time. On its publication, Allen, Lily, and their daughter Nora moved to the southern English coastal town of Ilfracombe, where he spent the remainder of his life. He wrote books at a remarkable pace, often more than one a year, producing nineteen works. Allen's days assumed a meticulous routine of meditating, writing, walking in nature, and gardening. His work habits never flagged. "Thoroughness is genius," he wrote in 1904.

For all of his creative output, Allen struggled with fragile health. Lily wrote of her husband faltering from an illness in late 1911. On January 24, 1912, Allen died at home in Ilfracombe at age forty-seven, probably of tuberculosis. In an obituary of January 27, the *Ilfracombe Chronicle* noted: "Mr. Allen's books . . . are perhaps better known abroad, especially in America, than in England."

Indeed, the twentieth century's leading American writers of motivational thought—from Napoleon Hill to Norman Vincent Peale—read and noted the influence of *As a Man Thinketh*. Dale Carnegie said the book had "a lasting and profound effect on my life." The cofounder of Alcoholics Anonymous, Bob Smith, called it a favorite. The black-nationalist pioneer Marcus Garvey embraced the book's do-for-self ethic and adapted the slogan "As Man Thinks So Is He" on the cover of his newspaper, *Blackman*. In years ahead, the book's influence showed up in myriad places: An adolescent Michael Jackson told a friend that it was his "favorite book in the world"; NFL Hall-of-Famer Curtis Martin credited *As a Man Thinketh* with helping him overcome pain and injury; businessman and Oprah Winfrey partner Stedman Graham said Allen's work helped him attain "real freedom."

Yet the full impact of *As a Man Thinketh* can best be seen in the successive generations of everyday readers who embraced its aphoristic lessons in directing one's thoughts to higher aims, and to understanding success as the outer manifestation of inner development. "Men do not attract that which they *want*," Allen told readers, "but that which they *are*." In that sense, Allen attracted a vast following of people who mirrored the ordinary circumstances from which he arose—and whose hopes for a better, nobler existence were reflected back to them in the example of his life.

"If the Workers of America Chose to . . ."

No figures in the mind-power culture were more explicit in uniting progressive and mystical impulses than an early-twentieth-century Indiana socialist named Wallace D. Wattles and his publisher, a suffragist activist named Elizabeth Towne.

Wattles's books were moderately popular during his lifetime, particularly his 1910 *The Science of Getting Rich*—an intriguing program to use the mind as a wealth tool. But his books fell into obscurity following his death in 1911, a period when the market was flush with New Thought titles, which came and went quickly. If you mentioned his name in most self-help circles at the start of the current century, you'd receive blank stares. But his work gained new dramatic new currency in 2006 when it reemerged as one of the central sources behind the blockbuster movie and book *The Secret*.

The following year, *The Science of Getting Rich*, almost a century after its initial publication, reached number one on the *BusinessWeek* bestseller list. To the entrepreneurial readers who rediscovered Wattles, however, the motivational hero's roots as a Christian socialist and radical social reformer were entirely unknown.

Wattles began his career in the 1890s as a Methodist minister in La Porte, Indiana. A student of the reformist minister George D. Herron, Wattles was a passionate exponent of the Social Gospel, a radical theology that emphasized Christ's teachings on social justice, particularly the equitable treatment of workers, immigrants, and the poor, and the imperative to redress vast imbalances in wealth. The Social Gospel attracted hundreds of thousands of sympathizers during Wattles's lifetime. In 1900, however, conservative members of his Methodist parish forced him from his pulpit after he opposed accepting collection-basket offerings from businessmen who used sweatshop labor. Wattles soon joined the more-liberal Quakers and began writing for a popular progressive and New Thought monthly journal called *Nautilus*.

Nautilus was the brainchild of Massachusetts suffragist and mind-power acolyte Elizabeth Towne. Beginning in 1898, its pages gave voice to a novel amalgam of worker's rights and mental science. Towne had once been Mrs. Joseph Struble, a Portland, Oregon, housewife and mother of two, who found herself in financial ruin after she and her husband separated in the late 1890s. Towne had quit school at age 14 to marry, but she was ardently self-educated and had taken classes from students of Emma Curtis Hopkins. Towne believed in the power of ideas—and in the fall of 1898 she hit upon a life-changing one.

Towne borrowed thirty dollars from her father and in the space of three weeks published her first issue of *Nautilus*. In a nation eagerly interested in New Thought culture, the journal quickly became a clearinghouse for ads from mental-healers, Christian Science practitioners, and those hawking a bevy of tonics, pills, and medical devices. In the late nineteenth century, ads for patent medicines were a cash cow for many magazines, not for New Thought journals alone. While some of the ads that populated the pages of *Nautilus* and other New Thought magazines were absurd or harmful, proffering narcotics or miracle cures, others offered more practical fare, such as botanical syrups or yogurt pills for digestion.

Within two years, Elizabeth obtained a formal divorce from her estranged husband. She asked for no alimony, having achieved a measure of financial independence through *Nautilus*. Legally freed from a marriage that had been marked by anger and fracture, Elizabeth, along with her teenage son and daughter, wound her way across the nation in spring 1900 to Holyoke, Massachusetts. Her journey east was intended to bring her closer to a New Thought book dealer, William Towne, with whom she had been corresponding. The couple quickly married—"the hour [we] first met," Elizabeth recalled. Together they prospered publishing *Nautilus*. Elizabeth was publisher and editor, and William was a columnist and treasurer, while her son, Chester, acted as managing editor.

The magazine and its book-publishing arm grew rapidly. In *Nautilus*'s first ten years of existence, its circulation shot from 3,400 to 35,000 (with reports in later years reaching 90,000). *Nautilus* remained in publication until 1953; it was one of the longest-running spiritual magazines in American history.

In addition to its writings on the uses of thought to "grow success," *Nautilus* abounded with tips on physical culture and exercise, including stretching, fresh air, deep breathing, and vegetarianism. Towne had no patience for those who drooped through life. She replied to an advice-seeker who signed his letter *A Weakling*: "The trouble with you and with all the other weaklings is that you sit still and let the thought-power evaporate through your skulls—and run off your tongues—instead of directing it down through the nerves and muscles of your bodies where it is needed and will do some good."

Along with mind-body therapeutics, Towne wrote on behalf of social reforms, calling for a universal five-dollar weekly wage for every man, woman, and child. Elizabeth and William were active in electoral politics, attending two conventions in 1912 where the Progressive Party was formed and Theodore Roosevelt was nominated to run for president. Towne became a force in local politics when she won a seat as Holyoke's first female alderman in 1926. Two years later she mounted an unsuccessful independent bid for mayor.

Towne discovered in Wallace D. Wattles a New Thought writer who, like her, advocated for working people. In 1908 and 1909, Wattles had made back-to-back runs for Congress and mayor of Elwood, Indiana— each time on the ticket of the Socialist Party of America. During his mayoral campaign, Wattles pledged his support to thirteen hundred striking tin workers in Elwood, while simultaneously completing his mind-power classic *The Science of Getting Rich*. It appeared in 1910 under the imprint of the Elizabeth Towne Publishing Company.

Embraced a century later by business go-getters, *The Science of Getting Rich*, on close reading, reveals the unmistakable mark of socialist language. Wattles did not endorse "getting rich" as a go-it-alone project. Rather, the reformer believed that workers could, through collective action and the prospering powers of the mind, create a new world of bounty, leisure, and equity—the same kind of gentle utopia foreseen in Edward Bellamy's 1888 novel, *Looking Backward*. As Wattles saw it:

> If the workers of America chose to do so, they could follow the example of their brothers in Belgium and other countries, and establish great department stores and co-operative industries; they could elect men of their own class to office, and pass laws favoring the development of such co-operative industries; and in a few years they could take peaceable possession of the industrial field.
>
> The working class may become the master class whenever they will begin to do things in a Certain Way . . .

To Wattles, the "Certain Way" meant using the mind as an occult force for attraction, the aspect of the book that interested creators of *The Secret*. And this highlights an important difference between Wattles and other early-twentieth-century writers on the character traits of success, such as Russell H. Conwell and Orison Swett Marden. Those writers endorsed the cultivation of willpower, optimism, and a can-do mind-set. They had no other social aims, and no belief in man's occult prowess. Wattles, on the other hand, popularized the notion, also seen in Prentice Mulford, that the mind possesses an actual ethereal power—a "thinking stuff" that could literally attract circumstances or manifest desires. This became a core belief of the positive-thinking culture and distinguished it from the earlier character-building literature.

In 1911, Wattles produced his final book, *The Science of Being Great*, also published by Towne. It remains the sole piece of American inspirational literature to celebrate the example of Socialist Party leader Eugene V. Debs. A hero to followers, Debs was sentenced in 1918 to ten years in federal prison for opposing the military draft during World War I. From his cell he won nearly one million votes for the presidency in 1920 (and probably more if voter suppression were factored in). Writing in 1911, Wattles counseled readers:

Think about the good side of men; the lovely, attractive part, and exert your will in refusing to think of anything else in connection with them. I know of no one who has attained to so much on this one point as Eugene V. Debs, twice the Socialist candidate for president of the United States. Mr. Debs reverences humanity. No appeal for help is ever made to him in vain. No one receives from him an unkind or censorious word. You cannot come into his presence without being made sensible of his deep and kindly personal interest in you. Every person, be he millionaire, grimy workingman, or toil worn woman, receives the radiant warmth of a brotherly affection that is sincere and true. No ragged child speaks to him on the street without receiving instant and tender recognition. Debs loves men. This has made him the leading figure in a great movement, the beloved hero of a million hearts, and will give him a deathless name.

In his speeches, Debs, too, encouraged a kind of working-class self-reliance, of both action and thought. "I would not lead you into the Promised Land if I could," he told audiences, "because if I led you in, some one else would lead you out. You must use your heads as well as your hands, and get yourself out of your present condition."

In early 1911 Wattles was preparing for another run for Congress on Debs's ticket. Wattles's daughter, Florence, a budding socialist orator and organizer, was assembling a ground operation for his next campaign in 1912. She insisted that his loss in the mayoral election had been due to fraud. The twenty-three-year-old Florence told a socialist convention in Kokomo, Indiana:

They voted not only the dead men in the cemeteries, but vacant lots as well. We were robbed of the election, but in 1912 we will carry the election. Mark that. And we'll get the offices, too. We mean to do it through a thorough and completely effective organization.

But her father, who extolled the healing properties of the mind, was frail and often in shaky health. Wattles died of tuberculosis that year at age fifty during a trip to Tennessee. The *Fort Wayne Sentinel* remembered him not for his mystical works but as "one of the best known socialists in Indiana."

Liberating Powers

In retrospect, the careers of Helen Wilmans, Elizabeth Towne, Wallace D. Wattles, and others can seem chimerical in their ideal of wedding social radicalism with the metaphysical powers of the mind. Yet their hopes reflected a brief moment in which avant-garde thinkers believed that human beings could develop and hone superior skills, and that life harbored unseen connections and channels of progress.

Indeed, Victorian-era men and women were enthralled with the theory of evolution, which, in the minds of figures like Wattles, seemed to promise that humanity was capable of orderly advancement in all areas of existence. Wattles and his contemporaries saw man as a psycho-spiritual being whose inner powers were as unrecognized as x-rays had once been in the farming towns where he was raised. Progress seemed to promise man's ability to continually improve his circumstances through the harnessing of natural and social laws, and Wattles believed that if such laws—including mental laws—could be properly understood, it followed that man's outer life could mirror the refinement of his inner state.

In this way, the possibilities of New Thought also touched the hopes of early-twentieth-century advocates for racial liberation. This was especially true of the black-nationalist pioneer Marcus Garvey, a man rarely perceived as having metaphysical affinities. Garvey, along with his

admiration for James Allen, punctuated his speeches and newspaper articles with telltale New Thought aphorisms, such as "Enthusiasm Is One
of the Big Keys to Success"; "Let us Give off Success and It Will Come";
and "always think yourself a perfect being." And he reminded his audiences of the need for "a universal business consciousness."

Garvey urged followers to take a "scientific" approach to religion—
by which he meant a mental-science, or New Thought, approach. In a
speech delivered in January 1928 in Kingston, Jamaica, Garvey told his
listeners that whites "live by science. You do everything by emotion.
That makes the vast difference between the two races. . . . Get a scientific
knowledge of religion, of God, of what you are; and you will create a
better world for yourselves. Negroes, the world is to your making."

Garvey seldom revealed his influences. But he made a rare exception
for two New Thought writers: Elbert Hubbard, whose work he recommended to followers, and Ella Wheeler Wilcox, the inspirational poet
who had studied with Emma Curtis Hopkins. Garvey read Wilcox's po-
etry aloud at rallies, including these lines:

> Live for something,—Have a purpose
> And that purpose keep in view
> Drifting like an helmless vessel
> Thou cans't ne'er to self be true.

Though not widely remembered today, Wilcox is still spoken of in
activist circles. The Reverend Al Sharpton told this story in 2011:

> When I was doing 90 days in jail in 2001, former [Atlanta]
> Mayor Maynard Jackson visited me, and he told me he read Ella
> Wheeler Wilcox's "Will" every day—that's how he became the
> first black mayor of Atlanta. It's very inspiring. It talks about
> how, no matter what, if you have strong will you can make it.

Divine Politics

Like Garvey, the messianic African-American religious leader Father Divine harnessed the positive-thinking gospel. The influential pre–civil rights era leader wove New Thought themes into speeches, hymns, and aphorisms to imbue his followers with a sense of their innate potentials. New Thought was an unseen source behind Father Divine's appeal.

Father Divine forged close ties to the New Thought world in the 1920s and 1930s. He especially liked the work of writer Robert Collier, a nephew of the publishing magnate P. F. Collier. Robert Collier had used mind-cure methods in the early 1920s when nothing else could be done to restore his health following a devastating bout of food poisoning. After recovering, Collier became an energetic advocate of New Thought, writing a highly influential 1926 book, The Secret of the Ages. Like the work of Wallace D. Wattles, it, too, became an inspiration behind the movie and book The Secret.

In The Secret of the Ages, Collier used engaging and deftly drawn anecdotes to argue that the powers of the mind were well known to the ancients but lost on modern people. Collier saw mind-power as the force that moved man out of the caves to build the ancient empires of Egypt, Greece, and Persia. To Collier, the power of mind formed the inner meaning behind every ancient parable, from genies in lamps to Christ walking on water. Father Divine liked what he read and gave away large numbers of Collier's books.

Beginning in the 1920s, Father Divine invited mind-power impresarios—including Collier's son, Gordon—to the elaborate banquets he hosted for followers at his Long Island home and ministry. Father Divine routinely treated acolytes to sumptuous, multicourse meals in a celebratory, revival-meeting atmosphere. His aim was to instill in them a consciousness of abundance. "This table," he told banquet-goers, "is but the outer expression . . . of the condition of the consciousness within. There is no limitation, there is no lack, there is no want."

He directed followers to repeat "it is wonderful" and "peace" as mantras of positivity. In addition to the books of Collier, Father Divine

gave banquet-goers works by mind-power authors Charles Fillmore and
Baird T. Spalding. Spalding was an eccentric gold prospector who, beginning in the mid-1920s, wrote a series of fanciful, and often enchanting,
mystical travelogues depicting himself as a student of hidden spiritual
masters and mystery schools in the Far East. Spalding borrowed his basic
mythos from Madame Blavatsky, but with a novel twist: His hidden masters taught principles that were very much in line with New Thought.

Around 1930, some white New-Thoughters joined Father Divine's
predominantly black movement. Eugene Del Mar, a prominent New
Thought lecturer who had studied with Helen Wilmans, became a dedicated supporter. The Anglo-American New Thought writer Walter C.
Lanyon grew deeply attached to Father Divine, dedicating books to him
and openly using Father Divine's language and letters in his books. Lanyon's 1931 work, It Is Wonderful, was titled after Father Divine's signature
mantra.

Father Divine's movement was not explicitly political. But in matters
of civil rights he encouraged followers in picketing, petition drives, and
letter-writing campaigns. In the 1930s his followers petitioned for an
antilynching bill, gathering some 250,000 signatures. Father Divine led
followers in hymns and prayers that combined a motivational tone with
calls for political progress. When Mississippi senator and Ku Klux Klan
member Theodore Bilbo filibustered antilynching legislation in 1938,
Father Divine's followers sang:

> D-O-W-N, down with Bilboism! Down! Down! Down!
> Up with Democracy! Let it flood city, village, and town;
> Let it sweep through the country
> And give its subjects the very Same Rights!
> Let every woman, man, boy, and girl,
> Help Democracy's banner to be unfurled,
> And clean out the Senate
> Of all lynch-mob violent leaders;
> And when they start to filibuster, don't allow them to talk;

Just snatch them off the floor and send them for a walk!
For Democracy shall flourish in the land of the free,
And its subjects shall have Life, Happiness, and Liberty!

Some scholars came to see Father Divine's organization as one of the precursors of the civil rights movement. Yet Father Divine often confounded journalists and critics with his claims to be God on earth and his encouraging of followers to "channel" his spirit for worldly success. Where outsiders saw audaciousness and megalomania, however, they missed the New Thought currents to which he belonged. Since the 1880s, Warren Felt Evans and Emma Curtis Hopkins had been telling of a "God-Self," or a divine power within. Robert Collier wrote: "Mind is God. And the subconscious in us is our part of Divinity." Father Divine saw positive thinking and, by extension, his own deific claims as a means of awakening followers to their holy inner-selves.

His methods could provide a startling uplift in an atmosphere of racial oppression. Scholar of religion Ronald Moran White noted that Father Divine's practices "undeniably" resulted in "a certain restructuring of his followers' attitudes toward themselves and the world."

Law of Attraction

Even as New Thought's most eloquent pioneers laid their hopes in a marriage of social reform and positive thinking, the link between mind-power and political protest showed signs of strain as the twentieth century progressed.

Concurrent with the rise of the prosperity gospel, an alluring new phrase began circulating in New Thought circles: *Law of Attraction*. The phrase grew familiar to millions of people who otherwise had little direct knowledge of the mind-power movement. In future generations, Law of Attraction got repeated throughout *The Secret*, ultimately becoming a better-known term than New Thought.

The theory behind the Law of Attraction is that the mind is constantly attracting circumstances to itself, and that through proper control of one's thoughts, this ever-operative principle of attraction could be used to attain one's desires—usually in the form of money, goods, or career advancement. As this concept caught on in the growing economy of the early twentieth century, many New Thought leaders began to place ever-greater emphasis on wealth building and individual advancement, while social concerns faded to a whisper. By the 1930s, the movement edged closer to what Charles Fillmore had once bemoaned: a spiritual school that viewed God largely as "a force of attraction."

It wasn't exactly that New Thought shed its liberal qualities. Sociologists Louis Schneider and Sanford M. Dornbusch made a broad survey of the inspirational and success books of the first half of the twentieth century and noted: "Racism and group-superiority themes are absent from the literature." Indeed, New Thought organizations, much like Unitarian-Universalist congregations, represented a popular alternative for seekers who rejected, or felt pushed from, mainline faiths. Artists, actors, gay and lesbian seekers, and a wide range of freethinkers were all heavily represented in the New Thought culture, and remain so.

But the movement began to emphasize a more self-involved vision. Increasingly, New Thought framed the problems of life—especially financial problems—in the same manner as it once had framed health: Everything depends on a person's intimate arrangements with the Divine Power within. The only reality that matters is that which the individual creates for himself.

In its original form, the Law of Attraction possessed a vastly different meaning from the one later attached to it by mind-power acolytes. The phrase first arose in the mid-nineteenth-century work of upstate New York medium Andrew Jackson Davis, the "Poughkeepsie Seer." Davis entered into medium trances from which he would dictate vast metaphysical lectures. Never being one to shy from loquaciousness, Davis in 1855 produced a six-volume treatise on metaphysical laws, *The Great Harmonia*. In volume 4, he described the Law of Attraction not as a principle of cause-and-effect thinking or as a method for using the mind to attract wealth, but, rather, as a cosmic law governing where a person's soul would dwell in the afterlife based on the affinities he had displayed on earth. In Davis's view, the Law of Attraction also governed the types of spirits that would be drawn to séances based on the character and intention of the people seated around the table.

In the vision of positive-thinking impresarios, the Law of Attraction took on different more distinctly material possibilities. The popular remaking of Davis's law began in 1892 in the final volume of Prentice Mulford's Your Forces, And How to Use Them. Mulford, who died the previous year, had written: "Such a friend will come to you through the inevitable law of attraction if you desire him or her . . ." In 1897, Ralph Waldo Trine used the term in his popular In Tune with the Infinite, and in 1899, Helen Wilmans invoked the Law of Attraction in her Conquest of Poverty. In June of that year, the New Thought leader Charles Brodie Patterson showcased the phrase in his influential article "The Law of Attraction," published in his journal, Mind. Patterson celebrated the Law of Attraction as a metaphysical super-law that dictated that everything around us is an out-picturing of what we dwell on most of the time in our thoughts. "Upon the recognition of this law depend health and happiness," Patterson wrote, "because neither can ensue unless in our thought we give out both."

No one on the early New Thought scene was more dramatic in illustrating the power of metaphysical laws than Chicago lawyer William Walker Atkinson. A student of Emma Curtis Hopkins and Helen Wilmans, Atkinson wrote dozens of books, which he published under his Yogi Publication Society. His 1902 book, The Law of the New Thought, devoted a chapter to the Law of Attraction. Atkinson often brought an exotic allure to his books by writing them under mysterious-sounding pseudonyms, such as Theron Q. Dumont and Yogi Ramacharaka. Writing in 1908 under the alias Three Initiates, Atkinson launched his most successful book, The Kybalion. The Kybalion, which seemed to be a Hellenic re-sounding of the term Kabbalah, presented itself as a modern commentary on an ancient work of lost Egypto-Greek esotericism by the mythical sage Hermes Trismegistus. *The Kybalion* framed the Law of Attraction as a tenet of ancient esoteric wisdom.

Though written in faux-arcane language, this work of Pseudo-Hermeticism did contain passages of surprising depth and substance. Atkinson located legitimate correspondences between New Thought and certain Hermetic ideas. These two philosophies, Hermeticism and New Thought, shared no actual lineage; but each believed in a universal over-mind, and Atkinson deftly traced those areas where they intersected. With its Hermetic reframing of the Law of Attraction, *The Kybalion* became a sensation among New-Thoughters, occultists, and even some black nationalists and Afrocentrists, who considered it an authentic retention of ancient Egyptian wisdom.

While it was an underground work, never registering in mainstream culture, *The Kybalion* became probably the bestselling occult book of the twentieth century. In later years, its influence showed up in surprising places. In 1982, *TV Guide* presented a rare profile of television star Sherman Hemsley, famous as TV's George Jefferson. Hemsley, who died in 2012, was intensely private and seldom gave interviews. *TV Guide* ran its piece under the headline "Don't Ask How He Lives or What He Believes In: A Rare View of *The Jeffersons* Star Who Works Hard to Hide an Unorthodox Lifestyle." The man who immortalized the cantankerous George obliquely credited a mysterious book and teacher with turning his life around as a young man. "Somewhere along the line," went the profile, "he met 'the man with the book'—although Sherman won't say which one. 'Don't want to advertise any book,' he grumbles. He is also very mysterious about exactly who the man was."

Hemsley's housemate, André Pavon, told *TV Guide* that the book was, in fact, *The Kybalion*. "He gave me that and others," Pavon said, adding, "It changed my life. He told me, 'You got to read it, man.'" Though sometimes depicted as a recluse, Hemsley simply lived by a different scale of values—those he derived from *The Kybalion*, as well as his interests in meditation and Kabbalah. Asked why he didn't frequent Hollywood parties and restaurants, he replied: "Nothing goes on there. The most exciting things happen in the mind." Although *The Kybalion* remained just off mainstream radar, Hemsley's comments exemplified the depth of dedication the occult work inspired among its fans.

In the years following *The Kybalion*, the Law of Attraction, whether seen as an ancient Hermetic idea or as a modern success formula, was embraced, extolled, and repeated as the keynote of mind-power spirituality. Its popularity brought the New Thought movement to a moral turning point: According to the logic of this super-law, the mind itself was an omnipotent force of attraction. A man's thoughts could assemble, disassemble, build up, or destroy. In essence, man was the Godhead. God may have existed both within and beyond man, but God the Creator, in this new formulation, was synonymous with the human imagination. Subtly, New Thought redirected its focus away from *opening man to the blessings of God* (a remnant of Mary Baker Eddy's theology), and toward *making man aware of this awesome, ever-operative inner power* that awaited his directions to bestow beauty, health, and plenty. Or to cause harm if one's mind unconsciously drifted to thoughts of illness, hatred, or despair.

In generations ahead, this radical metaphysic simultaneously popularized and burdened the positive-thinking movement. The Law of Attraction, however appealingly it promised material gain, dictated that man alone, through his thoughts, bore ultimate responsibility for everything that happened to him, whether good or bad. This was an ethical claim that future generations of positive thinkers weren't fully prepared to shoulder or defend.

chapter five

happy warriors

But to have done instead of not doing
               This is not vanity

—Ezra Pound, *Canto 81*

T
he rising tremors of the Great Depression did nothing to stem the progress of the positive-thinking movement. In times of economic calamity, mind-power philosophy not only continued to function as a source of innovation on the American scene but effectively issued a challenge to mainline religion that is still being felt today. The challenge was for churches to provide practical inspiration, usable advice, and psychological insights for dealing with the difficulties of daily life—or to risk irrelevance.

While most American churchgoers retained their ties to mainline congregations, worshippers from across the religious spectrum were increasingly familiar with New Thought's messages of spiritual self-help. They knew about books such as *As a Man Thinketh* and *In Tune with the Infinite*. Many people had taken the kinds of mail-order courses offered by Helen Wilmans or Elizabeth Towne, or knew someone who had. Christian Science churches sprouted up in some of the more affluent neighborhoods of New York, Boston, and Los Angeles. And mental healing was written about, sometimes critically but just as often approvingly, in national magazines. The message emerging from all these sources was that *religion could be useful*. Congregants from mainline churches increasingly demanded that problems with money, alcohol, marital relations, and self-image be addressed from the pulpit and in church programs. Otherwise, attendance would dwindle, as it did in the late 1920s and early 1930s.

The formula that revitalized the Protestant churches grew from the precedent laid down by New Thought—namely, that *faith ought to serve as a source of self-improvement*. This principle inspired mainstream spiritual programs in addiction recovery (such as Alcoholics Anonymous), physical healing (such as the Episcopal-based Emmanuel Movement), youth development (such as the Presbyterian Church's Camps Farthest Out), and an array of church-based support groups in marriage, grief, and career counseling.

Jewish congregations were touched as well. In the 1920s members of the Reform rabbinate made insistent pleas that rabbis be trained in mental therapeutics and taught to guide Jewish congregations in the use of healing prayers and inspirational religious readings. This resulted in the first pastoral counseling classes at rabbinical seminaries, a trend that quickly expanded to other denominations.

New Thought's most dynamic voices had long promoted a vision of therapeutic spirituality, and their efforts altered America's religious landscape—to the point where churches had to become forces not only for salvation but also for healing.

The Gospel of Usefulness

Americans of the early twentieth century were primed for this project—this quest to remake religion as useful—by their fascination with ideas and protocols that were deemed "scientific." For many people, the scientific method—by which a hypothesis could be tested through a set of repeated steps and empirical results—held out the hope of identifying the inner workings of life, and improving on them.

The Victorian age and the generation after were electrified by scientific advances. Louis Pasteur identified germs as the root cause of many diseases. Charles Darwin postulated the orderly development of biologic life. Albert Einstein probed the hidden mechanics behind energy, matter, and time. Sigmund Freud identified childhood traumas as the roots of adult neuroses. Even in politics, Karl Marx and Friedrich Engels argued that the hidden dynamics of life could be traced to economic exploitation, which resulted in inevitable patterns of class conflict.

All of these theories and outlooks shaped the central idea of modernity: That outer events possessed unseen yet knowable antecedents. Many social scientists, academics, and everyday people believed that through a proper grasp of natural laws—whether physical, social, or political—life's secrets could be unlocked and daily existence improved.

The modern faith in science and utility was felt in the realm of the spirit, too. In the years immediately following World War I, religious scholar Horatio Dresser wrote: "Our thought of God has become practical, concrete. This newer conception of God also belongs with the desire of modern man to test everything for himself, to feel in his own life whatever man claims to have felt in the past that exalted him."

Dresser, William James, and others wondered if certain spiritual practices could be shaped into a regimen that would produce observable, repeatable benefits. James had used the term "Gospel of Relaxation" to describe "certain psychological doctrines and show their practical applications to mental hygiene." He presented a set of mostly New Thought practices ("act and speak as if cheerfulness were already there"), which he believed could improve confidence, help deter illness, and create more easy-going relationships. Could this be the start of a modern, rationalist program for psychological and spiritual health?

Among New-Thoughters, the language for this project had long been in place. "We must deal scientifically with our faults," Emma Curtis Hopkins had written. Phineas Quimby had foretold a "science of health and happiness." Poet Ella Wheeler Wilcox wrote of "The Science of Right Thinking" and Wallace D. Wattles of "The Science of Being Great." By the early decades of the twentieth century, mind-cure and New Thought acolytes were eager to prove the efficacy of spiritual practice.

Heartland Rebels

At the forefront of this mission stood a group of "happy warriors"—a dynamic set of writers, teachers, and innovators who created the New Thought renaissance of the first half of the twentieth century. These impresarios shaped positive thinking as it is understood today: as a program to successful living. In most cases, they are little known; but these men and women articulated their ideals with such persuasiveness that their books, sermons, and spiritual regimens reshaped mainstream religion—and, eventually, much of modern life.

The happy warriors who ignited this revolution in practical spirituality had few ties to institutional faith. They were charismatic, independent teachers—many with their own original take on the positive-thinking creed. They had heartland names such as Frank B. Robinson, Glenn Clark, Ernest Holmes, and Roy Jarrett. In many cases, they were part of no historical religious tradition, although they repeatedly proved their ability to reach mainstream worshippers. They were often self-educated, with reading tastes that ran to Ralph Waldo Emerson, William Blake, Emanuel Swedenborg, Mary Baker Eddy, and Warren Felt Evans, as well as works of Theosophy and occultism, and the religious scriptures of the East. Indeed, these figures were probably the last leg of the positive-thinking tradition that had clearly imbibed the work of American meta-physicians such as Evans and Andrew Jackson Davis, whose names soon slipped into obscurity.

The new breed of positive thinkers increasingly borrowed, repro-cessed, and recirculated one another's phrases and concepts. There were times when some of them crossed into ethical lapses. Yet it would be a mistake to conclude that this generation lacked vision. Rather, in the grand tradition of American religious experimentation, these men and women distilled ideas from their own perspective, verified those ideas through their lived experience, and tested their utility before audiences at metaphysical churches, occult lodges, and big-city auditoriums. These early- to mid-twentieth-century teachers did not always use the term New Thought, but they very clearly saw themselves as apostles of a mind-power revolution.

No single chapter, or book, could encapsulate all of them. But the most dynamic among them, who appear in the pages that follow, bent modern culture to their passions.

DR. RICHARD C. CABOT:
PROBING MEDICINE AND THE MIND

In the wake of the medical licensing laws, the early twentieth cen-tury was not a propitious moment for religiously or psychologically oriented approaches to medicine. Most physicians regarded any form of positive-thinking or faith-based methods, even when used as com-plementary treatments, as smacking of Christian Science, a philoso-phy they considered cultish and dangerous. Protestant churches took a similar view. While Catholicism had long maintained a measured faith in healing miracles and shrines, most Protestant seminaries and pulpits saw religious healing as something that had ended with the apostolic era.

Indeed, during the Reformation, Protestant movements often cast aspersions on the healing claims of the Catholic Church, considering talk of medical miracles as nothing more than the church's attempt to shore up its role as the exclusive organ of God's word on earth. That attitude more or less prevailed at the start of the twentieth century.

A few early-twentieth-century physicians grudgingly used bread pills or sugar remedies to placate hypochondriacal patients, and some doctors recognized the usefulness of hypnosis as an analgesic. But any talk of using mental or faith-based treatments was considered heresy in the medical community.

Richard C. Cabot, a young, Harvard-educated physician at Massachusetts General Hospital, had a different take.

Born in Brookline, Massachusetts, in 1868, Cabot, from his earliest years, inhaled the atmosphere of New England Transcendentalism. His father, James, was an intimate friend of Ralph Waldo Emerson's, to whom he served as editor, literary executor, and early biographer. The Cabot family attended a liberal Unitarian church, and Richard studied at Harvard under William James and Idealist philosopher Josiah Royce.

William James was already devising the principles of the philosophy known as pragmatism. The heart of James's pragmatic outlook was that the measure of an idea's value was its *effect on conduct*. On this, James was uncompromising. To speak of allegiance to one creed or another was meaningless, he reasoned, unless you could demonstrate its impact on human behavior, "its *cash-value*, in terms of particular experience," he wrote in 1898.

Such thinking gave Cabot a framework for his own radical inquiries. He decided to become a medical doctor—but, crucially, he held to the belief that healing, like all facets of life, must be a composite. He believed that biologic cures in no way precluded, and often were aided by, the confidence of the patient, which could be fortified by faith, suggestion, and realistic, healthful self-belief. Taking a leaf from James's pragmatism, Cabot insisted that if a method healed, it was valid, whether the treatment was allopathic, alternative, spiritual, emotional, or any combination. While Cabot firmly believed that "spiritual healings" were really mental in nature, he conceded that the faculties at work were sometimes inscrutable, and warranted further study.

"It is a thousand pities that these dissensions—these sectarian dissensions—have occurred in medicine as well as in religion," Cabot wrote in 1908. "We ought to get together. There is truth in all the schools; indeed there is nothing more characteristic of the American spirit than the realization of that fact."

Cabot was a brilliant laboratory researcher—at age twenty-eight in 1896 he wrote the first English-language textbook on hematology. Yet he turned down an opportunity to become the first bacteriologist at Massachusetts General Hospital; two years later he accepted a less prestigious position in the outpatient department. Cabot was more interested in face-to-face treatment than in lab research. He believed that physicians were assuming an inappropriately distant and inflated role in the new century, and were neglecting the experience, emotions, social problems, and fears of the patient. In response, Cabot hired the nation's first medical social worker at Massachusetts General in 1905. The hospital administration disapproved of the move and refused to pay her. Cabot paid the salary himself.

The following year, Cabot joined forces with a controversial and intriguing healing program, which emerged from an Episcopal church in Boston's Back Bay. Called the Emmanuel Movement, for Emmanuel Church, which housed it, the project was a psycho-therapeutic clinic, presided over by the church's Reverend Elwood Worcester and his associate rector, Samuel McComb. The men sought to aid patients through prayer, support-group meetings, affirmations, hypnotic suggestion, and medical lectures delivered by Boston physicians.

The Emmanuel Movement sharply distanced itself from both Christian Science and mind-cure, insisting that its focus was limited to "functional nervous disorders," such as alcoholism, depression, migraines, chronic aches and pains, and digestive and bowel ailments. (This focus on "functional disorders" became a point of controversy, however, as the Emmanuel Movement also treated patients for tuberculosis, an infectious disease that then had no cure.) Further distinguishing itself from the mind-cure field, the Emmanuel clinic would see patients only on the referral and diagnosis of a physician. Reverend Worcester framed the clinic's activities not as an alternative to medicine but as a complement. The Emmanuel group received enormous, and often positive, media exposure, frequently from the nation's largest magazines, such as *Ladies' Home Journal* and *Good Housekeeping*.

Cabot became the Emmanuel Movement's chief medical advisor in 1906. He was intrigued not only by the relief that its methods seemed to bring, but by how the movement addressed a large number of ailments that, while real enough, didn't necessarily belong in the physician's examination room. "Now, without trying to limit the field precisely," Cabot wrote in 1908, "I should say that the diseases which are essentially mental or moral or spiritual in their origin should be treated (in part at least) by mental, moral and spiritual agencies. Cases of this type constitute in my experience about two-fifths of all the cases that come to an ordinary physician . . ." To Cabot the complementary approach was suited to disorders such as insomnia, digestive and bowel problems, and phantom aches and pains.

He felt, furthermore, that American medicine blinded itself with its specialized divisions. Every healer, from an osteopath to an allopath to a Christian Science practitioner, could speak of cure rates for those diseases *that came to them*, but not to the field of ailments in general. As Cabot saw it, medical professionals' frame of reference was too narrow, their willingness to collaborate too limited. Share patients and share data, he urged.

While Cabot believed in the efficacy of faith-based or mind-cure treatments, his support rested upon a strict distinction between "functional" and "organic" ailments. The mind-healing movements, he insisted, were highly capable of treating the kinds of *functional* diseases seen at the Emmanuel program—that is, bodily discomfort and stress-related disorders—which were not bacterial or structural. However, *organic* disease—biologic and organ-centered disorders—absolutely required standard medical care.

"Our friends the Christian Scientists," he wrote, "entirely ignore the distinction between organic and functional disease. I believe that organic disease is not helped to any extent by mental means, while functional disease has been helped a great deal by this means. Hence, there is nothing more important than to make clear this distinction."

Cabot's reasoning squares with the findings of today's most well-regarded placebo studies. The director of Harvard's Program in Placebo Studies and the Therapeutic Encounter, Ted J. Kaptchuk, told the *Wall Street Journal* in 2012: "Right now, I think evidence is that placebo changes not the underlying biology of an illness, but the way a person experiences or reacts to an illness." (It should be noted that Cabot considered placebos deceptive and he explicitly opposed their use; Kaptchuk's contemporary research, by contrast, centers on "transparent placebos," in which a patient knows he is receiving an inert substance. Kaptchuk's studies are considered later.)

For all the possibilities, Cabot and the Emmanuel Movement had limited success in winning the support of mainstream medicine. Cabot produced case studies and statistics showing traceable benefits from the Emmanuel program of prayer, encouragement, and religious counseling. Most medical professionals, however, turned up their noses. In journals and talks, physicians often complained that Emmanuel conflated the activities of doctors and clergy, and confused the public. (Cabot himself was never fully satisfied with the completeness of Emmanuel's record keeping.) "The Emmanuel movement," wrote physician Charles Dean Young in 1909 in the *Boston Medical and Surgical Journal*, "was and is, unquestionably well meant"—mental and spiritual healers had by this time come to realize that praise for good intent lined the steps to the guillotine—"but its originators are powerless to confine it within its legitimate bounds as the medical profession is powerless to prevent quackery, and, for some reason, the dear public does so love to be humbugged."

That same year Sigmund Freud visited America and, while he acknowledged knowing little about Emmanuel, the psychoanalyst told the *Boston Evening Transcript* on September 11: "This undertaking of a few men without medical, or with very superficial medical training, seems to me at the very least of questionable good. I can easily understand that this combination of church and psychotherapy appeals to the public, for the public has always had a certain weakness for everything that savors of mysteries . . ."

Ironically, the Emmanuel Movement, and other early strains of mind-cure, whetted the American appetite for Freud's theories of the unconscious. William James, who had contemporaneously labored to track the existence of a "subliminal mind," was dismayed by Freud's certainty that his psychoanalytic movement alone had science at its back. James wrote a colleague on September 28 that Freud had "condemned the American religious therapy (which has such extensive results) as very 'dangerous because so unscientific.' Bah!"

The controversies were no help to Cabot's career. In 1912, in what must have been a significant personal disappointment, Cabot was passed over for his expected appointment as Harvard's Jackson Professor of Medicine, one of the university's oldest medical professorships. Harvard instead opted for a professor who was more active in laboratory science. Cabot continued an important medical career, including as a director of battlefield medicine in France during World War I.

Following the war, Cabot launched a new campaign to urge American seminaries to train clergy in clinical and patient counseling. In 1925 he partnered with Anton Boisen, a minister who recovered following his institutionalization in a mental hospital to become one of the most eloquent voices for training seminary students in pastoral therapy. Cabot and his supporters met with measured success, helping to start pastoral training programs at Massachusetts General Hospital and Worcester State Hospital.

While widely copied in its early years, the Emmanuel Movement reached its end in 1929 with Reverend Worcester's retirement. There were no ready successors to his leadership. Indeed, none of Emmanuel's imitators were active for more than a few years. Emmanuel and its offshoots had petered out for reasons foreseen by Cabot: Ambitious clergy may have been willing to assume a counseling role, but they lacked training to sustain rigorous, ongoing programs. "The average clergy-man," wrote Carl J. Scherzer, a hospital chaplain who had studied Em-manuel, "was not academically trained to undertake such a healing program even though he possessed a personality that might predict a reasonable amount of success in it."

Cabot died in 1939, ten years after Emmanuel closed its doors.

Although Cabot and Emmanuel failed to win over mainstream phy-sicians, the movement proved a greater impact on the churches them-selves. In a national survey of liberal Protestant ministers in the early 1950s, more than one-third of respondents reported using methods of spiritual healing, which included affirmations, individual and group prayer, and acts of forgiveness—all elements of the Emmanuel program. This was a marked change from Protestant clergy's indifference toward such measures at the start of the century. And Cabot's calls for pastoral clinical training found new champions in the next generation.

RABBI LOUIS WITT:
"WE CANNOT HIDE THESE THINGS FROM THE WORLD"

When I was growing up as a teenager on Long Island, I once heard a young rabbi tell a religiously and politically conservative congregation that when we suffer inside we can also become deeper human beings. The formula for self-growth, he said, is "to turn your pain into a paint-ing." Some may have found it hokey, though judging from the silence in the room his remarks made an impact. I never forgot them.

Those words were a distant ripple from a Jewish spiritual-therapeutic movement that began in 1916 in response to the popularity of Christian Science among American Jews. In an echo of Mrs. Eddy's phrasing, it was called "Jewish Science." One of the motivational movement's most eloquent exponents was a St. Louis, Missouri, rabbi named Louis Witt. Though Witt disliked the term Jewish Science for its derivativeness, he ener-getically spread the movement's values into Judaism and other American faiths.

The Jewish Science movement was rooted in the early twentieth century, when American Jewish leaders worried over a steady inflow of Jewish converts into Christian Science. Though estimates widely varied, several thousand American Jews had joined Mrs. Eddy's healing movement by 1911. That year, the Jewish civic order B'nai B'rith was sufficiently concerned about the blurring lines between Judaism and Eddy's movement that it voted to exclude members who followed Christian Science practices.

It was not difficult to see the appeal of Christian Science to early-twentieth-century American Jews. The modern healing faith had none of the historical baggage of anti-Semitism. Christian Science literature was free of racially or religiously antagonistic language. Many Christian Science congregations were situated in upscale neighborhoods and, in the eyes of some, may have seemed like portals to assimilation and social acceptance. Most important, the rituals and liturgy that marked Jewish worship could, at times, seem formalized and empty to hungry seekers, who discovered a more intimate experience within the radical metaphysic and prayer treatments of Mrs. Eddy's church, with its promise of healing and a revelation of spiritual truth that soared beyond the bonds of the material world.

"May it be," wondered one Reform rabbi, Maurice H. Harris, "that we Jews—the rationalists of history—have been rational to a fault and have not realized sufficiently the value of the mystical in life?"

In 1916, Rabbi Alfred Geiger Moses, leader of a Reform congregation in Mobile, Alabama, conceived of a response. Moses attempted to devise a Jewish alternative in his book, *Jewish Science*, which gave the movement its name. While his ideas lacked the rigor of Mrs. Eddy's metaphysics of immaterialism, the rabbi sought to highlight what he saw as an authentic healing tradition tucked within the folds of Jewish history. Moses extensively revised his book in 1920 to reflect a more explicitly New Thought tone, with an emphasis on affirmations and denials, psychological insights, constructive optimism, and healing prayers. Moses drew his examples chiefly from Scripture—for example, he reframed the story of Jacob wrestling with an angel, and receiving his new name of "Israel," as a parable of man's quest for inner development.

"All human progress," Moses wrote, "has been accomplished by 'the Israelites' of humanity, who struggled with the forces of ignorance and wrong and mastered the laws of life and truth." The language of his 1920 book also reflected the work of New Thought author Ralph Waldo Trine, with its injunctions to "enter the silence"—Trine's signature phrase for communion with the infinite. *Jewish Science,* if not one of the best-remembered New Thought books, nonetheless had a distinctive and boldly experimental tone.

The book did not settle the question of how Judaism should respond to the mental-healing and Christian Science movements. Some rabbis wanted a more formal approach that specifically acknowledged and integrated mind-power methods. This was the position of Missouri rabbi Louis Witt, who in 1925 petitioned the Central Conference of American Rabbis (CCAR), the representative body of the Reform rabbinate, to authorize a committee to consider what Judaism could learn from the mental-healing movements.

At the group's 1925 annual meeting, Witt's proposal elicited caustic, even hostile, remarks. Rabbi Philip Waterman, of Kalamazoo, Michigan, lampooned the language of the "Cult of Jewish Science." From the convention floor he told Witt and the resolution's supporters: "Gentlemen of the Jewish Cult of Jewish Science, I want to say to you that humble as I am, I offer you this affirmation, I offer you this denial. Take it into the silence and let the silence be profound, let it be long."

Regardless, the conference did authorize Witt to chair a nine-person committee on "the Relationship of the Synagogue to Mental and Physical Healing."

Two years later, in June 1927, Witt was ready to present his committee's findings at a CCAR convention in Cape May, New Jersey. The committee itself was divided, 5 to 4, whether to even present its heterodox conclusions. With a slender majority at his back, Witt rose to deliver the findings on the final evening of the conference. Citing Richard C. Cabot's work in religion and health, the Witt report called for three basic reforms: (1) A rabbinical statement supporting "Spiritual Healing" in conjunction with mainstream medicine, as well as the promotion of "faith and prayer and higher forms of suggestion" to move a person's "indwelling divine energies into action." (2) The publication of booklets and periodicals to help congregants use Bible verses, rabbinical writings, and Jewish prayers for spiritual healing. (3) Establishing a course in "Reliotherapy or Spiritual Healing" at Hebrew Union College in Cincinnati, the Reform movement's seminary.

Witt knew he was facing opposition. In an era when most people still felt the chill of Victorian prohibitions against discussing matters of personal life, Witt delivered an extraordinarily intimate appeal from the convention floor. Speaking before three hundred conventioneers, he described how he and other rabbis were secretly sick at heart because of their disappointments in religion and their inability to help people in psychological anguish. As the St. Louis rabbi spoke, his words soared with such power that, at times, they seemed to emanate from the mouths of the reformist Hebrew prophets of antiquity:

> Now it has been said, to my utter amazement, that this report and this recommendation is a departure from Judaism. If it is a departure from Judaism then I wish I could be in something else than in the Jewish ministry. I claim this is the very essence of all that is fine and beautiful in Orthodox Judaism. It is that which haunts those of us who have been raised in Orthodoxy. Orthodox fathers and mothers did not have our rationalistic attitude. To them God was a reality. I tested out this recommendation in New York City last week. I asked a group of Orthodox Jews to give me some of their experiences. . . . I knew some of them very intimately. One of them told me that his daughter was very ill. He went to the Synagogue, he said, and

had a prayer offered for his daughter. When he came home his daughter said to him, "Papa, I had a dream; I dreamed that my bed was carried to the altar and I began to feel better."

The physician came the following day and although he had held out no hope the day before, he said, "Your child is going to get well."

I have gone into the hospitals; I have heard Orthodox Jews say, "God will help." This is what saved Judaism, it has been that personal attitude to a God who was very, very near, who could heal the sick, who was always present in time of trouble, who was always doing a spiritual healing. . . .

I am moved almost to smile—and if it were not so tragic I would smile—when I hear some of the rabbis say: Let us give the people more Judaism. You have been talking "more Judaism" ever since I have been a member of this Conference. What have you got? You have got nothing out of it because you have gone the wrong way. You are putting out new textbooks and you are giving more eloquent sermons on plays and novels and such things and you are talking before Rotary Clubs and on International Peace, and all those things. They are incidental to religion. . . .

A woman came to me three weeks ago, in the depths of melancholia. I did not know what to do for her. I talked as a doctor might talk—but I wanted to offer prayer for that woman and I wanted that woman to feel that I myself have been helped. I have gone through the period of melancholia. I have been a neurasthenic because of an utter disillusionment with regard to certain things in the Jewish ministry, and the things to which I dedicated my life, and many of you have confessed to me in past years, and some of you confessed to me last night and the night before, that you are suffering the same thing. We are hiding these things from the world . . . but the fact is that there is many a rabbi who is suffering from a sick soul and his soul is sick because life has meant frustration and disillusionment for him and we ourselves are not helped enough by the God that we preach—God is not near enough to us. . . .

I want this Conference to say that there is more power in religion than we are utilizing, and I want us then to proceed to utilize that power.

Witt's statement did not carry the day. His committee's recommendations were overwhelmingly voted down, 46 to 13. But a seed was planted. Ten years later, in 1937, the nation's Reform seminary, Hebrew Union College, acted on one of the committee's recommendations and inaugurated its first course in religious therapeutic training. The course later expanded to newly opened Hebrew Union campuses in New York and Los Angeles, and today is mandatory for Reform rabbis in America.

The same year the National Council of Churches formed a Commission on Religion and Health to promote therapeutic training among pastors. In 1949 the Lutheran Church formed an Advisory Council on Pastoral Care to promote clinical training of ministers. As the next decade opened, there existed two new and respected journals dedicated to ministerial counseling: the *Journal of Pastoral Care*, begun in 1946, and *Pastoral Psychology*, begun in 1950.

Yet the most decisive step in the mainstream acceptance of pastoral therapy grew out of the experience of World War II. Many of the eight thousand U.S. chaplains who went off to war discovered that soldiers were eager for counsel and solace. Sensing this gap in what servicemen wanted versus what they could offer, thousands of chaplains enrolled in courses on counseling. Harvard's Army Chaplains School, through which most military chaplains passed, established a curriculum in pastoral care in 1944. A study of American ministers conducted in the 1950s by the New York Academy of Sciences found that clergy often continued in this counseling role after the war, and that the wartime experience made them see pastoral therapy as a "special part" of their duties.

"By 1950," wrote religion scholar Rebecca Trachtenberg Alpert, "pastoral psychology was a routine part of the education of ministers."

Louis Witt, the Missouri rabbi who believed so deeply in the healing power of religion, is not widely remembered today. His name appears in few works of religious history. But Witt's ideals, and those of other rabbis loosely grouped within the movement of Jewish Science, formed a ripple. Joining with other influences, this ripple helped establish pastoral counseling as a mainstay of American religious life.*

BILL WILSON AND BOB SMITH:
HIGHER POWER FOR SELF-HELP

Many of the most effective purveyors of the positive-thinking gospel were figures only indirectly tied to its culture. Probably no other individuals in recent history were more consequential in shaping a mental-therapeutic spiritual program than Bill Wilson and Bob Smith, cofounders of Alcoholics Anonymous.

The Vermont-born men met in May 1935 in Akron, Ohio. Bill was a newly sober alcoholic traveling on business from New York. Alone at a hotel, he was desperate for a drink. He picked through a local church directory looking for a minister who could help him find another drunk to talk to. Bill had the idea that if he could locate another alcoholic to speak with, and to help, it might ease his own pangs for drink.

On that day, Bill found his way to Bob Smith, a local physician who had waged a long and losing battle with alcohol. Each man had spent years vainly trying out different ideas and treatments. When they met in Akron, however, each discovered that his inner resolve to stop drinking grew in proportion to his ability to counsel the other. Wilson and

---

* The Jewish Science movement remains active. The Society of Jewish Science maintains a congregation on Manhattan's East Side. That congregation's longtime religious leader, Tehilla Lichtenstein (1893–1973), was the first female head of an American Jewish congregation. She took over the pulpit from her husband, Rabbi Morris Lichtenstein, after his death in 1938. Like Emma Curtis Hopkins's seminary and other New Thought–inspired groups, Jewish Science evinced a notable pattern of early female leadership.

Smith's friendship resulted in the founding of Alcoholics Anonymous and the modern twelve-step movement.

Bill Wilson and Bob Smith appeared as all-American as their names. In their looks, dress, and politics, both men were as conservative as an old-fashioned banker, which Wilson actually was. But each man was also a spiritual adventurer, committed to traversing the terrain of metaphysical experience, from Spiritualism to New Thought to Eastern metaphysics in search of a workable solution to addiction. Together, they wove Christian, Swedenborgian, Jungian, Christian Science, and New Thought themes into the twelve steps of Alcoholics Anonymous.

Though initially designed for alcoholism, the AA approach gave birth to the modern recovery movement. Its twelve-step model was later used to treat problems encompassing drug addiction, compulsive gambling, weight control, excessive spending, and chronic anger. AA altered the language of American life, giving rise to expressions such as "easy does it," "one day at a time," "first things first," and "let go and let God." Its literature also popularized an ecumenical term for God: "Higher Power." This phrase appeared in the group's key principle that the alcoholic's "defense must come from a Higher Power," as Bill Wilson wrote in 1939. But Wilson and Smith insisted that twelve-steppers must form their own conception of God "*as we understood Him*," as the third step went. "Higher Power" neatly captured the radical ecumenism they were after.

The phrase Higher Power probably entered AA's lexicon through Ralph Waldo Trine's New Thought bestseller, *In Tune with the Infinite*, a favorite book of Bob Smith's. Trine repeatedly used the term, with particular reference to alcohol: "In the degree that we come into the realization of the higher powers of the mind and spirit . . . there also falls away the desire for the heavier, grosser, less valuable kinds of food and drink, such as the flesh of animals, alcoholic drinks . . ."

In a sense, Alcoholics Anonymous had its earliest beginnings with Bill Wilson's marriage in January 1918 to his wife and intellectual partner, Lois Burnham. Lois came from an old-line family with roots in Lancaster, Pennsylvania, and Brooklyn, New York. Her family had a deep commitment to the Swedenborgian Church, the congregation founded on the mystical philosophy of Emanuel Swedenborg. Lois's paternal grandfather was one of the nation's first Swedenborgian ministers. She and Bill got married at the Church of the Neighbor, a Swedenborgian congregation in Brooklyn. After that church's closing, Lois attended the New York New Church, a Swedenborgian congregation on Manhattan's East Side. Dating back to 1816, this congregation included Henry James Sr., the father of William and Henry James, and Helen Keller. It continues today. Lois was reticent about publicly expressing her Swedenborgian commitments—she wanted to avoid any appearance of religious favoritism after the founding of AA. Asked shortly before her death in 1988 whether Swedenborgianism had influenced the twelve steps, Lois replied that no particular faith should be singled out in AA. "If there was a connection," Lois said, "I wouldn't tell you anyway, for that very reason."

The Swedenborgian faith that ran through Lois's family does seem to have impacted Bill, especially when his binge drinking drove him to seek spiritual solutions. A key tenet of Swedenborgianism, later reflected in AA literature, was that man could serve as a vessel for higher energies. Swedenborg wrote of a "Divine influx" suffusing the material world. Ralph Waldo Trine called it a "divine inflow." This notion appears to have helped Bill define his own "awakening experience" in December 1934. At the time, Bill was laid up in Towns Hospital in Manhattan, a place where he frequently retreated to recover from benders. He was stuck in a cycle of binge drinking, drying out, and drinking again. Bill was in agony over being unable to control the alcoholism that was sending him down a path that would likely have ended in his death, due either to a drinking-related accident or illness, or to indigence.

"Lying there in conflict," Bill wrote, "I dropped into the blackest depression I had ever known. Momentarily my prideful obstinacy was crushed. I cried out, 'Now I'm ready to do anything . . .'" What happened next completely reordered his life:

> Though I certainly didn't really expect anything, I did make this frantic appeal: "If there be a God, will He show Himself!" The result was instant, electric, beyond description. The place seemed to light up, blinding white. I knew only ecstasy and seemed on a mountain. A great wind blew, enveloping and penetrating me. To me, it was not of air, but of Spirit. Blazing, there came the tremendous thought "You are a free man."

Bill had experienced something like the "Divine influx." The experience of religious awakening was confirmed for him several days later during a visit by his friend Ebby Thacher. Ebby was involved with a Christian evangelical fellowship called the Oxford Group. He gave Bill a book that became his closest companion and source of insight: *The Varieties of Religious Experience* by William James. "I devoured it," Wilson recalled. In James's case studies, Wilson recognized his own awakening episode. The philosopher had termed it a "conversion experience." The realization of a higher power, James wrote, often struck the believer with such clarity and power that it objectively altered the circumstances of his outer life. The conversion experience had done so for Bill; he never drank again.

In the years immediately ahead, Bill codified his experience into the first three steps of the twelve-step program. The first three steps were a kind of blueprint for a Jamesian conversion experience. They were written in such a way that the word *alcohol* could be replaced by any other compulsory fixation, such as *anger, drugs,* or *gambling*:

1. We admitted we were powerless over alcohol—that our lives had become unmanageable.
2. Came to believe that a Power greater than ourselves could restore us to sanity.
3. Made a decision to turn our will and our lives over to the care and direction of God *as we understood Him.*

Working as the chief writer, Bill published the twelve steps in 1939 in what became known as the "Big Book," *Alcoholics Anonymous*. While William James's work was central to Bill, many other influences shaped his book. Bill tore through spiritual literature, reading and rereading Mary Baker Eddy's *Science and Health*, alongside New Thought books such as Emmet Fox's *The Sermon on the Mount*, an interpretation of Christ's oration as a mental-manifestation philosophy. He also read Christian inspirational works, such as Scottish evangelist Henry Drummond's meditation on the transformative power of love, *The Greatest Thing in the World*.

Ebby Thacher also brought Bill to two additional philosophies that deeply impacted AA's development: the teachings of the Oxford Group and the spiritual outlook of Carl Jung. In a sense, all of these early influences—William James, the Oxford Group, and Jung—reflected vastly different thought systems. But their unifying core was the principle that the sensitive, searching mind could bring a person to an experience of a Higher Power.

The Oxford Group was an enterprising and profoundly influential evangelical movement in the first half of the twentieth century. Its teachings brilliantly distilled therapeutic and self-help principles from within traditional Christian thought. So named in 1929 because of its large contingent from Oxford University, the Oxford Group devised a protocol of steps and principles intended to awaken modern people to the healing qualities of God in a manner similar to that experienced by first-century Christians. These steps included radical honesty, stringent moral self-examination, confession, making restitution, daily meditation or "quiet time," and opening oneself to awakening or conversion experiences. Much of this was later reflected in the twelve steps.

To facilitate its program, the Oxford Group pioneered the use of group meetings or "house parties." These took place in an encounter-group atmosphere of confession, shared testimonies, and joint prayer. Mutual help and lay therapy were central to Oxford's program, and gave rise to a similar structure in AA.

Yet for some Oxford members, eventually including Bill and Lois

Wilson, the group-meeting atmosphere could deteriorate into a brow-beating, accusatory climate in which members were singled out for not sufficiently sharing personal intimacies or detailing their moral failings. Oxford's internal culture demanded a gung-ho approach—converts were often coached to be "maximum" in their commitment. This all-the-way style emanated from the group's founder, Frank Buchman, an American Lutheran minister who initiated its meetings in the early 1920s. Buchman was the organization's greatest asset and gravest failing.

A shrewd and impassioned organizer, Buchman built the group through a strategy of recruiting "key people." Such a figure might be a celebrity, a banker, or, on a college campus, the captain of the football team. A key person, in turn, attracted others into the fold. Buchman often organized his Oxford meetings at posh hotels or in the homes of well-to-do members—again making the group attractive by its sheen of success. Mary Baker Eddy probably devised a similar strategy in building her Christian Science churches, schools, and reading rooms in high-end neighborhoods. Even the Oxford Group's informal use of the great university's name (which it was later asked to discontinue) lent it an air of respectability.

In 1936 Buchman upset all of his carefully laid plans. The Lutheran minister ignited an international uproar when he apparently set his sights on attracting a unique key person: Adolf Hitler. During the 1930s, Buchman traveled to Germany, where he met with Heinrich Himmler (whose wife was reportedly in sympathy with the Oxford Group). Buchman vocally praised Hitler as a bulwark against atheistic Communism. ". . . think what it would mean to the world," he told a reporter for the *New York World-Telegram* in an interview published August 26, 1936, "if Hitler surrendered to the control of God. Or Mussolini. Or any dictator. Through such a man God could control a nation overnight and solve every last, bewildering problem."

The Oxford Group founder went further still, uttering his most notorious words: "I thank heaven for a man like Adolf Hitler, who built a front line of defense against the anti-Christ of Communism."

While Bill Wilson had wanted to save drunks, Frank Buchman said he wanted to save "drunken nations." Buchman's maximalist worldview held no appeal for Bill and Lois, who, after distancing themselves for some months following Buchman's announcement, pulled away from Oxford entirely by 1937. By the end of the decade most of AA's groups had stopped all cooperation with Oxford. Around that time the Buchman organization also lost some of its most thoughtful ministers and organizers, including the Reverend Sam Shoemaker, an Episcopal priest at New York's Calvary Church, who was a major influence on Bill.

Yet Bill's friend Ebby Thacher had also introduced Bill to another, very different stream of ideas: the psycho-spiritual theories of Carl Jung. Bill said the psychologist's role was "like no other" in the founding of AA. At the same time, Bill also praised William James as "a founder of Alcoholics Anonymous." Bill may have eagerly emphasized AA's debt to respected figures like Jung and James as a way of exorcising the shadows of Frank Buchman. Yet all of these influences could not be easily separated out, one from the other. As it happens, Ebby had been recruited into Oxford by a former patient of Jung's, a Rhode Island businessman named Rowland Hazard. Rowland's experiences, in turn, brought Jung's influence into AA.

Around 1931 Rowland visited the Swiss psychologist to seek help with his alcoholism. He reported leaving the doctor's care feeling cured, but suffered a relapse a few weeks later. Rowland returned desperate, pleading to know what could be done. Jung leveled with the American: He had never once seen a patient recover from alcoholism. "I can do nothing for you," the psychologist said. Rowland begged, surely there must be something? Well, Jung replied, there may be one possibility: "Occasionally, Rowland, alcoholics have recovered through spiritual experiences, better known as religious conversions." Jung went on: "All you can do is place yourself in a religious atmosphere of your own choosing"—here was the AA principle of pursuing God *as we understood Him*—and, Jung continued, "admit your personal powerlessness to go on living. If under such conditions you seek with all your might, you may then find . . ."

Jung's prescription matched what Bill had experienced at Towns Hospital. For Bill, it served as further confirmation of the need for a spiritual solution to addiction.

Years later, Bill finally wrote to Jung, on January 23, 1961, in the last months of the psychologist's life. Bill wanted to tell him how his counsel to Rowland had impacted the AA program. He also told Jung that "many AAs report a great variety of psychic phenomena, the cumulative weight of which is very considerable."

To Bill's delight, Jung responded with a long letter on January 30. The psychologist vividly recalled Rowland and what he had told him. Jung repeated to Bill his formula for overcoming alcoholism: *spiritus contra spiritum*. The Latin phrase could be roughly translated as: *Higher Spirit over lower spirits*, or alcohol. It was the twelve steps in a nutshell.

Although no vast religion of mental therapeutics ever appeared on the American scene, Alcoholics Anonymous, through its blending of ideas from Swedenborg, James, Oxford, Jung, and New Thought, created a home for the "religion of healthy-mindedness."

GLENN CLARK:
COACH OF THE SOUL

Mainline churches faced a crisis of mission in the 1920s and '30s when congregants demanded practical help with the problems of life. An answer came from Glenn Clark, a Presbyterian lay leader who devised a radical theory of prayer drawn from mind-power influences. Although this college educator and athletic coach didn't strictly consider himself part of the New Thought fold, he brought mental-therapeutic principles into the pews of mainline congregations. He also wrestled with ethical demons, which, at times, gained the better of his judgment.

Clark was born in 1882 to a large and devout Christian family in Des Moines, Iowa. He became a young literature professor and coach at

Macalester College, a Presbyterian liberal arts school in St. Paul, Minnesota. At Macalester, Clark developed ties to Christian Scientists and New-Thoughters, with whom he huddled in study sessions, prayer groups, and discussions.

Clark grew enamored of the ideas of an English scientist and spiritual seeker named F. L. Rawson, a follower of Mary Baker Eddy. Though Rawson later split with the Christian Science church, the English engineer continued searching for a methodical, even scientific, approach to prayer, an interest shared by Clark. When Rawson visited the United States in the early 1920s, Clark traveled to meet his British hero in Minneapolis. To Clark's chagrin, however, Rawson seemed more like a technician of the soul than a man driven by a passion for truth and goodness.

"I determined then and there not to be a mere follower of his," Clark wrote, "but to begin where he left off." This was Clark's strength: never to settle for an idea but always to look for ways to build on it.

Clark wanted a method of practical prayer—and he soon found it. In 1924 he realized that for two years straight he had experienced "an almost continuous stream of answered prayer." What caused it? Clark was an athlete, and he discovered that to pray effectively a person had to prepare for prayer in much the same way a winning athlete trained and drilled before a competition. Clark's prayer-preparation regimen included meditation, breathing exercises, and preliminary devotionals. With the proper degree of "warm up," inner reflection, and sincerity, Clark insisted, prayers were almost guaranteed to work. Clark gained a national audience for his ideas in the summer of 1924 when the *Atlantic Monthly* (a journal rarely given to practical theology) ran his hugely popular article on effective prayer, "The Soul's Sincere Desire."

Clark had a gift for blending Biblical and psychological concepts into meaningful self-help formulas. One of Clark's techniques came to him one day when he had a breakthrough in his understanding of the Biblical verse 2 Samuel 22:34: *He maketh my feet like hinds' feet; and setteth me upon my high places.* Clark saw the verse as a psychological allegory: "hinds' feet"—an animal's powerful rear legs—are the subconscious mind, which is man's

interior engine and spiritual center. Whoever can coordinate the workings of the subconscious with the strivings of the conscious mind—just
as an animal coordinates its rear and front legs—is "most certain to
reach the heights in life," Clark wrote.

As a college varsity coach, Clark cultivated a backslapping rapport
with young people. He wanted to find ways of instructing them in constructive prayer and practical Christianity. This coach of the soul found
his answer in opening a network of Christian youth camps, Camps Farthest Out. The idea for the camps came to him in a dream in 1929. He
dubbed them "laboratories for experimentation in the art of praying."
After the first camp launched on Lake Koronis in central Minnesota in
1930, Camps Farthest Out set the mold for twentieth-century programs
in Christian youth development. They remain popular around the world
today.

Clark's first camps attracted a wide range of Christians, along with
some Jews and nonreligious campers. AA cofounder Bob Smith attended
retreats at Camps Farthest Out and spoke of Clark as one of his favorite
authors. Clark also maintained ties in the New Thought world, delivering talks at conventions of the International New Thought Alliance.

Clark believed in the power of prayer to cure illness, manage ad-
dictions, improve relationships—and even end war. That last conviction figured into a troubling aspect of his career. During World War II,
Clark tended toward a myopic view of using prayer and thought-power
to compel Hitler to halt his Blitzkrieg. While this approach was hardly
troubling in itself, Clark believed in it so completely that his political
outlook verged on appeasement. Clark was convinced that his prayer
groups had slowed Hitler's march into Poland in 1939 (rather than the
recent signing of the Polish-British Common Defense Pact). Even after
the war, Clark believed in Hitler's transparently propagandistic demand
that Poland could have settled matters "peacefully" by handing over the
Danzig Corridor to the Third Reich. "What he [Hitler] asked for," Clark
wrote, "merely the Danzig Corridor and a little more, was a fraction of
what, when provoked to war, he finally did take. In other words, all he

asked for were territories which many neutral authorities thought it only just for Germany to have. Think what this offer meant!" Such convictions were tempered by neither time nor perspective—Clark wrote this following the war in 1949, seven years before his death.

Writing in 1940, Clark described having a spiritual vision of Mussolini bending his head and lowering into a devout kneel "until his forehead touches the ground." Soon after Clark said that, he received a newspaper clipping from his Boston publisher, Little Brown, reporting that Mussolini had written to the company to purchase Clark's book, *The Soul's Sincere Desire*, and had paid for it with "his *personal* check."

One wants to believe Clark when he wrote in the same piece: "I do not believe in appeasement or compromise of any sort" toward the Axis. And in his heart he meant this. But Clark went beyond endorsing the uses of prayer and thoughts of love to influence Hitler; he made concrete and ardently felt policy prescriptions that amounted to the very thing he claimed to be set against. The spiritual visionary was so desperate to see the light that he was blinded to darker realities.

Other New Thought leaders, who will soon be met, raised their voices against fascism before the war and held rallies for Allied victory. Bill Wilson tried (and was deemed too old) to register for military service at the start of the conflict. Christian Scientists sent chaplains and service members to the front lines. In the positive-thinking culture Clark was a political outlier. Nonetheless, the question stands: Was Clark's blindness endemic to the positive-thinking philosophies? The final chapter will more fully consider how New Thought and positive thinking responded to evil, or, as in Clark's case, failed to.

ERNEST HOLMES:
NEW THOUGHT AMBASSADOR

Ernest Holmes was a Maine Yankee who remade himself as a California mystic—and became one of New Thought's greatest shapers and popularizers. While never widely known, Holmes stood at the center of Hollywood's mystical scene in the first half of the twentieth century, attracting admirers from Cecil B. DeMille to Elvis Presley. If New Thought had an ambassador, Holmes was it.

Born in a dingy Maine farmhouse in 1887 and never formally educated, the young Ernest devoured works by Ralph Waldo Emerson, Mary Baker Eddy, Scottish evangelist Henry Drummond, and British judge Thomas Troward, who published an ambitious series of lectures on the logic behind creative-mind principles.

Ernest grew especially fond of Transcendentalism, particularly as expressed in Emerson's classic "Self-Reliance." Emerson's most famous essay was also his least understood. While critics saw "Self-Reliance" as a paean to go-it-alone individualism, Ernest perceived its deeper truth: We all have within us a true self, free of conformity and conditioning; to live from this personal core is what alone makes a man great. It set Ernest's mind on fire.

At the start of World War I, Ernest relocated from New England to Venice, California, where his older brother, Fenwicke, was already settled. Fenwicke shared his brother's interests and became Ernest's intellectual partner. The two began filling lecture halls as early as 1916 with their metaphysical talks. Roundish and twinkle-eyed, Ernest shined before audiences. He exuded an unlikely charisma—as well as a shrewd command of different spiritual philosophies and religious systems. He spoke with clarity and total confidence, rarely using notes. His philosophy held that the images in our mind constantly out-picture into reality; we can direct the mind's forces and achieve our ideals, or we can passively be pulled along by an undisciplined rush of thoughts; either way we are in the gravitational tug of our ideas.

The young metaphysician's following grew as he performed "treatments"—or prayer and mind-power healings—on visitors to the office where he worked as a purchasing agent for the city of Venice. After travels to New York and other cities, where he road-tested his message among different listeners, Ernest molded his ideas into the philosophy called "Science of Mind" or "Religious Science." His movement developed into a thriving network of positivity-based churches:

the United Church of Religious Science. This proved an ill-fated choice of words, which in later decades served to confuse his movement with the more visible and entirely unrelated Church of Scientology. (In 2011 the Holmes congregations reorganized under the new name Centers for Spiritual Living.)

Ernest Holmes's comprehensive grasp of Scripture and world religious traditions, and his serious yet personable style, seemed, at least in his person, to nudge New Thought into a territory of intellectual and ethical solidity. His brother and collaborator Fenwicke presented a shakier history.

In 1929, Fenwicke, then a Congregationalist clergyman and Divine Science minister, came under investigation from the New York state attorney general for a stock-peddling scheme. Fenwicke purportedly pushed worthless mining stocks on congregants at his Divine Science congregation in New York as an adjunct to his prosperity teachings. The attorney general got an injunction barring Fenwicke and another Holmes sibling, William, from selling securities pending trial.

Watson S. Washburn and Edmund S. De Long, investigators for the attorney general, wrote about the Fenwicke Holmes affair in their 1932 book, *High and Low Financiers*:

> Five million dollars' worth of stock was sold by the Holmes brothers during the period commencing in 1920 and ending in 1929 when William and Fenwicke were enjoined from further stock-selling activities . . . a trial which has not yet been held. None of this stock ever paid a cent in interest or dividends.

The authors may have been exercising a certain degree of prosecutorial zeal. They worked for the man who pursued Fenwicke, New York State Attorney General Hamilton Ward, to whom they dedicated their book. Washburn and De Long were likely settling a score on a case that never made it through the courts. A trial had been scheduled for May 1930 but apparently never happened. State and federal court records show no decisions with Fenwicke's name attached. The likelihood is that a plea deal was struck, probably with Ward's successor, as Ward's term ended that same year.

Fenwicke managed to escape the legal cloud. He became a formidable force in spreading the positive-thinking gospel, including to Japan, where it spawned a popular counterpart to the Science of Mind movement: *Seicho-No-Ie*, or Home of Infinite Life, Truth, and Abundance. He also made a decisive impact on the influential mythologist Joseph Campbell, who attended Fenwicke's lectures in New York in the late 1920s. Fenwicke gave the young seeker an exercise to discover what he really wanted out of life: "One should jot down notes for a period of four or five weeks on the things that interest one. It will be found that all the interests tend in a certain direction." Campbell used this technique to reach his decision to become a scholar of myth. Fenwicke's advice seemed to echo in Campbell's famous maxim: "Follow your bliss."

Ernest Holmes narrowly eluded the vortex of his brother's legal problems. Investigators Washburn and De Long maintained that while Ernest was living in Venice Beach around 1917 he "was already engaged in a small way in the lucrative business of selling questionable stocks." They offered no evidence for the assertion and Ernest's name appeared in none of the news coverage that dogged Fenwicke. In fact, the younger brother had stopped working with Fenwicke in 1925—the reasons were never publicly discussed. They reunited in 1958, two years before Ernest's death, to collaborate on an epic poem, *The Voice Celestial*.

Ernest lived long enough to see his Science of Mind churches spread across the nation, encompassing more than 100,000 congregants. But his final years also saw his movement riven by a factional split. In a dispute over whether the churches would be self-governed, a cluster of ministries broke away in 1957 to form their own organization. The rift was bridged in 2011 when the two Holmes-based ministries, the United Church of Religious Science and the smaller Religous Science International, formally reunited.

Holmes's chief legacy was less as a congregational organizer than as a public voice. A formidable figure in the spiritual culture of Southern California, he attracted acolytes from Cary Grant to Peggy Lee to Cecil B. DeMille. His key text, *The Science of Mind*, became a favorite of Elvis Presley's and is found today in the library of George Lucas. As will be seen, Holmes made a major impact on Rev. Norman Vincent Peale. More recently, his books were named as an influence by major-league pitcher Barry Zito and by Martin Luther King Jr.'s eldest daughter, Yolanda, who called Science of Mind her core religious commitment shortly before her death in 2007.

While Ernest Holmes was never as well known as some of those who drank from his ideas, he was the closest New Thought had to an ambassador of the positive.

CHRISTIAN D. LARSON:
SOARING LANGUAGE, ETHICAL PITFALLS

While displaying a serene demeanor and a relentlessly upbeat tone, Christian D. Larson pursued a dual existence as both a visionary writer who shaped the language of self-help, and a businessman who pushed ethical boundaries in his publishing empire.

Born to Norwegian immigrant parents in the near-wilderness of northern Iowa in 1874, Larson had planned on a career as a Lutheran minister. But after a year at a Lutheran seminary in Minneapolis in 1894, he grew interested in Unitarianism, Transcendentalism, and the new mind-power philosophies. In 1898 Larson moved to Cincinnati, where he began writing and publishing New Thought tracts—and soon became a prolific and dynamic author.

Some of his earliest works featured phrases that became widely known, though rarely credited back to Larson. They include "live the simple life," "make yourself over," "live in the present only," and "attitude of gratitude"—the last made famous by Oprah Winfrey. Larson also coined the term "be all that you can be" generations before it became

the advertising slogan of the U.S. Army. His work "Promise Yourself"—
a verse meditation on the power of determined cheerfulness—gained
worldwide notice in 1922 when it was adopted as the credo of Optimist
International, a philanthropic club similar to the Jaycees or Rotarians.
The verse work became known ever after as "The Optimist Creed."

For a time, Larson was also enormously successful at publishing his
own widely read books and magazines at his Chicago-based Progress
Company. His magazine, *Eternal Progress*, which he launched in 1901, grew
by the end of the decade into a beautifully produced, socially progressive journal that combined the ideals of mind-power metaphysics with
articles and photographs highlighting the growth of the nation.

Alongside articles heralding New Thought's emergence as "a universal religion," *Eternal Progress* abounded with reportage and illustrated
spreads on great dams, railroads, skyscrapers, and other engineering
marvels that were bringing optimism about the future in the early twentieth century. In a typical issue, *Eternal Progress* chronicled the rebuilding
of San Francisco after the 1906 fire and earthquake, and the beauty and
growing economy of the Pacific Northwest, with its logging and fishing
enterprises. Larson also ran articles calling for universal suffrage and the
establishment of programs to educate and reform prisoners.

Even more than Elizabeth Towne's *Nautilus*, and probably unlike any
other magazine in American history, *Eternal Progress* captured all the hall-
marks of the Progressive Era: bounding commerce, scientific advances,
working-class struggles, social reforms, and the appeal of the new mental therapeutics. This zeitgeist of unlimited potential was captured in
Larson's March 1909 issue in the poem "Eternal Progress" by Townsend
Allen:

> From the first primeval atom,
> Upward, upward is the trend;
> Greater out of lesser growing.
> Ever to the perfect end.

Upward, onward, each to-morrow
Should be better than the past;
God's work in His creation;
All who will may win at last.

To broaden the magazine's appeal beyond the metaphysical, Larson shortened its name to *Progress* in June of that year.

For all of Larson's ideals, the visionary writer had a checkered business history. On July 25, 1911, the U.S. District Court for Northern Illinois declared Larson's Progress Company in "involuntary bankruptcy" following complaints from creditors who were owed $300,000. The court ordered a receiver to take control of the company's plants and holdings, and suspended publication of Larson's 250,000-circulation magazine. By August Larson had left town for Los Angeles. He later told an interviewer that his Chicago printing plant had burned down and, rather than rebuild, he decided to follow the country's momentum and move west. At the time of the Progress Company's receivership in 1911, however, creditors estimated that the company continued to hold plant and printing assets of about $100,000—a surprisingly robust sum for a business that Larson said was lost in a fire. Closer to the truth may be that Larson, facing a mountainous debt and with creditors at his heels, decided to act on his principle to "make yourself over" and left his liabilities behind to "reinvent" himself in Southern California.

Once in Los Angeles, Larson covered his tracks. He took one of the last books published in 1910 by his Progress Company, *Your Forces and How to Use Them*—he had taken the title from Prentice Mulford's signature work—and reissued it, switching the copyright year from 1910 to 1912 and changing the name of the copyright holder from the Progress Company to himself. He probably did this to shield the book from his Chicago creditors.* Larson repeated the practice with several other works.

---

* This book contained Larson's "Optimist Creed." His switch in the copyright dates, from 1910 to 1912, created the lasting misimpression that the world-famous meditation appeared two years later than it actually did.

In 1912, he reverted the name of his magazine back to its original title, *Eternal Progress*, and resumed publication. Larson hadn't lost his taste for social relevancy, as the renewed publication was heralded by an essay contest that offered a hundred-dollar prize for the best article on "The Cure of Poverty."

Larson's career exemplified the conflicting ideals that could mark the early New Thought movement.

Seen from one perspective, Larson meant what he wrote about the power of the mind to impact events, which he articulated in more than forty books until his death in 1962. Critics sometimes failed to appreciate the depths of passion and sincerity that were necessary for any writer to energetically produce that kind of output—much of it, in Larson's case, delightfully readable. When Larson's message reached people who had been raised in religiously repressive settings, or amid the peer pressure of small towns, it could arrive as a vivifying gospel of self-will.

Yet Larson also displayed a quality seen in Fenwicke Holmes (who cited Larson as a key influence) and in other mind-power acolytes who made ethical compromises on the path to self-improvement. And this was Larson's unnerving ability to avert his gaze so completely from the pale side of life, as in his debt-ridden Chicago past, that his sunny metaphysics served to conceal a lack of personal accountability. This moral ambiguity intermittently colored positive thinking for decades ahead.

ROY HERBERT JARRETT:
SALESMAN AS SEEKER

A popular New Thought voice of the 1920s and '30s sought to resolve the moral conundrums of self-affirming metaphysics. He concealed his identity behind the initials R.H.J., which stood for Roy Herbert Jarrett. By profession Jarrett was a salesman of typewriters and office printing machines. But this salesman accomplished what few ministers or practical philosophers ever did: He worked out an ethical philosophy of personal success and higher living, and couched it in everyday, immensely persuasive language. At age fifty-two Jarrett brought his message to the world with a self-published, pocket-sized pamphlet called simply: It *Works*.

Published in 1926, Jarrett's twenty-eight-page pamphlet has never gone out of print. It has sold over 1.5 million copies and remains popular—for good reason. It *Works* is one of the most beguiling and infectious books ever written on mental manifestation. Anyone who wants to taste (or test) such ideas can finish Jarrett's pamphlet during a lunch break. And many people did so. Americans who had never before given much thought to metaphysical ideas wound up buying and often giving away large numbers of It *Works*, sending grateful testimonials to the address that Jarrett printed inside.

As the legend goes at the front of the booklet, Jarrett had sent his short manuscript to a friend for critique. Jarrett identified the friend only by the initials "J.F.S." The helper returned it with the notation: "IT WORKS," which Jarrett decided to use as his title. The legend is true. The friend was Jewell F. Stevens, owner of an eponymous Chicago advertising agency, which specialized in religious items and books. In 1931, the advertising executive Stevens hired Jarrett to join his agency as a merchandising consultant and account manager. For Jarrett, the new position was deliverance from a tough, working-class background, and years of toil in the Willy Loman–domain of sales work. Jarrett became the example of his own success philosophy.

Roy Herbert Jarrett was born in 1874 to a Scottish immigrant household in Quincy, Illinois. His father worked as an iceman and a night watchman. Roy's mother died when he was eight. By his midtwenties, Roy was married and living in Rochester, New York, working as a sales manager for the Smith Premier Typewriter Company. His first marriage failed, and by 1905 he returned to the Midwest to marry a new wife and live closer to his aged father. In Chicago, Jarrett found work as a salesman for the American Multigraph Sales Company. It was the pivotal move of his life.

American Multigraph manufactured typewriters and workplace printing machinery. In a sense, the printing company was the Apple

Computer of its day. The company's flagship product, the Multigraph, was an innovative, compact printing press. It took up no more space than an office desk and could be operated without specialized knowledge. The Multigraph was the first generation of easy-to-use printing devices, allowing offices to produce their own flyers, mailers, and newsletters. Its manufacturer possessed a sense of mission. American Multigraph had a reputation in the printing trade for its gung-ho culture and pep-rally sales conventions.

"For years," wrote the industry journal *Office Appliances* in September 1922, "a feature of every convention has been an address on 'The Romance of the Multigraph' by Advertising Manager Tim Thrift." On the surface, Thrift told salesmen, the Multigraph could print labels, newsletters, and pamphlets—but one must peer into "the soul of what to some appears as a machine." The Multigraph, he said, was "not a thing of metal, wood and paint; a mere machine sold to some man who can be convinced he should buy it. Ah, no! The Multigraph is a thing of service to the world . . ."

Cynics could laugh, but for Jarrett the company's motivational tone, combined with the magical-seeming efficiency of modern printing, helped launch him on the idea of It *Works*.

Jarrett's belief in inspirational business messages dovetailed with his interest in autosuggestion and mental conditioning. Such ideas reached Jarrett through the work of a French pharmacist and self-taught psychologist named Emile Coué, who had visited Chicago. Jarrett's vision grew from a cross-pollination of American business motivation and the ideals of the French mind-power theorist.

Born in Brittany in 1857, Emile Coué developed an early interest in hypnotism, which he pursued through a mail-order course from Rochester, New York. Coué more rigorously studied hypnotic methods in the late 1880s with physician Ambroise-Auguste Liébeault. The French therapist Liébault was one of the founders of the so-called Nancy School of hypnotism, which promoted hypnotism's therapeutic uses. While working as a pharmacist at Troyes in northwestern France in the early 1900s,

Coué made a startling discovery: Patients responded better to medications when he spoke in praise of the formula. Coué came to believe that the imagination aided not only in recovery but also in a person's general sense of well-being. From this insight, Coué developed a method of "conscious autosuggestion." It was a form of waking hypnosis that involved repeating confidence-building mantras while in a relaxed or semiconscious state.

Coué argued that many people in life suffer from a poor self-image. Our *willpower*, or drive to achieve, he said, is constantly overcome by our *imagination*, by which he meant a person's unconscious self-perceptions. "When the will and the imagination are opposed to each other," he wrote, "it is always the *imagination* which *wins* . . ." By way of example, he asked people to think of walking across a wooden plank laid on the floor—obviously an easy task. But if the same plank is elevated high off the ground, the task becomes fraught with fear even though the physical demand is the same. This, Coué asserted, is what we are constantly doing on a mental level when we *imagine* ourselves as worthless or weak.

Coué's method of *autosuggestion* was a model of simplicity. He told patients to repeat the confidence-building mantra: *Day by Day, In Every Way, I'm Getting Better and Better.* It was to be recited twenty times each morning and evening, just loud enough to hear, while lying in bed upon awakening and before going to sleep, with eyes closed and the mind focused on what you desire. He advised using a string with twenty knots to count off the repetitions, as if counting rosary beads.

In the early 1920s, news of Coué's method reached America. The "Miracle Man of France" briefly grew into an international sensation. American newspapers featured *Ripley's-Believe-It-Or-Not*-styled drawings of Coué, looking like a goateed magician and gently displaying his knotted string at eye level like a hypnotic device. In early 1923, Coué made a three-week lecture tour of America. One of his final stops in February was in Jarrett's hometown, where the Frenchman delivered a talk at Chicago's Orchestra Hall.

In a raucous scene, a crowd of more than two thousand demanded that the therapist help a paralytic man who had been seated onstage. Coué defiantly told the audience that his autosuggestive treatments could work only on illnesses that originated in the mind. "I have not the magic hand," he insisted. Nonetheless, Coué approached the man and told him to concentrate on his legs and to repeat, "It is passing, it is passing." The seated man struggled up and haltingly walked. The crowd exploded. Coué rejected any notion that his "cure" was miraculous and insisted that the man's disease must have been psychosomatic.

To some American listeners, Coué's message of self-affirmation held special relevance for oppressed people. The pages of Marcus Garvey's newspaper, Negro World, echoed Coué's day-by-day mantra in an editorial headline: "Every Day in Every Way We See Drawing Nearer and Nearer the Coming of the Dawn for Black Men." The paper editorialized that Marcus Garvey's teachings provided the same "uplifting psychic influence" as Coué's.

Coué took a special liking to Americans. He found American attitudes a refreshing departure from what he knew back home. "The French mind," he wrote, "prefers first to discuss and argue on the fundamentals of a principle before inquiring into its practical adaptability to every-day life. The American mind, on the contrary, immediately sees the possibilities of it, and seeks . . . to carry the idea further even than the author of it may have conceived."

The therapist could have been describing the salesman-seeker Roy Jarrett. "A short while ago," Jarrett wrote in 1926, the year of Coué's death, "Dr. Emile Coué came to this country and showed thousands of people how to help themselves. Thousands of others spoofed at the idea, refused his assistance and are today where they were before his visit." But Jarrett saw the potential.

Taking his cue from the ease of Coué's approach, Jarrett devised "Three Positive Rules to Accomplishment" in It Works. In summary, they went:

1. Carefully write a list of what you *really* want in life—
    once you are satisfied with it, read it three times daily:
    morning, noon, and night.
2. Think about what you want as often as possible.
3. Keep your practice and desires strictly to yourself.
    (This was intended to prevent other people's negative
    reactions from sullying your inner resolve.)

Just as Coué had observed about American audiences, Jarrett boldly
expanded on the uses of autosuggestion. In the steps of the American
metaphysical tradition, Jarrett believed that subconscious-mind training
did more than recondition the mind: it activated a divine inner power
that served to out-picture a person's mental images into the surrounding
world. "I call this power 'Emmanuel' (God in us)," Jarrett wrote.

With its ease of methods, the self-published pamphlet quickly found
an audience and ran through multiple printings. Many readers swore by
it, and wrote in for additional copies to give away to friends (something
Jarrett encouraged with a bulk-order form). But Jarrett felt incomplete.
It wasn't that he chafed at using mind-power for material ends. Indeed,
he urged readers to use the book for money, possessions, or just about
anything they wanted. But he believed that many had missed the book's
deeper point. "Merely giving you the simple rules to accomplishment,
with brief instructions as to their use," he wrote several years later,
"while beneficial, is not satisfying."

Jarrett's deeper purpose in It *Works* was only hinted at by a mysterious
symbol he placed on its cover. Below the title It *Works* appeared a simple
drawing of a cross, with its bottom bent at a right angle. The square-and-
cross appeared on every copy of the little red book until 1992, when a
later publisher removed it. That symbol, wrote Jarrett's friend Stevens,
"was really the undisclosed reason for the book."

What was this beguiling square-and-cross, which some readers
ignored, some wondered at, and a publisher later cut? Five years after
producing It *Works*, Roy Jarrett made a little known and final foray into

publishing. In 1931, he produced a thoughtful and ambitious work, The *Meaning of the Mark*. The longer volume served as an inner key to It *Works*—it explained his strange symbol and dealt directly with the moral quandaries of success-based spirituality.

Jarrett explained that the cross-and-square was his personal symbol of spiritual awakening. Its meaning, he hoped, would be intuitively felt by readers. The square represented earthly values, particularly the need to treat others with the respect one seeks for oneself, which Jarrett saw as the hidden key to achievement. But there was another part to the matter. Personal attainment could find its lasting and proper purpose only when conjoined to the cross, the presence of God. Together, individual striving and receptivity to the Divine would bring man into the fullness of life. Jarrett wrote:

> The definition of correct thinking for our purpose is: "thoughts which are harmoniously agreeable to God and man as a whole." Thoughts agreeable to God come to you through the intuitive messages from your soul, often intensified by the senses. Thoughts agreeable to man come to you more frequently through the senses and are often intensified by intuition.

By dwelling on the meaning of the square-and-cross, he reasoned, the reader could be constantly reminded to unite the two currents of life.

The success of It *Works* helped Jarrett attain a lifestyle that, while not extravagant, went beyond anything his laborer father could have hoped for. Jarrett and his wife retired to a sunny hacienda-style bungalow in a tidy middle-class section of Beverly Hills. But their California idyll was fated to be short-lived. Jarrett died there in 1937 at age sixty-three of leukemia. He had been diagnosed three years earlier.

Jarrett didn't embark on his career as a writer until the final years of his life. He produced both of his books while in his fifties. His success arose not despite the lateness of his start but *because* of it. Like James

Allen and the best New Thought pioneers, this self-educated man from ordinary life devised a philosophy that had been tested by the nature of his own personal conduct and lived experience. Only then did he deem it worth sharing.

FRANK B. ROBINSON AND THE FILLMORES:
PIONEERING MEDIA MINISTERS

No set of figures in the New Thought tradition could seem more different than Frank B. Robinson and the husband-wife team of Charles and Myrtle Fillmore.

A Stetson-wearing pitchman, Robinson grew up as an orphaned knockabout in the American West and went on to operate his own mail-order religion during the Great Depression. The Fillmores were a solidly midwestern married couple who lived by values of thrift, accountability, religious devotion, and their own carefully honed message of Christian healing, which they spread through their Unity ministry.

Yet Robinson and the Fillmores, preaching their own distinctive versions of the New Thought gospel, pioneered the uses of mass media—including advertising, radio, and mailings—to spread a mystical message to vast numbers of people. These positive thinkers were the first media ministers of the twentieth century.

Robinson's religion-by-mail was known by the enticingly modern name of *Psychiana*, which Robinson said came to him in a dream. It was a subscription-based faith that he began in the late 1920s from his home in Moscow, Idaho. Through national print and radio ads, Robinson sold sets of digest-sized correspondence lessons on how to use the reality-shaping powers of the mind.

"And the best thing about it," he told a wire-service reporter, "is that we guarantee results or your money refunded. I guess it's about the only 'money-back' religion in the world." Critics scoffed, but the Psychiana movement grew so large during the Great Depression that it could have been considered the eighth-largest religion on earth.

Robinson was born in 1886 into a household in northern England headed by an abusive Baptist minister. Frank lost his mother to pneumonia when he was eight. Six years later, when Frank was fourteen and his younger brother Sydney was twelve, their father kicked the boys out of their home. Wanting a fresh start with his new wife, the minister shipped his sons off to Canada, with no plans for their care. When they reached the door of an Ontario preacher with whom their father had supposedly made arrangements, the man turned them onto the streets.

Robinson bounced around in different jobs. He joined the Royal Canadian Mounted Police, as well as the U.S. Army and Navy, but each time he was discharged for drunkenness and bad conduct. Nonetheless, the handsome Robinson showed an innate and keen grasp of religious topics; he attracted benefactors in Toronto who enrolled him in McMaster University's Bible Training School. As a student, however, Robinson refused to accept the premise that Christianity, or any religion, had a monopoly on truth. He argued with students and teachers that all religions had the same basic structure and myths. Yet no religion, he insisted, gave man anything practical or real to hang on to. His sponsors cut him off.

The former Bible student made his way to Oregon, where he married and finally settled into steady employment as a druggist. A new job took him to Los Angeles. There, at age forty-two, Robinson returned home depressed one Sunday afternoon following a Methodist church service in Hollywood. He was disappointed with the listless service, and he felt that his personal search for a real, verifiable God had gone nowhere. He pleaded to be shown something more—and challenged God to reveal himself. "Oh, God," he cried, "if I have to go to hell, I'll go with the consciousness that I went there earnestly trying to find you, God." Suddenly, Robinson felt his entire body pulsing with life; something alive and creative seemed to be coursing through him. His mood lifted, and his mind grew clear and focused.

What Robinson discovered that afternoon, he said, is that the power of God pulses through the human mind, waiting to do man's will. "The creative God-law of the universe . . . is all around you and in existence for the fulfilling of your every right desire," he wrote.

Though his conclusions radically differed from Alcoholics Anonymous cofounder Bill Wilson's, Robinson, like Wilson, described what William James had termed a "conversion experience." Wilson and Robinson depicted it in parallel terms. Yet while Bill Wilson saw God as a source of refuge and help for recovery, Robinson believed that his spiritual realization revealed to him a universal "God Law." This metaphysical law meant, in short, that *the imagination of man is God.* While religionists had been seeking God on crosses or in the heavens, Robinson said, the "God Law" was really one and the same as the human mind. He had finally discovered "a workable, useable God."

With ideas bursting in his head, Robinson moved with his wife and young son to the small town of Moscow, Idaho—for the sole purpose of accepting a job at a pharmacy that closed at 6 p.m. Leaving work early allowed the druggist to begin writing the lessons that would become the basis for his "new psychological religion."

One Saturday in 1928, Robinson sat down at a borrowed typewriter for thirty-six hours, laying out the lessons that would deliver his "God Law" into the hands of ordinary people. His written work completed, Robinson pulled together four hundred dollars and began taking out ads in newspapers, detective pulps, romance magazines, and on matchbook covers. Robinson's sales pitches were as audacious as the man himself. "I TALKED WITH GOD," his ads read. "Yes I Did—Actually and Literally . . . You too may experience that strange mystical power which comes from talking with God." Twenty dollars bought twenty lesson pamphlets on how to use the applied power of thought to bring success, money, jobs, and anything that was needed. People replied, first by the thousands and soon tens of thousands, and a new religious movement was born.

Though disparaged in the press as a "mail-order prophet," Robinson provided something of a lifeline to his subscribers, who sent him thousands of grateful letters. The standard religious institutions were paying no attention to their psychological despair. Robinson, on the other hand, thundered against the dithering of mainline churches and urged his followers to shift their mind-sets, open themselves to fresh ideas, and believe in the promise within themselves.

Charges of charlatanry inevitably swirled around Robinson, yet surviving financial records show that the "Miracle Man of Moscow" profited to no unusual degree from Psychiana. He and his wife, son, and daughter lived in a comfortable if ordinary upper-middle-class house in the Idaho town, where his printing and mail-order businesses became the largest local employer outside the University of Idaho during the Great Depression. Robinson drew a standard white-collar salary, while continually putting money back into his business, which required constant advertising to stay afloat.

In the 1940s, Robinson struck up a friendship with Science of Mind founder Ernest Holmes. At a time when many American churches were segregated, Holmes and Robinson conducted a series of racially integrated prayer crusades in Los Angeles. At the September 1941 meetings, the two metaphysical teachers delivered rousing calls for racial equality and led prayers for the victory of democracy on the eve of America's entry into World War II. During the war Robinson cabled Finland's president and urged him to fortify his embattled nation's military defenses with a daily affirmation to be recited by the Finnish army, cabinet ministers, and Psychiana members in America: *The power of God is superior to the powers of war, hate, and evil.* Finland's president, probably with tongue in cheek, wired back that he would act on Robinson's idea as soon as "practicable."

Though powerfully built and energetic, Robinson had a weak heart. The mail-order prophet died of heart failure on October 19, 1948. Sacks of cards and telegrams poured into the Psychiana offices—distraught followers wondered, who would replace the man who talked with God? The helm briefly went to Robinson's son, Alfred, a thoughtful and earnest Stanford graduate who had served as a fighter pilot in World War II. But Alfred acknowledged lacking his father's passion. With debts mounting, the Robinson family in 1952 shut down Psychiana—its once-busy print shops quiet and its remaining brochures, magazines, pamphlets, and lesson plans carted away.

Robinson's story is more than one of fame found and quickly lost. At a time when traditional congregations were shrinking, Robinson pointed the way to reaching people by speaking to their most practical concerns, and doing so through methods of national advertising. Even while declaring Robinson a "religious racketeer," mainline congregations copied his outreach methods. Today, Robinson's techniques—including national ads, broadcasts, direct-response mailings—are standard fare, particularly among evangelical ministries.

But that influence does not wholly capture Frank B. Robinson. Robinson was a classic American religious discontent—a man who built his own path to higher realization when the existing ones didn't work for him. He never sought to appeal to the churches for respectability. He wanted to create a faith that was entirely free of them. After the Psychiana founder's death, his friend and chronicler Marcus Bach eulogized him:

> Men who have never had to struggle against want and need and have never had to fight for a place in life, men to whom success comes easily or who follow a prescribed pattern for their careers, cannot understand Robinson and should not be expected to understand him. He was a soul in unrest whom the churches never sought and never found and never cared about. In retaliation he never sought the churches, and paradoxically he generated much of his phenomenal determination and accomplishment because of his revolt against them.

Charles Fillmore died the same year as Frank B. Robinson, in 1948. Fillmore's wife and close collaborator, Myrtle, had passed away years earlier, in 1931. Eschewing Robinson's personal flamboyance and magical tone, the Fillmores built their Unity movement on a similar campaign of national media, as well as an innovative distance-prayer ministry. The Fillmores perfected the media methods that Robinson had only begun.

Unlike the flameout of Psychiana, Unity grew into a long-reigning force on the national scene, and remains so today.

The Fillmores had an extraordinary personal rise. Charles Fillmore was born in 1854 on a Chippewa reservation near St. Cloud, Minnesota. His father, Henry, was a trader with the Native Americans and lived in close proximity to the Chippewa and the Sioux. There were periods of tension. When Charles was two, he was seized from his home by a Sioux band, probably in a business dispute. Henry managed to secure his return. Henry cared little for education, and Charles and his young brother spent only a few terms at a rural schoolhouse. For Charles, life was given over to trapping, hunting, storing up supplies, and wandering the range.

At age ten, Charles suffered a serious injury to his hip while ice-skating. His mother, Mary, could find little medical care, and the injury never properly healed. Charles struggled with years of pain and discomfort, and by adulthood his right leg was about four and a half inches shorter than his left. He had to walk with an iron leg brace. A childhood virus had left him deaf in his right ear.

As a teenager, Charles, not unlike other people dwelling on the prairie, took an interest in Spiritualism, or talking to the dead, which in the years of mourning following the Civil War was sweeping the nation. Charles also expressed interest in "Hermetic philosophy," by which he meant mail-order occult courses. The teenage Charles found work with a printer, and at age twenty-two in 1876 he was employed as a railroad clerk in east Texas, an area growing with the addition of new rail lines. There Charles joined local reading clubs and discussion groups, at which he met Myrtle Page. A teacher at a private school, Myrtle was ten years older than he. Charles followed her back to her home in Clinton, Missouri, where they married in early 1881. Myrtle was an intellectually vibrant woman who had spent a year at Oberlin College. But, like Charles, she had suffered childhood illnesses that trailed her into adulthood.

"It was a strange combination," wrote historian James W. Teener. "Charles, twenty-six years of age, small of body and slightly stooped, with a decided limp because of his shortened leg, suffering from curvature of the spine and deafness in the right ear; Myrtle, ten years his senior, and, according to her claims already a victim of tuberculosis."

Charles discovered a talent for real estate and began prospering in the Missouri market. In 1884 the couple again moved, now with two sons, to Kansas City. The western city had doubled in population in the previous decade and was in the midst of a real-estate boom. Charles and Myrtle financially thrived, but their physical health deteriorated. Charles was experiencing discomfort from his iron brace, and he discovered that the sight in his right eye was failing. Myrtle, already in tenuous health, was diagnosed with malaria. Nothing seemed to help her. Then in the spring of 1886 the Fillmores learned of a mental-healer coming to the city, Eugene B. Weeks. Like many early mind-healing figures, Weeks called himself a Christian Scientist, but he adhered to the New Thought philosophy taught by Emma Curtis Hopkins. Weeks gave Myrtle an affirmation that began her journey back to health: "I am a child of God and therefore I do not inherit sickness." Myrtle ardently repeated these words until they struck her with the force of a conversion.

She and Charles studied everything they could find on mental healing, also expanding their studies to Buddhism, Hinduism, Theosophy, hypnotism, and various forms of Christian mysticism. They later took classes in Kansas City from Hopkins herself. Like Myrtle, Charles began to feel physically improved. "My chronic pains ceased," he wrote. "My hip healed and grew stronger." He reported being able to walk without his brace, and said his right leg grew fuller and more muscular. Charles also claimed that hearing began returning to his right ear and sight to his right eye.

Eager to share their discoveries, the couple formed Kansas City prayer and discussion groups. Drawing upon Charles's printing background, they launched the magazine Modern Thought in April 1889. It was dedicated to metaphysical healing, New Thought, and Christian Science, and also to occult philosophies and methods, such as Mesmerism, Spiritualism, Theosophy, clairvoyance, astrology, and palmistry—topics that Charles later sharply rejected. *Modern Thought* marked the beginnings of the Unity School of Practical Christianity. In years ahead, Charles insisted that the school was explicitly Christian—based in *"Pure Mind Healing* only," and not the occult subjects that had once moved him.

Magazines, pamphlets, correspondence courses, and mail-order prayer services quickly followed. In a crucial move in 1890, the Fillmores formed the Society of Silent Unity, a distance-prayer service whose workers prayed for anyone who wrote in. Silent Unity quickly became the signature Fillmore operation. In 1907, Charles added telephone technology to Silent Unity, staffing the phone lines with trained, round-the-clock prayer attendants. Unity was probably the first ministry to use the phones in this way.

People called in for help, first in the thousands and then hundreds of thousands. They rang from farms, cities, small towns, and overseas—making prayer requests for healing, marital strife, loneliness, or financial needs. Countless callers felt some solace from the sympathetic voice on the other end of the phone who answered: "This is Silent Unity. How may we pray with you?" Silent Unity remains a popular service, handling thousands of calls a day. It is not a money-raising outfit or a faith-healing operation, but a confidential prayer service run with dignity and sensitivity. Silent Unity was the type of prayer program that physician Richard C. Cabot would have found an appropriate complement to medical treatment.

In 1919 Charles began using his real-estate savvy to acquire land near Kansas City, which took shape as the fourteen-hundred-acre Unity Village. This campus housed the Fillmores' publishing operations, distance-prayer ministry, radio broadcasts, churches, meeting spaces, hotel rooms, and residential quarters.* Continually expanding

---

* For many years, Unity's residential housing was segregated. Unity's black ministerial students and guests were denied residency until 1956, when Johnnie Colemon, an African-American female ministerial student from Chicago, embarked on a successful petition drive to open campus housing. Colemon became founding minister of one of the nation's largest New Thought congregations, the Christ Universal Temple, in Chicago.

their media operation, the Fillmores exposed hundreds of thousands of American households to mind-power metaphysics through their magazine *Unity* and their children's periodical, *Wee Wisdom*, which also launched the literary career of novelist Sidney Sheldon. It published the ten-year-old's first poem in 1927 and sent him five dollars.

All of this occurred in an era before the nation's vast media ministries had taken root. The pioneering televangelist Oral Roberts did not publish his first pamphlet-sized work until 1947, the year before the deaths of Charles Fillmore and Frank B. Robinson. At a time when America's evangelical revivals were still held in large tents, the Fillmores had already completed a model of the ministry as a clearinghouse for magazines, pamphlets, advice books, radio shows, and prayer requests. In 1948, journalist Marcus Bach, the friend to Frank B. Robinson, visited Unity Village and was astonished at how the Missouri operation dwarfed even Robinson's own:

> As I walked through the mailing rooms at the plant in Kansas City, I could believe what I had been told; an average of four thousand pieces of mail was leaving Unity every day. Many of these were heavily stuffed envelopes from Silent Unity, a prayer room equipped with a telephone. The attendant who answers . . . relays the requests to a group of Unity believers who pray without ceasing. Someone is at the altar of Silent Unity day and night; receiving requests, tuning in on God, and stuffing envelopes with a mimeographed letter, a booklet of testimonials, and a printed affirmation, "The healing power of God, through Christ, is now doing Its perfect work in me, and I am made whole." The output of Unity's efficient publicity machine is astounding: a million monthly periodicals, thousands of tracts, pamphlets, pocket-sized editions of daily devotions, and numerous books written by the Fillmores. To an amazingly varied clientele they bring a realization of the "Christ within."

This was the first full-scale realization of the modern media ministry, built on positive-thinking ideals.

NEVILLE GODDARD:
MAN AS CREATOR

Perhaps the most intriguing and substantive teacher of New Thought in the years immediately following World War II was an Anglo–West Indian dancer and stage actor who cultivated a mysterious biography and went by the singular name Neville.

Born in 1905 in Barbados to an English family, Neville Goddard arrived in New York in the early 1920s to study theater. His ambition for the stage faded as he came in contact with various mystical and occult philosophies. By the early 1930s he embarked on a new and unforeseen career as a lecturer and writer of mind-power metaphysics. In lectures, Neville often referred to an enigmatic, turbaned black man named Abdullah who he said tutored him in Scripture, number mysticism, Kabbalah, and Hebrew.

Whatever the source of Neville's education, his outlook not only reflected the most occultic edge of New Thought but also the philosophy's most intellectually stimulating expression. Neville saw each individual as a potential God, who could select from among a universe of infinite realities, all brought into existence by a mixture of our mind's-eye imagery and emotive states. *That which we think, feel, and see to be true,* Neville taught, *literally is true.* In Neville's viewpoint, our active imagination—that is, our thoughts and corresponding feelings—creates reality. (I consider the implications of Neville's ideas further in the final chapter.)

In public talks, Neville made extravagant claims—such as his use of mental visualizations to win himself an honorable discharge from the U.S. Army after being drafted at the height of World War II. In actuality, such a sudden discharge did occur. Neville entered the army on November 12, 1942, obligated to serve for the duration of the war. But military records show that four months later, in March 1943, the mystic and Greenwich Village aesthete was "discharged from service to accept employment in an essential wartime industry." Neville resumed his "essential wartime" job as a metaphysical lecturer. A profile in *The New Yorker* of September 11, 1943, described the handsome speaker back at the lectern before swooning (and often female) New York audiences. It is unclear why Neville, a lithe man in perfect health, would have been released from the military at the peak of the war. "Unfortunately," an army public affairs officer said, "Mr. Goddard's records were destroyed in the 1973 fire at the National Personnel Records Center."

Neville also made bold claims about the prosperous rise of his family's food-service and retail businesses in Barbados—claims that likewise conform to public records. Even Neville's tales about the mysterious Abdullah, as will be seen, are far from dismissible.

Yet other stories surrounding Neville are shakier. In 1955, Hollywood gossip columnist Jimmie Fidler described the young Neville as "enormously wealthy," his family possessing "a whole island in the West Indies." In actuality, Neville's material existence as a young man was precarious, a fact he never disguised. While he landed roles on Broadway and toured as part of a ballroom dancing duo, Neville lived hand-to-mouth, working for a time as an elevator operator and a shipping clerk. In pursuit of spiritual awareness, the young man experimented with ascetic living, including swearing off meat, dairy, tobacco, and alcohol. At one point, his weight dropped from 176 to 135 pounds.

By 1930 Neville felt physically unwell and was no closer to peering into life's mysteries. But he experienced a dramatic turnaround upon meeting his mysterious spiritual mentor named Abdullah. In Neville's recollection, his first meeting with Abdullah had an air of kismet:

> When I first met my friend Abdullah back in 1931 I entered a room where he was speaking and when the speech was ended he came over, extended his hand and said: "Neville, you are six months late." I had never seen the man before, so I said: "I am six months late? How do you know me?" and

he replied: "The brothers told me that you were coming and you are six months late."

Writing about Neville in the 1940s, the occult philosopher Israel Regardie called Abdullah an "eccentric Ethiopian rabbi." The description stuck, and Neville's apprenticeship under an "African rabbi" became part of his mythos.

Following this fateful encounter, Neville said he and Abdullah together studied Hebrew, Scripture, number symbolism, and mystical religions for five years—planting the seeds of Neville's philosophy of mental creativity. Neville recalled first grasping the potential of creative thought while he was living in a rented room on Manhattan's Upper West Side in the winter of 1933. The young man was depressed: his theatrical career had stalled and he was broke. "After twelve years in America, I was a failure in my own eyes," he said. "I was in the theater and made money one year and spent it the next month." The twenty-eight-year-old ached to spend Christmas with his family in Barbados, but he couldn't afford to travel.

"Live as though you are there," Abdullah told him, "and that you shall be." Wandering the streets of New York City, Neville adopted the *feeling state* that he was really and truly at home on his native island. "Abdullah taught me the importance of remaining faithful to an idea and not compromising," he remembered. On a December morning before the last ship that year was to depart for Barbados, Neville received a letter from a long-out-of-touch brother: Tucked inside were fifty dollars and a passenger ticket.

By the mid-1950s, Neville's life story exerted a powerful pull on a budding writer whose own memoirs of mystic discovery later made him a near-household name: Carlos Castaneda. Castaneda told his own tales of tutelage under a mysterious instructor, in his case a Native American sorcerer named Don Juan. Castaneda first discovered Neville through an early love interest in Los Angeles, Margaret Runyan, who was among Neville's most dedicated students. A cousin of American story-teller Damon Runyon, Margaret wooed the stocky Latin art student at a friend's house, slipping Carlos a slender Neville volume called *The Search*, in which she had inscribed her name and phone number. The two became lovers and later husband and wife.

Runyan spoke frequently to Castaneda about her mystical teacher Neville, but he responded with little more than mild interest—with one exception. In her memoirs, Runyan recalled Castaneda growing fascinated when the conversation turned to Neville's discipleship under an exotic teacher:

> . . . it was more than the message that attracted Carlos, it was Neville himself. He was so mysterious. Nobody was really sure who he was or where he had come from. There were vague references to Barbados in the West Indies and his being the son of an ultra-rich plantation family, but nobody knew for sure. They couldn't even be sure about this Abdullah business, his Indian teacher, who was always *way back there* in the jungle, or someplace. The only thing you really knew was that Neville was here and that he might be back next week, but then again . . .

"There was," she concluded, "a certain power in that position, an appealing kind of freedom in the lack of past and Carlos knew it."

Both Neville and Castaneda were dealing with the same basic idea, and one that had a certain pedigree in America's alternative spiritual culture: tutelage under hidden spiritual masters. It was a concept that the Russian mystic Madame H. P. Blavatsky ignited in the minds of Western seekers with her late-nineteenth-century accounts of her mentorship to unseen *Mahatmas,* or Great Souls. Blavatsky aroused a hope that invisible help was out there; that guidance could be sought from a difficult-to-place master of wisdom, someone who might arrive from an exotic land, or another plane of existence, and who could dispense illuminated knowledge. Indeed, the Abdullah story as told by Neville might be dismissible as a tale borrowed and retouched from Blavatsky—except for another, better-known figure in the positive-thinking tradition who, toward the end of his life, made his own claims of mentorship under the turbaned Abdullah.

The Irish emigrant writer Joseph Murphy arrived in New York City in the early 1920s with a degree in chemistry and a passion to study metaphysics. Murphy is widely remembered for his 1963 megaseller *The Power of Your Subconscious Mind*. The book remains one of the most engaging and popular works of mind-power philosophy. Shortly before his death in 1981, Murphy, in a little-known series of interviews published by a French press in Quebec, described his own encounter with the mysterious Abdullah. Interviewer Bernard Cantin recounted the tale in his 1987 book of dialogues with Murphy:

> It was in New York that Joseph Murphy also met the professor Abdullah, a Jewish man of black ancestry, a native of Israel, who knew, in every detail, all the symbolism of each of the verses of the Old and the New Testaments. This meeting was one of the most significant in Dr. Murphy's spiritual evolution. In fact, Abdullah, who had never seen nor known the Murphy family, said flatly that Murphy came from a family of six children, and not five, as Murphy himself had believed. Later on, Murphy, intrigued, questioned his mother and learned that, indeed, he had had another brother who had died a few hours after his birth, and was never spoken of again.

Was there a real esoteric teacher named Abdullah who taught Neville and Murphy? A plausible candidate exists. He is found in the figure of a 1920s- and '30s-era black-nationalist mystic named Arnold Josiah Ford. Like Neville, Ford was born in Barbados, in 1877, the son of an itinerant preacher. Ford arrived in Harlem around 1910 and established himself as a leading voice in the Ethiopianism movement, a precursor to Jamaican Rastafarianism. Both movements held that the East African nation of Ethiopia was home to a lost Israelite tribe that had preserved the teachings of a mystical African belief system. Ford considered himself an original Israelite, and a man of authentic Judaic descent. Like Abdullah, Ford was considered an "Ethiopian rabbi." Surviving photographs show Ford as a dignified, somewhat severe-looking man with a set jaw and penetrating gaze, wearing a turban, just like Neville's Abdullah. Ford himself cultivated an air of mystery, attracting "much apocryphal and often contradictory speculation," noted Randall K. Burkett, a historian of black-nationalist movements.

Ford lived in New York City at the same time that Neville began his discipleship with Abdullah. Neville recalled his and Abdullah's first meeting in 1931, and U.S. Census records show Ford was living in Harlem on West 131st Street in 1930. (He was also at the same address in 1920, shortly before Joseph Murphy arrived.) Historian Howard Brotz, in his study of the black-Jewish movement in Harlem, wrote of Ford: "It is certain that he studied Hebrew with some immigrant teacher and was a key link" in communicating "approximations of Talmudic Judaism" from within the Ethiopianism movement. This would fit Neville's depiction of Abdullah tutoring him in Hebrew and Kabbalah. (It should be noted that early-twentieth-century occultists often loosely used the term *Kabbalah* to denote any kind of Judaic study.)

More still, Ford's philosophy of Ethiopianism possessed a mental metaphysics. "The philosophy," noted historian Jill Watts, ". . . contained an element of mind-power, for many adherents of Ethiopianism subscribed to mental healing and believed that material circumstances could be altered through God's power. Such notions closely paralleled tenets of New Thought . . ." Ford was also an early supporter of black-nationalist pioneer Marcus Garvey and served as the musical director of Garvey's Universal Negro Improvement Association. Garvey, as noted earlier, suffused his movement with New Thought metaphysics and phraseology.

The commonalities between Ford and Abdullah are striking: the black rabbi, the turban, the study of Hebrew, mind-power metaphysics, the Barbados connection, and the time frame. All of it point to Ford as a viable candidate for the mysterious teacher Abdullah.

Yet there are too many gaps in both Neville's and Ford's backgrounds to allow for a conclusive leap. Records of Ford's life grow thinner after 1931, the year he departed New York and migrated to Ethiopia. Ethiopian emperor Haile Selassie, after his coronation in 1930, offered land grants to any African Americans willing to relocate to the East African nation. Ford accepted the offer. The timing of Ford's departure is the biggest single blow to the Abdullah-Ford theory. Neville said he and his teacher had studied together for five years. This obviously would not have been possible with Ford, who had apparently left New York in 1931, the same year Neville said that he and Abdullah first met.

In a coda to Ford's career, he journeyed to Africa, along with several other American followers of Ethiopianism, to accept the land grants offered by Haile Selassie. Yet Ford's life in the Ethiopian countryside, a period so sadly sparse of records, could only have been a difficult existence for the urbane musician. Here was a man uprooted from metropolitan surroundings at an advanced age to settle into a new and unfamiliar agricultural landscape. All the while, Ethiopia was facing the threat of invasion by fascist Italy. Ford died in Ethiopia in September 1935, a few weeks before Mussolini's troops crossed the border.

While Ford's migration runs counter to Neville's timeline, there are other ways in which Ford may fit into the Abdullah mythos. Neville could have extrapolated Abdullah from Ford's character after spending a briefer time with Ford. Or Abdullah may have been a metaphorical composite of several contemporaneous figures, perhaps including Ford.[*] Or, finally, Abdullah may have been Neville's invention, though this scenario doesn't account for Murphy's record.

The full story may never be knowable, but the notion of two young

---

[*] Neville may have hinted as much, especially in light of his love for Hebrew symbolism. He affectionately called Abdullah "Ab" for short—a variant of the Hebrew *abba* for "father." Neville may have fashioned a mythical "father mentor" from various teachers.

metaphysical seekers, Neville and Murphy, living in pre–World War II New York and studying under an African-American esoteric teacher, whether Ford or another, is itself wholly plausible. The crisscrossing currents of the mind-power movement in the first half of the twentieth century produced collaborations among a wide range of spiritual travelers. Such figures traversed the metaphysical landscape with a passion for personal development and self-reinvention.

Success and Setback

All of these determined seekers compelled mainstream spiritual culture to adapt itself to New Thought's innovations. But the positive-thinking movement failed in one key respect. And that was in the ideal hoped for by Richard C. Cabot: To marry the possibilities of mind-power methods to rationalism; to devise a metaphysical therapeutics that could find allies among medical authorities and scientists.

The possibilities had once seemed promising. In the early 1950s, Ernest Holmes shared a congenial dinner with Albert Einstein at Caltech. Holmes said that Einstein agreed with his premise "that permanent world peace is not an illusion but a potential possibility and an evolutionary imperative, and that science will *aid* in that evolution." As late as 1969, the *New York Times* respectfully covered a meeting of the International New Thought Alliance under the headline "Mental Power as Force for Peace Tied to Man's Triumph in Space."

But the push to find common ground between mind-power and science puttered out, and would not be heard again for another generation. New Thought books were considered too miraculous in tone, and too magical in their claims, to win attention from scientists, physicians, or literary and journalistic arbiters of opinion.

Medical researchers, however, did begin turning new attention to the placebo effect after World War II. The impetus arrived when caregivers at an Allied battlefield hospital in southern Italy eased pain among injured soldiers by telling them that the saline solutions they were receiving were morphine, a substance of which the hospital had run short. Yet even as civilian researchers reconsidered the possibilities of mind-body medicine, they did so without a nod toward, or even any historical awareness of, the claims of the mental-healing movement. No new intellectual champion, akin to Cabot or William James, emerged to draw correlations between modern medical questions and the experiences that mind-cure advocates had reported since the late nineteenth century.

The mind-power movement was invisible within the intellectual culture. In a sense, this absence reflected the movement's second historical failure. The first had occurred earlier in the twentieth century when progressive figures such as Helen Wilmans, Wallace D. Wattles, and Elizabeth Towne found themselves unable to sustainably wed mind-power culture to movements for social reform.

Even as New Thought's intellectual and social aims floundered, however, its popularity soared. Or, rather, the popularity of its *methods* did. The term *New Thought* was only occasionally heard. Positive-thinking ideas, stripped of mystical language, congregational labels, and any historical moorings, began flowing into mainstream culture—and not just the religious culture: sales conferences, board rooms, dinnertime conversations, therapy offices, and even political campaigns began buzzing with the metaphysics of optimism.

This development arrived after World War II, when a newer and less overtly mystical generation of positive-thinking teachers made their impact felt. These newcomers had taken careful measure of New Thought's successes and failings. They meticulously distanced themselves from the occult language and miraculous claims that could turn away mainstream people. This fresh breed of thought-crusaders finally, and permanently, transformed positive thinking into the philosophy of American life.

chapter six

the american creed

Nothing is impossible.

—Ronald Reagan

n the 1920s two revolutionary self-help authors arrived on the American scene. The two men had never collaborated but they possessed a shared instinct. By stripping New Thought of its magical language, they reconfigured mind-power principles into a secular methodology for personal achievement. Each went on to write landmark books whose titles and bylines became synonymous with success: *Think and Grow Rich* by Napoleon Hill and *How to Win Friends and Influence People* by Dale Carnegie.

Hill was more clearly a product of the mind-power culture. His first book, in 1928, was an eight-volume opus called *The Law of Success*, a title borrowed from Prentice Mulford. Like Mulford, Hill believed that the mind possessed clairvoyant energies and forces. In particular Hill emphasized the existence of a "Master Mind," an over-mind of shared human consciousness, which reveals itself to us in moments of intuition, in hunches, or in prophetic dreams. Tapping into the Master Mind became the centerpiece of his work.

Hill jettisoned any vestige of the mind-power movement's earlier social consciousness. "I gave a beggar a dime," he wrote, "with the suggestion that he invest it in a copy of Elbert Hubbard's *Message to Garcia*." Hill was referring to Hubbard's famous 1899 essay about an American soldier who displayed remarkable drive in carrying a message behind enemy lines to a Cuban rebel leader during the Spanish-American War. *Message to Garcia* was Hubbard's paean to self-will and personal accountability. Hubbard's social outlook, however, wasn't quite what Hill's tribute implied.

When not praising the rugged virtues admired by Hill, Hubbard had produced articles on the horrendous working conditions in southern cotton mills, helping instigate some of the nation's first child labor laws. Hubbard and his wife Alice, a suffragist and New-Thoughter, were killed on a peace mission to Europe in 1915 to protest World War I to the German Kaiser. A German U-boat torpedoed their passenger liner, the *Lusitania*, off the Irish coast. They died with nearly twelve hundred other civilians. "Big business has been to blame in this thing," Hubbard had written of the war before his journey, ". . . let it not escape this truth— that no longer shall individuals be allowed to thrive by selling murder machines to the mob."

Hill overlooked that side of Hubbard's work. Instead, he geared his appeal to the modern striver who wanted to get ahead. This focus probably grew from the influence of the man Hill came to idolize, and whose ideas undergirded his own: the industrialist Andrew Carnegie.

The Gospel of Wealth

Napoleon Hill became interested in the science of success in 1908 while working as a reporter for *Bob Taylor's Magazine*, an inspirational journal founded by the ex-governor of Hill's home state of Virginia. The publisher, Bob Taylor, took a particular interest in up-by-the-bootstraps life stories of business leaders. Through Taylor's connections, Hill was able to score the ultimate "get": an interview with the steel magnate Andrew Carnegie.

Hill described his first encounters with Carnegie—"the richest man that the richest nation on earth ever produced"—in terms that brought to mind Moses receiving the tablets on Mount Sinai. Whatever impression Hill left on Carnegie, the industrialist made no mention of the younger man in his writings. Nonetheless, Carnegie's memoirs do paint the image of himself as a man who enjoyed discussing the metaphysics of success.

In his 1920 autobiography, which appeared the year after his death, Carnegie recalled that as an adolescent he "became deeply interested in the mysterious doctrines of Swedenborg." A Spiritualist aunt encouraged the young Carnegie to develop his psychical talents, or "ability to expound 'spiritual sense.'"

Carnegie's earliest writings probed whether there are natural laws of success, a theme that reemerged in Hill's work. In 1889, Carnegie published his essay "Wealth"—which might have gained little note if not for its republication by England's *Pall Mall Gazette* under the more provocative title by which it became famous: "The Gospel of Wealth." Taking a leaf from the neo-Darwinian views of philosopher Herbert Spencer, Carnegie described a "law of competition" that he believed brought a rough, necessary order to the world:

> While the law may be sometimes hard to the individual, it is
> best for the race, because it insures the survival of the fittest
> in every department. We accept and welcome, therefore, as
> conditions to which we must accommodate ourselves, great

inequality of environment, the concentration of business, industrial and commercial, in the hands of a few, and the law
of competition between these, as being not only beneficial
but essential for the future progress of the race.

Where Wallace D. Wattles had extolled creativity above competition,
Carnegie welcomed "laws of accumulation" as necessary means of sepa-
rating life's winners from losers. But Carnegie's essay had an interesting
wrinkle. He counseled giving away one's money in acts of philanthropy
as the legitimate culmination of worldly success. And if the rich didn't
find a way to disperse their fortunes through philanthropy, Carnegie
called for a nearly 100 percent estate tax to settle the matter for them.

At their 1908 meeting, Hill eagerly questioned Carnegie about his
success-building methods. The steel manufacturer urged the reporter to
speak with other captains of commerce to determine whether a defin-
able set of steps led to their accomplishments. Carnegie offered to open
doors for Hill. Hill spent the next twenty years studying and interview-
ing businessmen, diplomats, generals, inventors, and other high achiev-
ers in an effort to map out their shared principles. He finally distilled
seventeen traits or habits that these outliers seemed to have in common.
They included concentrating your energies on *one definite major aim*; doing
more work than you are paid for; cultivating intuition, or a sixth sense;
showing persistence; reprogramming your thoughts through autosuggestion; practicing tolerance of opinion; gaining specialized knowledge;
and convening around you a collaborative Master Mind group, whose
members could blend their mental energies and ideas.

In the years following his meeting with Carnegie, and after his study
of the success methods of other industry titans, Hill embarked on a series of articles and books, which culminated in *Think and Grow Rich* in
1937. Hill's books never attracted serious critical attention—other than
to be dismissed or waved aside for vulgar shallowness. Indeed, New
Thought and self-help literature became a category of book that went
unread by its detractors. But Hill was often subtler, shrewder, and surer

in his understanding of human nature than many scoffers supposed. Yet his career also revealed the kind of yes-man corporatism that increasingly marked the motivational field in the twentieth century.

In his autobiographical writings, Hill showed a repugnant lack of moral feeling as a young man by helping local businessmen conceal the killing of a black bellhop in Richlands, Virginia. The episode occurred in 1902. The black hotel worker died after a drunken bank cashier—an employee of Hill's boss at the time—dropped a loaded revolver, which went off, killing the bellman. The nineteen-year-old Hill sprang into action as the consummate fixer, coaxing local authorities to label the criminally negligent death as "accidental," and getting the victim quickly buried. The town's "big men" rewarded Hill by naming him the manager of an area coal mine—the youngest such manager in the nation, Hill proudly reckoned.

The episode reflected the troubling pattern of Hill's life: He identified with power so strongly that he never questioned the decency, ethics, and general outlook of the man in the corner office. Nowhere in his accounts of high climbers is there any countervailing consideration of cunning, ruthlessness, or amorality—or, for that matter, of the kind of corrupt obsequiousness that Hill showed back in Richlands. Even in his elderly years, prior to his death in 1970, Hill remained oddly attached to his image as a "promising young man" set on charming industrial giants.

"I Know! I Know!! I Know!!!"

A similar outlook prevailed in the work of Dale Carnegie. Like Hill, Carnegie possessed an innate grasp of how to get men in power to open up to him: Just ask them how they overcame their early hardships. But this method of gaining access—in which the questioner always dotes and never challenges—also left Carnegie with the perspective that corporate chieftains are always ready with a put-'er-there-pal handshake and an abundance of helpful advice. The question of corruption or backbiting never seemed to enter Carnegie's mind. He believed that the men on top deserved to be there—and his level of introspection on the matter went no further.

Yet Carnegie, like Hill, proved a pioneering observer of human nature, and a genius of communication. He had a key message and he understood how to convey it to a vast range of people. It was this: *Agreeable people win*.

Growing up in Missouri, Dale Carnegie began his career as a salesman and traveling stage actor. In the years immediately preceding World War I, he realized that the rules of business had changed. America had entered an age in which communication skills were—for the first time ever—the foundation of success. As Carnegie saw it, the ability to speak clearly and convincingly, to tell stories and jokes, and to connect with one's bosses, workmates, and customers was a vital tool. He further believed that the power of persuasion could be learned through study, drilling, and practice. In 1912 Carnegie convinced the manager at the New York YMCA where he was living to allow him to deliver a series of lessons in the art of public speaking. In an era in which image mattered, the young instructor altered the spelling of his surname from the less-elegant *Carnagey* to *Carnegie*.

Carnegie worked tirelessly to build his following as a speaking coach. In future years he was anointed with his own appearance in *Ripley's Believe-It-Or-Not*, which reported that Carnegie had personally critiqued 150,000 speeches. In 1926, Carnegie outlined his formula in his first book, *Public Speaking: A Practical Course for Businessmen*. It remains probably the best volume ever produced on the topic. Carnegie devised a near-airtight template for how to deliver a good talk, including the proper use of stories and parables, the need for *over-preparation*, how to memorably deploy numbers, the use of good diction, and the right tonality of the voice.

His real breakout, however, occurred in 1936 with the landmark *How to Win Friends and Influence People*. Two years earlier, an executive at Simon & Schuster, Leon Shimkin, had enrolled in a fourteen-week course of Carnegie's lectures on public speaking and human relations. The

Brooklyn-born Shimkin was a dedicated self-improver. He had talked his way into publishing on the vow that he could do everything from bookkeeping to answering phones to stenography. He took Carnegie's classes out of genuine personal interest—and was immediately sold on the success coach's potential as an author. Not every literary tastemaker agreed. Social critics such as H. L. Mencken heaped scorn on self-help, and most of the lettered classes wanted no part of it. But Shimkin saw the potential in figures like Carnegie.

For his part, Carnegie was cool to the prospect of Simon & Schuster as his publisher. The still-new press had previously rejected two of Carnegie's manuscripts. Carnegie resented it and was hesitant to pursue a project with them. Plus, he doubted that his lectures on how to cultivate a pleasing personality would even translate into a good book. Shimkin persisted. He arranged to have Carnegie's talks transcribed, and urged the speaking coach to massage the transcripts into proper chapters. Carnegie's work-in-progress arrived with the quiet title "The Art of Getting Along with People." It evolved into "How to Make Friends and Influence People"—but, still, it wasn't quite right. Under Shimkin's guidance "Make Friends" became the more fetching "Win Friends"—and one of history's best-known titles was born.

How to Win Friends and Influence People became the bible of self-advancement, and it remains so. Carnegie, like no other writer, understood the foibles of human nature: He noted how we love being flattered, hearing the sound of our own name, and talking about ourselves; conversely, we hate being told we are wrong or hearing the words "I disagree." *The New York Times* detected "a subtle cynicism" in the Carnegie approach. But few could deny that Carnegie understood how to get things done within organizations, including the kinds of large companies in which Americans were increasingly employed. He innately grasped how to ease the frictions of personality that stymied careers and projects. And Carnegie told the blunt truth about human affairs: We tend to self-idealize; so if you want to win someone's cooperation, avoid offending his sense of vanity.

Carnegie didn't write in the typical New Thought vein. He rarely made spiritual references. Yet he very definitely saw the mind as a tool that wielded power over people and circumstances, including physical health. In his 1944 book, *How to Stop Worrying and Start Living*, Carnegie wrote: "You are probably saying to yourself right now: 'This man Carnegie is proselytizing for Christian Science.' No. You are wrong. I am not a Christian Scientist. But the longer I live, the more convinced I am by the tremendous power of thought. As a result of many years spent in teaching adults, I know men and women can banish worry, fear, and various kinds of illnesses, and can transform their lives by changing their thoughts. I know! I know!! I know!!!"

The Untroubled Mind

Not all therapeutic writers were as exclamatory as Dale Carnegie. A more somber metaphysical literature briefly won public acclaim. The top-selling and most influential spiritual writer in America immediately following World War II was an erudite Boston rabbi named Joshua Loth Liebman. Liebman's surprise bestseller, *Peace of Mind*, appeared in 1946, shortly after the war ended. The book spent a remarkable fifty-eight weeks at number one on the *New York Times* bestseller list, a record for its time. *Peace of Mind* sought to diagnose the angst and fears of a postwar world in which physical survival was no longer at risk, but boredom, ennui, and depression seemed everywhere on the rise.

Liebman was no success guru. Early in his book he devised a prayer for the self-aware modern man: "God, Lord of the universe, heap worldly gifts at the feet of foolish men. But on my head pour only the sweet waters of serenity. Give me the gift of the Untroubled Mind." Yet Liebman also wrote in the vein of mind-power theology. His writing echoed the tone of Jewish Science, the early-twentieth-century metaphysical movement that formed a Jewish alternative to Christian Science. (Liebman's *Peace of Mind* was preceded by a 1927 work of the same title by a leading Jewish Science rabbi, Morris Lichtenstein.) In particular, Liebman's prayer for modern people seemed inspired by the work of S. Felix

Mendelsohn, a Reform rabbi from Chicago who was active in Jewish Science. Foreshadowing Liebman's work, Mendelsohn deftly blended explicit modern psychological language with the positive-thinking ideal in his 1938 "Daily Prayer for the Modern Jew":

> Help me, O God, realize my potentialities for noble and creative endeavor. . . . Grant that I gain a thorough insight into my personality and that I see myself as I really am. Help me not to waste my energies but to labor diligently with cheerful heart and mind. Let happiness pervade my every thought and deed and enable me to enjoy good health and to dispel fear and anger from my consciousness. May I realize the eternal character of my soul which partakes of Thine ever-existing presence.

Liebman took this psychological tone further. He wanted man to awaken to unseen neuroses, and to achieve a credible self-love, while acknowledging dark emotions as an inevitable part of life. In his 1946 book, the rabbi intrepidly updated William James's "religion of healthy-mindedness" with this variant: "All men today need the healthy-mindedness of Judaism, the natural piety with which the Jew declares, 'One world at a time is enough.'" Liebman was not addressing himself exclusively to Jews; he was redefining Jewish ethics and psychoanalytic traditions as universal guideposts to healing.

Liebman saw psychological awareness as a necessary adjunct to the sin-and-repentance model of traditional religion. Indeed, postwar Americans of all backgrounds seemed to find succor in Liebman's assurance that depression, addiction, infidelity, jealousy, and other modern maladies were not causes for guilt or shame, but were disorders of the psyche and the soul that could be treated through an improved sense of self-worth and a willingness to evaluate one's personal desires in light of classical ethics.

Liebman didn't run from contemporary issues. Both as a clergyman and in his personal life he dealt forthrightly with the scars of the Holocaust. It was a topic that virtually none of the positive-thinking teachers even touched. After the war, Liebman's family had adopted a Polish-Jewish orphan—an adolescent girl who had survived Auschwitz. The therapist-rabbi saw in the war an enduring tragedy that demanded acknowledgment. In January 1948, he told *Ladies' Home Journal*: "Mine has been a rabbinate of trouble—of depression. Hitler's rise, world crisis, global war, the attempted extermination of my people." Yet Liebman believed that such circumstances required a constructive response among survivors and mourners, who were also obligated to pursue meaningful, productive lives. To them and others, Liebman wrote:

> For those who have lost loved ones during the tragic war, all of the rest of life will be but a half loaf of bread—yet a half loaf eaten in courage and accepted in truth is infinitely better than a moldy whole loaf, green with the decay of self-pity and selfish sorrow which really dishonors the memory of those who lived for our up building and happiness.

Spirited Communication

Liebman keenly understood how to bring moral seriousness to a discussion of people's personal needs. He possessed a gift for language and phraseology that could universalize his psycho-spiritual message. The bestselling rabbi's instincts for literary popularity, however, were not always razor-sharp—at least not on the first try.

When Liebman initially submitted his manuscript in 1945 to Simon & Schuster (ever since Dale Carnegie the publisher had developed a reputation for self-help) it arrived with the languid title "Morale for Moderns." That didn't sound to anyone like a bestseller. After coming under the tutelage of editor Henry Morton Robinson, himself an author and a former editor of *Reader's Digest*, Liebman's ethical tract reemerged with the friendlier title "Peace of Mind"—an aim to which everyone could aspire. And here was another gift of the early self-help writers and their editors: The ability to render a title in terms that were clear, plain, and self-evidently desirable. Students of publishing, politics, and advertising could benefit from noting the phraseology of these men and women: every book and article announced its aim clearly, often employing phrases such as "how to" or "the power of," and promising a definite benefit, whether in money, mental relaxation, or relationships. For Liebman, such language provided the framework to explore tender psychological issues while courting the broadest reach of people.

Some Christian leaders, such as Billy Graham and Monsignor Fulton Sheen, were overtly disdainful of Liebman's psychological augmentation of Scripture. Sheen was particularly bellicose, satirizing Liebman's approach to prayer in terms that purposely picked at the rabbi's modernist voice: " 'I thank Thee, O Lord, that my Freudian adviser has told me that there is no such thing as guilt, that sin is a myth, and that Thou, O Father, art only a projection of my Father complex. . . . Oh, I thank Thee that I am not like the rest of men, those nasty people, such as the Christian there in the back of the temple who thinks that he is a sinner . . .' "

Others, including Rev. Norman Vincent Peale, not yet famous as the ambassador of the positive, were deeply excited by Liebman's message. Peale enthusiastically recommended the rabbi's book. In 1946, the *Federal Council of Churches Bulletin* hailed Liebman for writing "in the best manner of the Jewish prophets" and urged churches not to repeat the mistakes of the past by opposing the insights of the "psychological clinic." It was a moment of remarkable openness on the American religious scene.

Two years after his book appeared, Liebman died suddenly of heart failure at age forty-one. Though young and boundlessly energetic, he had maintained a frantic—and frantically ambitious—schedule of talks, sermons, articles, and radio addresses. Having addressed the pressures of modern living, Liebman died of modernity's most common disease: stress.

At the time of Liebman's death, the Bible alone surpassed *Peace of Mind* as the top-selling spiritual book of the twentieth century. But *Peace of Mind* would soon be eclipsed by the work of one of the rabbi's closest admirers: a man who saw the potential for reaching great masses of people through a mystical program couched in reassuringly familiar terms.

Apostle of Happiness

Four years after Liebman's death, the driving idea behind all the self-help movements of the postwar era appeared in the title of Norman Vincent Peale's 1952 *The Power of Positive Thinking*. The book broke Liebman's record, spending an unprecedented ninety-eight weeks at number one on the *Times* bestseller list. And it made positive thinking into an everyday, every-man-and-woman philosophy. The Protestant minister's outlook was electrifying and freeing to people who had been raised on religion as a punitive institution. Peale's core message, recalled his longtime friend and co-minister the Reverend Arthur Caliandro, was this: "Not only can you be forgiven, but you could achieve, you could accomplish."

Raised in Ohio, Peale was placed in charge of Marble Collegiate Church on Manhattan's East Side during the Great Depression. Though Marble Collegiate was one of the nation's oldest pulpits—with roots extending to 1628 and its Fifth Avenue church building dating to 1854— the Dutch Reformed congregation was ailing and shrinking when Peale took over in 1932. The buoyant young minister quickly attracted new congregants. His appeal stemmed from his interest in the therapeutic power of prayer. At the Manhattan church, Peale struck up a partnership with a psychoanalyst, Smiley Blanton, who had studied with Sigmund Freud and been psychoanalyzed by the master himself. Peale and Blanton believed that religion and psychiatry could complement one another. Peale emphasized that the modern minister should be considered a professional, "a scientist of the spiritual life," and a figure as capable, in his own way, of providing counsel as a doctor or analyst. Blanton compared the awakening of the unconscious to William James's "conversion experience." The psychiatrist felt that the airing of repressed wishes and memories could, like a religious conversion, "transform the person's life."

In 1937, Peale and Blanton opened the Religio-Psychiatric Clinic in the church basement. Patients received care from either a minister or a therapist, or both. The church clinic was similar to the Emmanuel Movement, though it focused strictly on anxious minds and troubled hearts. By 1952, the Religio-Psychiatric Clinic and its support staff, which it drew from area hospitals, therapy offices, and clinics, saw some three thousand patients annually; ten years later the number swelled to an extraordinary twenty-five thousand.

While Peale and Blanton closely collaborated, Peale's interests branched off in more mystical directions. The minister developed his own ideas about the force of "prayer power" to magnetically attract circumstances, and the mind's ability to aim suggestions and influences at other people. Blanton, until his death in 1966, maintained his partnership with Peale, and their clinic continues today as the Blanton-Peale Institute and Counseling Center. Blanton, however, often kept his written work distinct and remained aloof from his friend's metaphysical theories.

In 1952, fifteen years after opening the Religio-Psychiatric Clinic, Peale reached into every corner of America, and many other parts of the world, with his manifesto, *The Power of Positive Thinking*. It became the kind of book that could be found in households everywhere, including those where there were few other books. It was not Peale's first book. In the late 1930s, he had written quieter, more modest-selling works that depicted religion less as a philosophy of practical solutions than as a refuge from the torrents of life. Peale's tone began to change in 1948 with his first self-help bestseller, *A Guide to Confident Living*, which more fully enunciated his positive-thinking themes. Four years later *The Power of Positive Thinking* took Peale's methods to their most practical edge and overshadowed everything that came before it.

Peale's innovation was to craft a system that reprocessed mind-power teachings through Scriptural language and lessons. In actuality, Peale's techniques came straight from New Thought. They included visualizations, affirmations, inducements to action of the *leap-and-the-net-will-appear* variety, formulas for manifestation ("1. PRAYERIZE 2. PICTURIZE 3. ACTUALIZE"), and assertions of self-belief backed by religious faith. Peale's approach *was* New Thought—but stripped of most magical terminology.

The minister used Biblical references and practical, everyday anecdotes that were reassuringly familiar in tone to the churchgoing public. (Though Peale did let slip a few telltale pieces of occult phraseology, as will be seen.) *The Power of Positive Thinking* was the most accessible expression of mind-power philosophy since Ralph Waldo Trine's *In Tune with the Infinite* and James Allen's *As a Man Thinketh*—but it surpassed even the combined influence of those two works through Peale's story-telling abilities and his insight into human character, gleaned from years of experience at the Religio-Psychiatric Clinic.

Peale generally deflected questions about his intellectual or spiritual sources. He often said his insights came squarely from Scripture. In his 1984 memoir, *The True Joy of Positive Living*, Peale identified Ralph Waldo Emerson and the Roman philosopher-king Marcus Aurelius as his "lifelong teachers." It was the kind of benign claim that Peale typically used to maintain his image as nothing more than an Ohio minister's son with a penchant for age-old advice. But Peale's life and career were run through with a complex web of mystical and political influences. Beneath his sunny exterior there existed a surprisingly complicated man.

"You Can If You Think You Can"

In a little-known interview in 1987, six years before his death, Peale made a rare disclosure about where his ideas came from, and how he related to the spiritual and intellectual trends around him. Peale described the influence he found in California mystic Ernest Holmes. Indeed, the Peale-Holmes relationship reveals how the vision of early New Thought gave rise to the broader American culture of motivational philosophy and therapeutic spirituality.

Peale and the Science of Mind founder Holmes had met just once, in Los Angeles in the summer of 1940. At the time, each went to hear the other deliver a talk. But Holmes's work had already reached Peale when he was younger. "Ernest came into my life long before we actually met," Peale said, "before I even decided to be a minister, when I was a vacillating, insecure, twenty-year-old." These weren't empty words. Peale did suffer from a lifelong sense of inferiority, especially after his reputation as a minister of practical wisdom made him a target of mockery among critics and intellectuals, who saw him as a simplistic purveyor of feel-good nostrums. Yet this feeling of inferiority was also his lifelong link to other people. Only someone who knew what it meant to feel inferior could relate to people in need.

Peale recalled that when he took his first job, as a reporter at the *Detroit Journal* in 1920, his editor detected the young man's "paralyzing fear of inadequacy." As the minister recounted, "He took me aside and handed me a book, *Creative Mind and Success* by Ernest Holmes." It was Holmes's second book, written in 1919. "Now I want you to read this," the editor told him. "I know this fellow Holmes. I've learned a lot from him, and so can you." What did Peale learn? "Love God, love others, you can if you think you can, the proper control and use of the human mind, drop your limited sense of self and gain true Self-Reliance." Holmes's slender volume of essays and affirmations opened Peale to new possibilities of what a religious message could be. Peale entered Boston University Seminary soon after finding it. "There is no question in my mind that Ernest Holmes's teachings had helped me on my way," he said.

Peale's writing and sermons reflected mind-power influences beyond Holmes. Reverend Caliandro, who succeeded Peale at the pulpit of Marble Collegiate when the minister retired in 1984, recalled Peale's deep attraction to Napoleon Hill ("he was really after that same form"), Dale Carnegie, Charles Fillmore, and Emmet Fox. Peale adopted the mind-power movement's phraseology, including "Law of Attraction."

He echoed New Thought concepts that had their earliest inception in Mesmerism, such as the notion that the mind emits a tangible, magnetic *prayer power.* "The human body's magnetic power has actually been tested," he wrote in *The Power of Positive Thinking.* "We have thousands of little sending stations, and when these are turned up by prayer it is possible for a tremendous power to flow through a person and to pass between human beings."

Peale also used phrases such as "in tune with the infinite" (from Ralph Waldo Trine) and "music of the spheres" (a Hermetic-Pythagorean theory of harmonious proportions among the orbits of planets); and he urged people to observe and listen to nature, syncing one's personality with the tempo of the natural world, which he considered the tempo of God-in-man. "All of the universe is in vibration," Peale wrote in *The Power of Positive Thinking.* ". . . The reaction between human beings is also in vibration. When you send out a prayer for a person, you employ the force inherent in a spiritual universe." This wasn't exactly the language of a conservative Dutch Reformed minister.

That observation about vibrations seemed to enter Peale's writing through the work of Florence Scovel Shinn, an artist and mystic whose books Peale praised later in his life. She was among the most alluring and unusual New Thought figures of the early twentieth century. Florence was born in 1871 in Camden, New Jersey, and in 1898 married American realist painter Everett Shinn. They were part of the Ashcan School of American artists, a cohort known for depicting street scenes, urban life, and the immigrant experience. Florence Shinn worked as an artist and illustrator of children's literature in New York City before writing her 1925 New Thought classic, *The Game of Life and How to Play It.* Unable to interest New York presses, she published the book herself. Shinn quickly became a popular New Thought teacher and lecturer, bringing a unique warmth and amiability to mystic-occult ideas. Her writing often described universal "vibrations"—an idea that entered her books, before entering Peale's, through the occult work *The Kybalion,* which Shinn avowedly admired.

Yet it would be an error to assume, as some fundamentalist critics have charged, that Peale was some kind of occultist in vestments. He was not. In many regards Peale was, in fact, the midwestern Methodist he presented himself as. He labored to find a Scriptural antecedent to the ideas he wrote about. In the truest sense, Peale was a great synthesizer. He once recalled his father telling him—quite rightly:

> Norman, I have read and studied all your books and sermons and it is clearly evident that you have gradually evolved a new religious system of thought and teaching. And it's O.K., too, very O.K., because its center and circumference and essence is Jesus Christ. There is no doubt about its solid Biblical orientation. Yes, you have evolved a new Christian emphasis out of a composite of Science of Mind, metaphysics, Christian Science, medical and psychological practice, Baptist evangelism, Methodist witnessing and solid Dutch Reformed Calvinism.

Ministry of Success

For all of Peale's spiritual adventurousness, the minister was most at home among business elites and corporate climbers. Reverend Caliandro remembered an elderly Peale's attraction to Donald Trump upon first seeing the real-estate magnate on television. Peale was always "very impressed with successful people" and self-promoters, Caliandro recalled. "That was a weakness."

Peale acknowledged his tendency to kowtow to the powerful. He once obligingly invited success author Dale Carnegie to deliver a talk at the Religio-Psychiatric Clinic—a move that disturbed Smiley Blanton, who couldn't see what Carnegie's self-salesmanship had to do with the clinic's therapeutic work. Peale admitted that he often evinced an "all-things-to-all-men attitude," and he reluctantly withdrew the invitation.

Peale gamely courted corporations, penning a *Reader's Digest* article in 1950, "Let the Church Speak Up for Capitalism." U.S. Steel soon became a major supporter of Peale's motivational digest, *Guideposts*, which had struggled at its inception in 1945. In the early 1950s, the steel giant purchased monthly subscriptions for all of its 125,000 employees. The following decade, some 762 American businesses were ordering company-wide subscriptions to *Guideposts*.*

Beyond his business contacts, Peale maintained a network of conservative political friendships. Beginning in World War II, he began a lifelong relationship with Richard Nixon, who attended Peale's Marble Collegiate Church while he was temporarily stationed in the city during the war. Nixon continued to attend Marble Collegiate after moving to Manhattan in the early 1960s, following his unsuccessful run for governor of California. Shortly after Nixon took the White House in 1968, Peale performed the marriage ceremony of Nixon's daughter Julie to former president Dwight Eisenhower's grandson David, at his New York pulpit with the two presidential families looking on. (Dwight Eisenhower was hospitalized at the time and watched on closed circuit TV.) Peale remained close with Nixon and became the president's spiritual counselor during Watergate.

In recognition of Peale's influence as an ambassador of encouragement, Ronald Reagan awarded him the Presidential Medal of Freedom in 1984. Reagan hailed Peale for devising "a philosophy of happiness." Peale's White House ceremony, and publication of his memoirs that same year, marked the culmination of decades that he had spent burnishing his image as the minister to whom all aspiring Americans could relate. "A crustless sandwich nowadays is more controversial than Norman Vincent Peale," *People* magazine wrote in 1982.

Yet Peale had once been seriously damaged by political embarrassment. More than two decades before he stood with Reagan, Peale was

---

* While *Guideposts* exemplified mainline business and Cold War values, it was a maverick voice in covering issues ranging from addiction to depression. The magazine also intrepidly introduced readers to developments in psychical research.

the subject of controversy and scorn for his political alliances within some of the darkest precincts of right-wing activism.

"A Sinister Shadow"

Contrary to his persona, Peale never stood aloof from partisan politics. Indeed, he had a history of sharp-edged political statements. In 1934, he warned congregants that "a sinister shadow is being thrown upon our liberties," a thinly veiled reference to the New Deal. In 1952, he supported an archconservative movement to draft General Douglas MacArthur to run for president. In 1956, Peale used his pulpit to criticize Democratic presidential candidate Adlai Stevenson for being divorced.

But it was in the fall of 1960 that Peale ignited a storm of controversy. During the Nixon-Kennedy campaign, Peale publicly aligned himself with a group of conservative Protestant ministers who opposed the presidential candidacy of John F. Kennedy on the grounds that Kennedy, as a Roman Catholic, would ultimately prove loyal to the pope. The benignly named Citizens for Religious Freedom said in a statement: "It is inconceivable that a Roman Catholic president would not be under extreme pressure by the hierarchy of his church to accede to its policies . . ." Conspiracists feared that the young senator was, in effect, a Vatican "Manchurian Candidate."

In early September, Peale cochaired a Washington meeting of Citizens for Religious Freedom and addressed reporters afterward as its spokesman. While journalists were being handed copies of the Committee's anti-Catholic position paper, Peale absurdly (and unconvincingly) characterized the meeting as a mere "philosophical" discussion of "the nature and character of the Roman Catholic Church." (It was a discussion to which no Catholics had been invited.)

An immediate flood of negative coverage led to calls for Peale's resignation from his pulpit, and several newspapers dropped his syndicated column. In statements that followed, Peale tried to play down his advocacy. He attempted to further dampen his characterization of the group's Washington meeting as a gathering to merely discuss "the general subject of religious freedom." Eventually he claimed to have no idea there was any further agenda to the conference that he cochaired—and certainly none pertaining to politics. These positions were clearly contradicted by the group's earlier statements about the unfitness of a Catholic to serve as president.

In the weeks immediately following the Washington meeting, Peale succeeded in convincing his parishioners that he had simply wandered, Forrest Gump–style, into a situation of which he had no foreknowledge. Speaking in *"who me?"* tones from his Marble Collegiate pulpit, Peale said of his decision to attend the meeting: "I never been too bright, anyhow." The line elicited sympathetic laughter from the pews. Within Marble Collegiate, the rift had been healed.

But a darker Peale emerged in private. In a 1960 letter to a female supporter, Peale wrote: "I don't care a bit who of the candidates is chosen except that he be an American who takes orders from no one but the American people." He went on to ask her how a "dedicated Protestant as yourself could so enthusiastically favor an Irish Catholic for President of our country which was founded by Calvinistic Christians?" Upon Kennedy's electoral victory, a despondent Peale wrote to friends: "Protestant America got its death blow on November 8th."

To Peale's critics, the minister's attack-and-deny tactics on Kennedy came as no surprise. Detractors saw him as a smiley-faced cipher—a propagator of happiness with no ethical core. Indeed, it must be acknowledged that Peale's philosophy of positivity and self-worth was incapable of meeting life in all of its difficulties and tragedies. His outlook did not include a theology of suffering. Peale seemed incapable of persuading readers, as his hero Emerson once did, that the individual facing illness, tragedy, and death could find dignity and purpose only by seeing himself as part of the cycles of creation, in which loss plays an inevitable part.

It must also be said, however, that if those intellectuals who rolled their eyes at Peale's gospel of affirmation had taken the care to read his books they would have discovered a wealth of serviceable ideas. Peale's outlook could ford a river—his advice could prevent a marriage from crumbling when an unspeakable criticism, of the kind that can never be rescinded, was uttered in the heat of an argument. Peale's integration of psychology into church life dramatically lessened the 1950s stigma of seeing a psychiatrist. Indeed, Peale was the best-known clergyman to embrace psychotherapy—the literature from his Religio-Psychiatric Clinic told of the "sacredness of human personality." And Peale encouraged the faith traditions to stretch and grow in order to stay relevant. Four years after taking the pulpit at Marble Collegiate, he privately wrote a congregant: "As time passes men's ideas change; their knowledge is enlarged; and before long a creed leaves much to be said and says some things that are no longer tenable."

Peale possessed spiritual depth—though "the world did not see that depth," Caliandro recalled. Still, supporters and critics alike harbored questions both about Peale's theology and, in the wake of the Kennedy debacle, his innermost judgment.

Delusion and Deliverance

The chief criticism of Peale's work arose from his principle that self-assurance brings accomplishment. Critiquing this modern urge to self-belief, philosopher George Santayana noted: "Assurance is contemptible and fatal unless it is self-knowledge." The philosopher's observation highlights a contradiction in Peale's approach—which is that blindly self-confident people, rather than accurately assessing their strengths and achieving their ends, are often dangerously delusive.

Yet the part of the equation that Santayana and other critics missed is that the pursuit of self-belief *can itself become a form of self-inquiry*. Peale didn't promulgate a conceited idealism that deterred self-questioning. What Peale understood—and this is a key facet of the positive-thinking approach that detractors overlooked—is that only by a coordinated effort of thought could an individual begin to grasp or question what he actually wants from life and who he really is.

Consider how rare it is for us to make a meaningful, sustained observation of our likes and dislikes. Of course, we routinely complain, grasp, go along, fight—but we rarely ask ourselves, in a protracted and serious way: *What would create purpose or contentment for me? What would I really like to be doing right now—and in whose company?* We seldom ask, with deadly seriousness, who we want as intimates; where we physically and morally wish to dwell; and what we want to *do* with ourselves.

Once we persistently ask these things, we may be forced to acknowledge unclaimed desires, including those that we may not like discovering. Someone who has outwardly shrugged at money may find that such attainments really matter to him. Or the realization of a cherished desire may fail to satisfy, forcing someone who yearned for a certain status or recognition to take a second look at things. Whatever happens, the scrutinizing of our assumptions always places us before a deepened question.

The individual who possesses authentic and healthful self-belief is, in actuality, easily distinguishable from the person who harbors the fatal self-delusion noted by Santayana. Self-delusiveness always exposes itself in one telltale character trait: that of the person *who places chronic demands on others.* The seemingly self-assured man who persistently makes claims on the energies and attention of other people is not expressing self-sufficiency but, rather, fear and defensiveness. His false sense of security constantly requires propping up. *The deluded self-striver is characterized by his inability to leave other people alone.*

Seen in proper perspective, Peale's outlook demanded a personal inventory: a reckoning of one's abilities and wishes, a responsibility for choosing one's associates, and a clear self-sense of how one relates to others—none of which is guaranteed to increase one's portion but will increase awareness. And the individual, armed with that awareness, must possess a willingness to leap a chasm when life demands. That, finally, is what Peale's work pushes a mature reader toward.

As a seeker, Peale was engaged in all facets of mental life. He exchanged admiring letters with Duke University psychical researcher J.B. Rhine. He cultivated dialogue with other religious leaders. He regularly referred Jewish advice-seekers to Tehilla Lichtenstein, the pioneering female leader of the Jewish Science movement. Peale considered her a friend. The board of his Religio-Psychiatric Clinic was religiously diverse. All of this, finally, turns us back on the question: Where did Peale's anti-Catholic bigotry come from? Friends and colleagues were mystified. Reverend Caliandro, a minister of depth and sensitivity who knew Peale for decades, could only shake his head in wonder.

One possibility is that Peale suffered from a form of prejudice that remains common today: When a member of a minority group is a friend or coworker, all is well; but when that same figure is a president or authority figure, fears of a changing social order begin to rise; code words get used. For Peale, it was fine, even desirable, to break bread with Catholics and Jews; but he simply couldn't picture an America, in the form of a Kennedy presidency, that looked different from the one he grew up in.

Seen from this perspective, Peale, as a man, was less than his work. Yet there is probably not an ethical philosopher, political reformer, or religious figure of whom this cannot be said.

In the decades following the Kennedy debacle, Peale was more circumspect about his public affiliations. "You couldn't get me near a politician now," he said in 1982. Peale's caution extended not only to politics but also to his connections with the New Thought world. He wanted no controversial associations, and he cultivated his latter-day image for the broadest possible appeal. Referring to the New Thought community in an interview in 1989, four years before his death, Peale said: "They think I am one of them, but I am not." He added as an afterthought: "Actually I am not opposed to it."

The Aquarian

The nation's most fateful evangelizer of the positive in the latter half of the twentieth century was neither a mystic nor a minister. Like many of the shapers of positive thinking, he had a modest formal education, possessed a self-devised philosophy of life, and showed a willingness to experiment with a wide range of religious ideas. Friends and adversaries alike experienced a sense of wonder that he became the twentieth century's most influential president next to Franklin Roosevelt. This was Ronald Reagan.

Every historical writer who has approached the life of Reagan experiences the same sense of perplexity over who the man really was. Pulitzer-winning biographer Edmund Morris was so confounded by his subject that in his epic biography, *Dutch*, the writer made himself a character, finding it more useful to chart Reagan's influence on those around him than to part the curtain on the man himself. (Morris wondered if there even was a man behind the curtain.) Many biographers were left to plumb Reagan's movies, his penchant for homegrown wisdom, and his bevy of moralistic stories for keys to the man's outer actions—such as his stare-down of the Soviet Union (followed by his role-reversal as a peacemaker); his chimerical (though to the Soviets alarming) pursuit of "Star Wars"; and his bread-and-butter conservatism (clung to even though his family was rescued by the New Deal). In every respect, Reagan was a pairing of opposites.

The skeleton key to Reagan's career is not found in his films, his flights of idealism, or the pivoting of his internal moral compass, though each of these things is important. To be finally understood, Reagan must be seen as a product of the positive-thinking movement. Indeed, it was Reagan's song of the positive—as articulated in thousands of speeches as a conservative activist, California governor, and U.S. president—that, more than any other factor, made the principle of brighter tomorrows and limitless possibilities into the idealized creed of America.

The code in which Reagan spoke is the key to the inner man—a fact sensed by President Gerald Ford, who called Reagan "one of the few political leaders I have ever met whose public speeches revealed more than his private conversations." (Reagan, it should be noted, had produced his own political speeches starting in the 1950s, and, as president, crafted the basic boilerplate and stories for many of his talks.)

In a 2010 reassessment of Reagan, Newsweek erroneously called him a born-again Christian. For all the admiration that born-again Christians felt for Reagan, and he for them, he cannot be described in that way. Ronald and Nancy Reagan's proclivity for astrology is already well known, but it is just one branch from a larger tree. One of the most overlooked facets of Reagan's career, and an aspect of his life with which few admirers have come to terms, is the strain of avant-garde thought and mysticism that touched him as a young man, and Reagan's enduring taste for the New Age spirituality of his Hollywood years.

Reagan didn't experience Hollywood as an interlude in his life. He spent nearly three decades of his adulthood there; it was, in all its facets, an integral part of him. He complained to biographer Lou Cannon about "this New York Times kind of business of referring to me as a B-picture actor." In a late-night discussion, after speaking with Cannon about his string of substantial film roles, Reagan concluded somewhat sheepishly, "I'm proud of having been an actor." He was similarly proud of being part of that community's spiritual and social customs.

One of his closest friends in California was astrologer Carroll Righter, who in 1969 became the first and only astrologer to appear on the cover of Time magazine. In Reagan's best-known movie, Kings Row from 1942, he costarred and became friendly with actress Eden Gray, who went on to write some of the twentieth century's most popular guides to Tarot cards. (Gray recalled Reagan gamely reading aloud from his horoscope and those of other actors before shoots.) And when Reagan began his political rise in the 1950s, his early speeches, and those he later delivered as president, featured themes and phrases that can be traced to the writings of a Hollywood-based occult philosopher, Manly P. Hall.

None of this was a source of embarrassment to Reagan. Throughout his life he was at ease discussing premonitory dreams, astrology, number symbolism, out-of-body experiences, and his belief in UFOs, including personal sightings in the 1950s and '70s.

During his 1980 presidential campaign, he sat for a three-hour interview with journalist Angela Fox Dunn, the daughter of Malvina Fox Dunn, Reagan's drama coach at Warner Brothers in the 1930s. Reagan never opened up so much as when he was around people with ties to his movie days. With surprising frankness, the Republican nominee expounded on topics ranging from the astrological signs of past presidents, to his mother's religious beliefs, to the prophetic qualities of psychic Jeane Dixon, another old Hollywood friend. While Dixon was "always gung ho for me to be president," Reagan related, in the "foretelling part of her mind" the prophetess didn't see him in the Oval Office. (A prediction that, more or less, squared with Dixon's record.) He also boasted to Dunn of being an Aquarius, the most mystical of all the zodiac signs. "I believe you'll find that 80 percent of the people in New York's Hall of Fame are Aquarians," he said.*

At the back of his personality, Reagan was the man he proudly described to Dunn: an Aquarian. He was influenced by various mystical and mind-power cultures, whose mark he left permanently stamped on America.

"Child of Destiny"

Long before his life in Hollywood, Reagan was at home with various blends of American mysticism. A combination of the conventional and otherworldly characterized his childhood.

"The best part," he recalled, "was that I was allowed to dream. Many the day I spent deep in a huge rocker in the mystic atmosphere of Aunt Emma's living room with its horsehair-stuffed gargoyles of furniture, its

---

* It is not clear what Hall of Fame Reagan was referring to—it may have been the Hall of Fame for Great Americans at New York's Bronx Community College. If so, he would have been disappointed to learn that Aquarians are not overrepresented among its inventors, statesmen, and scientists.

shawls and antimacassars, globes of glass over birds and flowers, books and strange odors . . ."

His mother, Nelle, was, by turns, religiously conservative, but she also infused her sons with a freethinking streak, telling Ron and his brother to address their parents by first names. In a progressive viewpoint that wouldn't gain currency until many years later, Nelle told the boys that their father's alcoholism was really a disease. Nelle was committed to seeing her sons well rounded, and she took them to plays, recitals, and lectures. One biographer called her a "determined improver." Another noted that she "encouraged positive thinking." Nelle wrote a poem for her Disciples of Christ church newsletter, "On the Sunnyside":

> Think lovely thoughts, ennobling the soul
>   Keeping them from strife. . . .
> The sunnyside's the only side
>   Full of graces divine
> Sometimes too bright for us to scan
>   I'd seek to make them mine.

Nelle doted on Ron as her favorite. "Within the Reagan household," observed biographer Lou Cannon, "and perhaps in Ronald Reagan's heart, there was an early sense that he was a child of destiny." By the time Reagan arrived at Eureka College in central Illinois in 1928, he was comfortable with this perspective. He fondly recalled a French professor with a reputation as a psychic who forecast his greatness. "This is a class of destiny," she announced at the start of the term, and he felt she was speaking directly to him.

Reagan's break into radio came in 1932, when he was hired by the Palmer family, who were proprietors of an Iowa radio station. The Palmers were also a clan of Spiritualists, mystics, high eccentrics, and visionaries. The family patriarch, D. D. Palmer, was the founder of chiropractic healing in the late nineteenth century. A Mesmerist and Spiritualist, D. D. Palmer said that the chiropractic method was transmitted to him from "an intelligence in the spiritual world" during an Iowa Spiritualist convention.

D.D.'s son and successor, "Colonel" B. J. Palmer—the man who hired young Reagan as a broadcaster—developed his own variant of mind-power philosophy. Colorful and fearless, B.J. expanded the college of chiropractic and mental healing, which his father had founded in Davenport, Iowa. This was where Reagan walked the halls and grounds as an employee at the radio station called WOC, for "World of Chiropractic." Its programming promoted the school but also featured standard broadcasts of sports, news, and music.

Part showman, B. J. Palmer created a strange otherworld on the campus, which had an adjacent mansion and gardens nicknamed "A Little Bit O'Heaven." B.J. festooned the Iowa property with curios from his world travels: statues of the Hindu gods Kali and Ganesha, massive Buddha heads and shrines, Chinese Foo Dogs, bronze and marble renderings of Venus, Japanese temple gates, and a truly eerie, enormous stone mosaic of a coiled, fanged serpent. ("The serpent was cast out of heaven," B.J. explained in a visitors' guide.)

Reagan spent his working hours at the college's rooftop station and joined the chiropractic students for meals in the basement cafeteria. Making his way from the roof to the basement, Reagan recalled seeing the hallways of the Palmer School of Chiropractic emblazoned with bits of B.J.'s philosophy, such as: "THINK! SPEAK! ACT, POSITIVE! I AM! I WILL! I CAN! I MUST!" Like many mental mystics, B.J. believed that man possessed an inner divine sense, a branch of the "Universal Intelligence," which he termed Innate. "INNATE," Palmer wrote, "is the ONE eternal, internal, stable, and permanent factor that is a fixed and reliable entity . . . the same capable INNER VOICE that is capable of getting any sick organ well."

To Reagan, B. J. Palmer's world was neither shocking nor surprising. It primed him for the spiritual culture he soon discovered in Hollywood. During his film career, Reagan encountered a mystical influence that left its mark on his political vision.

The President and the Occultist

Reagan often spoke of America's divine purpose and of a mysterious plan behind the nation's founding. "You can call it mysticism if you want to," he told the Conservative Political Action Conference in 1974, "but I have always believed that there was some divine plan that placed this great continent between two oceans to be sought out by those who were possessed of an abiding love of freedom and a special kind of courage." These were remarks to which Reagan often returned. He repeated them almost verbatim as president before a television audience of millions for the Statue of Liberty centenary on July 4, 1986.

When touching on such themes, Reagan echoed the work, and sometimes the phrasing, of occult scholar Manly P. Hall.

From the dawn of Hall's career in the early 1920s until his death in 1990, the Los Angeles teacher wrote about America's "secret destiny." The United States, in Hall's view, was a society that had been planned and founded by secret esoteric orders to spread enlightenment and liberty to the world.

In 1928, Hall attained underground fame when, at the remarkably young age of twenty-seven, he published *The Secret Teachings of All Ages*, a massive codex to the mystical and esoteric philosophies of antiquity. Exploring subjects from Native American mythology to Pythagorean mathematics to the geometry of ancient Egypt, this *encyclopedia arcana* remains the unparalleled guidebook to ancient symbols and esoteric thought. *The Secret Teachings* won the admiration of figures ranging from General John Pershing to Elvis Presley. Novelist Dan Brown cites it as a key source.

After publishing his "Great Book," Hall spent the rest of his life lecturing and writing within the walls of his Egypto–art deco campus, the Philosophical Research Society, in LA's Griffith Park neighborhood. Hall called the place a "mystery school" in the mold of Pythagoras's ancient academy.

It was there in 1944 that the occult thinker produced a short work, one little known beyond his immediate circle. This book, *The Secret Destiny*

of *America*, evidently caught the eye of Reagan, then a middling movie
actor gravitating toward politics.

Hall's concise volume described how America was the product of
a "Great Plan" for religious liberty and self-governance, launched by a
hidden order of ancient philosophers and secret societies. In one chapter, Hall described a rousing speech delivered by a mysterious "unknown speaker" before the signing of the Declaration of Independence.
The "strange man," wrote Hall, invisibly entered and exited the locked
doors of the statehouse in Philadelphia on July 4, 1776, delivering an
oration that bolstered the wavering spirits of the delegates. "God has
given America to be free!" commanded the mysterious speaker, urg-
ing the men to overcome their fears of being hanged or beheaded, and
to seal destiny by signing the great document. Newly emboldened, the
delegates rushed forward to add their names. They looked to thank the
stranger only to discover that he had vanished from the locked room.
Was this, Hall wondered, "one of the agents of the secret Order, guard-
ing and directing the destiny of America?"

At a 1957 commencement address at his alma mater Eureka College, Reagan, then a corporate spokesman for General Electric, sought
to inspire students with this leaf from occult history. "This is a land of
destiny," Reagan said, "and our forefathers found their way here by some
Divine system of selective service gathered here to fulfill a mission to
advance man a further step in his climb from the swamps." Reagan then
retold (without naming a source) the tale of Hall's unknown speaker.
"When they turned to thank the speaker for his timely words," Reagan
concluded, "he couldn't be found and to this day no one knows who he
was or how he entered or left the guarded room." Reagan revived the
story in 1981, when *Parade* magazine asked the president for a personal
essay on what July 4 meant to him. Presidential aide Michael Deaver delivered the piece with a note saying, "This Fourth of July message is the
president's own words and written initially in the president's hand," on
a yellow pad at Camp David. Reagan retold the legend of the unknown

speaker—this time using language very close to Hall's own: "When they turned to thank him for his timely oratory, he was not to be found, nor could any be found who knew who he was or how he had come in or gone out through the locked and guarded doors."

Where did Hall uncover the tale that inspired a president? The episode originated as "The Speech of the Unknown" in a collection of folkloric stories about America's founding, published in 1847 under the title *Washington and His Generals, or Legends of the Revolution* by American social reformer and muckraker George Lippard. Lippard, a friend of Edgar Allan Poe, had a strong taste for the gothic—he cloaked his mystery man in a "dark robe." He also tacitly acknowledged inventing the story: "The name of the Orator . . . is not definitely known. In this speech, it is my wish to compress some portion of the fiery eloquence of the time."

For his part, Hall seemed to know almost nothing about the story's point of origin. He had been given a copy of the "Speech of the Unknown" by a since-deceased secretary of the occult Theosophical Society, but with no bibliographical information other than its being from a "rare old volume of early American political speeches." The speech appeared in 1938 in the Society's journal, *The Theosophist*, with the sole note that it was "published in a rare volume of addresses, and known probably to only one in a million, even of American citizens."

There are indications that Reagan and Hall may have personally met to discuss the story. In an element unique to Hall's version, the mystic-writer (dubiously) attributed the tale of the unknown speaker to the writings of Thomas Jefferson. When Reagan addressed the Conservative Political Action Conference in Washington on January 25, 1974, he again told the story, but this time cited an attribution—of sorts. Reagan said the tale was told to him "some years ago" by "a writer, who happened to be an avid student of history. . . . I was told by this man that the story could be found in the writings of Jefferson. I confess, I never researched or made an effort to verify it."

Whether the president and the occultist ever met, it is Hall's language that unmistakably marks the Reagan telling.

Biographer Edmund Morris noted Reagan's fondness for apocryphal tales and his "Dalíesque ability to bend reality to his own purposes." Yet he added that the president's stories "should be taken seriously because they represent core philosophy." This influential (and sometimes inscrutable) president of the late twentieth century found an illustration of his core belief in America's purpose within the pages of an occult work little known beyond its genre.

"Anything Is Possible"

During the 1980 president campaign, many Americans were electrified by Reagan's depiction of America as a divinely ordained nation where anything could be willed into existence.

In announcing his candidacy in 1979, Reagan declared: "To me our country is a living, breathing presence, unimpressed by what others say is impossible. . . . If there is one thing we are sure of it is . . . that nothing is impossible, and that man is capable of improving his circumstances beyond what we are told is fact." It was a vastly different kind of political oratory than the restrained, moralistic tones of his opponent, Jimmy Carter.

Through his reiteration of this theme of America's destiny, and his powers as a communicator, Reagan shaped how Americans *wanted* to see themselves: as a portentous people possessed of the indomitable spirit to scale any height. This American self-perception could bitterly clash with reality in the face of a declining industrial base and falling middle-class wages. Nonetheless, the image that Reagan gave Americans of themselves—as a people always ushering in new dawns—formed the political template to which every president who followed him had to publicly adhere.*

---

* It can seem as if songs of the affirmative have always marked presidential oratory—but not exactly. Accepting the Democratic nomination in 1960, John F. Kennedy spoke in terms that could hardly be imagined today: "There has also been a change—a slippage—in our intellectual and moral strength. . . . Blight has descended on our regulatory agencies—and a dry rot, beginning in Washington, is seeping into every corner of America—in the payola mentality, the expense account way of life, the confusion between what is legal and what is right."

After Reagan, virtually every major campaign address included pae-
ans to better tomorrows, from Bill Clinton's invocation of "a place called
Hope" (and his use of Fleetwood Mac's "Don't Stop Thinking About
Tomorrow"), to Barack Obama's "Yes, we can." In his 2011 State of the
Union address, Obama echoed one of Reagan's signature lines when he
declared: "This is a country where anything is possible." The one recent
president who complained that he couldn't master "the vision thing,"
George H. W. Bush, was not returned to office.

Political Psychology

In Reagan's private life, positive thinking didn't always allow for deep
relationships. Reagan's campaign aides and White House staffers were
sometimes seriously hurt by the manner in which he would forget all
about people and relationships that no longer suited a new phase or role
in which he found himself. This was his habit in all areas of life—and it
layered him with a kind of emotional buffer. While recovering from an
operation for colon cancer in 1985, Reagan pointed out to Time magazine
that he did not "have cancer"—rather he was a man who "had cancer,"
past tense. "But it's gone," he explained, "along with the surrounding
tissue. . . . So I am someone who does not have cancer."

That is how Reagan dealt with almost every challenge: He found the
terms to conceptualize himself in the strongest possible manner based on
the demands of the moment. That talent could make him seem shallow
and insincere, yet it allowed him to adapt in unexpected ways. Just as the
young New Dealer of the 1930s transformed into the law-and-order conservative of the 1960s, so did the man who campaigned as a flinty Cold
Warrior transform into a global peacemaker during his second term.

In the latter years of his presidency, Reagan was one of the few world
figures who not only believed in the authenticity of *glasnost* and *perestroika*
in the Soviet Union (as most conservatives at the time did not) but who
possessed a vision of what the post-Soviet era would look like (as most
liberals then did not). In a mixture of dream making and idealism, Rea-

gan firmly believed that his "Star Wars" initiative would rid the world of the nuclear threat and open the borders of all nations to peaceful commerce and exchange.

For those who looked carefully, his global outlook had been foreshadowed during his Hollywood career. Soon after World War II, Reagan joined a group called the United World Federalists. The organization advocated a worldwide government organized along a United Nations–style system of rule making and dispute resolution. It was precisely the kind of "big picture" idea that excited Hollywood politicos of the mid-twentieth century (and that evokes deep suspicion in Tea Party activists of the twenty-first century). Globalist peacemaking touched something in Reagan's earliest ideals. "I went through a period in college," he later recalled, "in the aftermath of World War I, where I became a pacifist and thought the whole thing [i.e., the war] was a frame-up."

Reagan's penchant for science fiction has been widely noted. The United World Federalists could seem like the kind of universal government that sometimes showed up in sci-fi entertainment, like the United Federation of Planets in *Star Trek*, or the Galactic Republic (replaced by the evil Galactic Empire) in the *Star Wars* movies. Perhaps not coincidentally, Reagan also spoke openly of his belief in UFOs for much of his life. According to family friend Lucille Ball, Reagan insisted in the 1950s that he and Nancy had a close brush with a flying saucer while they were driving down the coastal highway one night. The couple, Ball recalled, arrived almost an hour late for a Los Angeles dinner party at the home of actor William Holden. They came in "all out of breath and so excited" and proceeded to tell shocked friends about witnessing a UFO. As president, Reagan more than once assured Soviet premier Mikhail Gorbachev that an interstellar threat would unite U.S. and Soviet societies. Gorbachev honestly seemed perplexed as to whether Reagan was kidding, but ultimately decided he was not.

Reagan's Irish ancestors might have called that side of him "barmy." But this aspect of Reagan should not be dismissed as shallowness or mental weakness. Reagan thought in epic, picturesque terms—about the Soviet Union as "evil," about himself as a man of "destiny," about the mission of America as "mystical." Reagan's mother, Nelle, left him with a sense of enchantment about the power of big ideas. One of the ironies of twenty-first-century politics is how the nationalistic, anti-immigration activists of the Tea Party often extol Reagan as their hero. However passionately Reagan favored tax cutting or getting rid of "government waste," his outlook was fundamentally globalist and even a touch utopian.

Reagan also inherited his mother's passion for self-improvement. As a boy, he learned to read before starting school. He mastered scripts and later policy papers with rapidity. Critics thought Reagan was not a details man, but that wasn't exactly correct. Reagan could voraciously digest information that tapped his enthusiasm; he ran on enthusiasm, and without it he was adrift. In adulthood he maintained reading habits that extended to seven daily newspapers. Reagan would never be caught dead on camera, unlike his avowed admirer Sarah Palin, unable to cite a daily paper he read or to identify a favorite Founding Father. Part of Reagan's ire toward student activists while he was governor of California stemmed from how the small-town college boy in him felt an Oz-like wonder toward the University of California and the motto on its coat of arms: "Let There Be Light." He resented those who he believed desecrated its intellectual opportunities.

It must also be said, however, that Reagan's style was to read selectively and to question narrowly. As soon as he homed in on a position—such as his belief in massive welfare fraud—he would constantly happen upon fact after fact, usually in the form of stories or an offbeat statistic, to buttress his conviction. Campaign aides told of sometimes "misplacing" the chief's favorite magazines in order to avoid his glomming on to a factoid—such as trees causing air pollution—that would later prove an embarrassment. If there is an adjunct to Reagan's credo "Nothing is impossible," it might be: *If I believe it that makes it so.* That outlook may have helped a poor Depression-era boy adopt a powerful (and needed) faith in self. But it could reflect a dangerous self-indulgence in the realm of policy making.

Reagan, Peale, Hill, Carnegie, and other positive thinkers had so thoroughly, and subtly, convinced the public over the course of decades that what you think is what matters most that by 2010 few objected or even noticed when New York's Democratic senator Charles Schumer defended a scaled-down jobs creation bill by claiming that it was the very act of passage, rather than the policy particulars themselves, that made the difference: ". . . the longer I am around, I think it's the market's psychology that matters dramatically." In substance, it was not much different from mental healer Phineas Quimby concluding a century and a half earlier: "Man's happiness is in his belief."

chapter seven

the spirit of success

I, so far as I can sense the pattern of
my mind, write of the wish that comes
true, for some reason a terrifying concept,
at least to my imagination.

—James M. Cain, preface to *The Butterfly*, 1946

The era of the mind-power pioneers reached a close by the Age of Reagan. The "philosophy of happiness," as Reagan called it, appeared everywhere; the landmark texts had been written; the theology had been dispersed across mainline churches or secularized within business culture; and much of the public viewed a "positive attitude" as a naturally desirable, if elusive, aim.

As it happens, the year Reagan took office in 1981 marked the passing of New Thought minister and metaphysical writer Joseph Murphy, who was the last real innovator from the field's formative years. Murphy formed a link to the generation of American mystical thinkers who were unchurched, self-schooled, and made a comfortable, though not lavish, livelihood from book royalties, speaking fees, and the collection-basket offerings at metaphysical churches and meeting halls. Murphy's death concluded the period in which New Thought was shaped by itinerant figures who lacked a significant business apparatus.

The motivational up-and-comers of the 1970s and 1980s, by contrast, were not classifiable by any one philosophy, and were far more plugged in to the business of publishing, weekend seminars, audio programs, and for-profit teaching institutes. They included sales coaches Zig Ziglar and Og Mandino; human-potential author Stephen Covey; management experts Ken Blanchard and Spencer Johnson; metaphysical publisher Louise Hay; inspirational writers Jack Canfield and Richard Carlson; life coaches Anthony Robbins and Brian Tracy; plus a wide range of spiritual self-help authors, including Wayne Dyer, Jean Houston, and Marianne Williamson (who got her start as a Unity minister).

There were also prominent voices on the evangelical circuit, often reaching millions of people, such as the spiritual healer and televangelist Oral Roberts and the provocatively audacious prosperity minister Reverend Ike, who became a media sensation in the 1970s with his claim that "God wants you to be rich." The New Thought movement's indispensable phrase, Law of Attraction, was retooled by Rev. Pat Robertson as Law of Reciprocity, and by popular Korean evangelist David Yonggi Cho as Law of Incubation. This concept, which began with Spiritualist medium Andrew Jackson Davis, became a staple of New-Agers and evangelical media ministers alike.

The most distinctive evangelical figure who spread motivational philosophy in the 1970s and '80s was Hour of Power television host and Norman Vincent Peale protégé Rev. Robert H. Schuller. From the pulpit of his massive, glass-paneled Crystal Cathedral in Garden Grove, California,

Schuller preached a philosophy he called "possibility thinking." He eschewed the politics of evangelism. As a result, Schuller attracted a following among both mainline Christians and New-Agers. He was one of very few figures of whom this was true.

Yet Schuller's retirement in 2006 brought disorder and financial chaos to the Crystal Cathedral organization, which filed for bankruptcy in fall 2010. The once-formidable ministry had built too ambitiously and suffered a drop in broadcast audiences. Facing a $43 million debt, the megachurch was forced to rely on volunteers to landscape its forty-acre campus.

In 2011 the Schuller ministry announced the sale of its grounds and the 10,664-windowed Crystal Cathedral to the Catholic Church. The landmark structure, which had been designed as a four-pointed star by architect Philip Johnson, was redubbed Christ Cathedral by its new owners. In early 2012 Robert Schuller cut ties with the church amid board disputes, and most other Schuller family members departed in an atmosphere of power struggles and accusations. The remaining ministry struggled to maintain a sizable audience for the once-popular *Hour of Power* show.

While the fortunes of individual figures could rise and fall, the business of motivation, from the broadcasts of Oprah Winfrey to a wide-ranging network of multimedia seminars and workshops, was a staple of the American scene by the late twentieth century. The persona of the motivational coach was sufficiently recognizable to be routinely satirized in movies and on television, including in *Saturday Night Live* actor Chris Farley's 1990 sendup of motivational speaker "Matt Foley," who bellowed: *You're gonna end up livin' in a van down by the river!* Either as sources of inspiration or as objects of derision, empowerment coaches became an American archetype.

In actuality, the motivational field as a modern business phenomenon received its start from a man of reserved character and dignity. He neither charged around stages, waved his arms, nor raised his voice above the tone that one might expect from a trusted family physician.

His work ignited the business motivation genre at a time when the television and recording industries were in their infancy.

The Strangest Secret

The emergence of business motivation as a field—one that played out in books and convention halls and also became a powerful electronic medium, first on vinyl albums and audio tapes, and then later on television, DVDs, the Internet, and apps—can be traced back to the experience of a child of the Great Depression. He was a Marine who survived the attack on Pearl Harbor, a successful broadcaster and salesman, and, above all, a relentlessly curious man who yearned to know what set apart successful people. His deep, sonorous voice became familiar to millions after he recorded "the secret" to success on a vinyl record in 1956. His name was Earl Nightingale.

Nightingale was born in 1921 in Long Beach, California. By the time Earl was twelve, in 1933, his father had abandoned the family. Earl, his mother, and two brothers lived destitute in a "tent city" near the Long Beach waterfront, a home to people displaced in the Depression. Earl's mother supported the family by working as a seamstress in a WPA factory. The adolescent Earl despaired not only of the family's poverty but also of the people he came in touch with. Everyone around him seemed backbiting, sullen, and directionless.

"I started looking for security when I was 12," Nightingale recalled. What he specifically meant was that he wanted to determine why some people were poor while others thrived. He hungered to be a member of the latter group. As a twelve-year-old, he ignored broader socioeconomic factors. This may have reflected a certain blindness to the larger mechanics of life, not dissimilar to the outlook found in a young Ronald Reagan. But the wish to succeed also drove him to read voraciously in search of "the answer." He haunted the Long Beach Public Library, poring over every available work of religion, psychology, and philosophy.

At the age of seventeen, Earl was no closer to solving his riddle.

Yearning for independence and needing three meals a day, he joined the U.S. Marine Corps on the eve of World War II. In 1941, he became one of twelve survivors out of a company of a hundred Marines aboard the U.S.S. *Arizona* during the attack on Pearl Harbor. Nightingale made it through the war, emerging not only with his physical well-being but also with the full maturation of a personal gift. He possessed a remarkable speaking voice—rich, deep, sonorous. His intonation was flawless. When stationed after the war as an instructor at Camp Lejeune in North Carolina, Nightingale moonlighted as an announcer with a local radio station. From there he found radio jobs in Phoenix and then at a CBS affiliate in Chicago.

At CBS in 1950, the twenty-nine-year-old became the voice of the aviator-cowboy adventurer Sky King on a radio serial of the same name. It was the type of rock-'em-sock-'em role in which Reagan had once excelled.

But a more fateful development happened in Nightingale's life around that time. He finally discovered his secret to success.

After reading hundreds of works of psychology, religion, mysticism, and ethics, the ex-Marine and radio announcer underwent a revelation. It came while he was reading Napoleon Hill's *Think and Grow Rich*. Nightingale realized that in the writings of every era, from the Taoist philosophy of Lao Tzu to the Stoic meditations of the Roman emperor Marcus Aurelius to the Transcendentalist essays of Emerson, the same truth appeared, over and over. He had been reading it for years and simply not seeing it. It came down to six words: *We become what we think about.*

That was it. *We become what we think about.* It was the "answer" for which he had been searching.

Nightingale left the CBS station, though he remained the voice of Sky King for several years. He moved to a new radio gig, which allowed him to write his own spots. At Chicago's WGN, Nightingale not only wrote and hosted his own hour-and-a-half talk show—where he was able to expound on bits of philosophy, stories, and slice-of-life anecdotes—but he also worked out a deal to profit from products he sold on the air.

He promoted *Think and Grow Rich* through a local bookstore and received a cut of every copy sold. He followed suit with other products, literally from soup to soap. He soon began pitching retirement-insurance policies sold by the Franklin Life Insurance Company. This enterprise was less successful. Nightingale's pitches moved few policies. Then he seized upon a different idea: Rather than selling policies, he would recruit salesmen for the company.

"If you, my listener, are a sales person or a wife of a sales person and your husband is making less than twenty thousand a year, I came across an idea that is fantastic," Nightingale intoned. He asked people to mail in cards with their addresses, and he invited respondents to recruitment meetings for Franklin Life. Nightingale brought top salesmen into Franklin's fold that way. Some of them remained with the firm for decades, a Franklin executive recalled. Nightingale was a pitch artist—but he sold a fair deal.

The radio announcer discovered that he was better at recruiting and revving up salesmen than at selling goods or policies himself. From that time forward, Nightingale's number-one product became motivating other people. In the mid-1950s, Nightingale purchased his own franchise office of Franklin Life, an idea probably put to him by a new friend, W. Clement Stone, a highly successful Chicago insurance man who had collaborated on books with Napoleon Hill.

Nightingale got into a routine of delivering inspiring talks to his salesmen. One day in 1956, before taking a long vacation from the office, Nightingale privately recorded a motivational message for the men to hear in his absence. His thirty-minute message told the story of his discovery of the six-word formula: *We become what we think about.* He called the presentation "The Strangest Secret." In clear, simple terms Nightingale described how this formula was the fulcrum on which all practical philosophies rested. It was a "secret," he explained, only insofar as we overlook it, just as we undervalue or ignore those things we are given freely: love, health, sensations, and, above all, the uses of our minds.

"The human mind *isn't used*," he said, "merely because we take it for granted."

The vinyl phonograph record electrified everyone who heard it. It got passed around, shared, and borrowed. Nightingale returned home surprised by the demand for it. No commercial advice record had ever before been produced. But the pitchman saw the possibilities. Calling on friends in the record business, Nightingale made a professional version of "The Strangest Secret," and Columbia Records agreed to distribute the album. *The Strangest Secret* became the first spoken-word album to receive a Gold Record, for sales in excess of one million copies.

With orders booming, Nightingale partnered in 1959 with another Chicagoan, a direct-mail advertiser named Lloyd Conant. Together they formed Nightingale-Conant, which became the nation's first recording company focused on motivational fare. The company offered Nightingale's recordings, first on vinyl and later on cassettes. In decades ahead its catalogue expanded to include self-help figures such as Anthony Robbins, Robert Kiyosaki, and Deepak Chopra.

Nightingale had minted an industry. And in his search for the truth about human nature, he had stumbled upon a new kind of product: *selling people on the promise within themselves*. He made himself the field's first marketer and promoter. Like the radioman that he was, Nightingale performed and produced the early merchandise, first in the form of *The Strangest Secret*, and later in his widely syndicated radio program, *Our Changing World*, which he wrote and narrated beginning in 1959.

Nightingale was evangelizer, philosopher, and pitchman rolled into one. In partnership with mail-order expert Conant, he also became manufacturer, fulfillment manager, and catalogue retailer. Nightingale's business model was simple: Do it all.

Nightingale's commercial outlook was more than the result of Depression-era determination and personal guile. Critics of Nightingale and other motivational pitchmen often made the mistake of contrasting selling with believing, as though one must naturally preclude the other. Nightingale was, above all, a believer. To listeners eager for his message,

Nightingale's voice and viewpoint were sincere, deeply affecting, and practical. He encouraged the honing of individual ability. He read voraciously and urged his listeners to do the same. He inveighed against the conformity and thoughtlessness that characterized many human lives.

By the time Nightingale received his Gold Record in 1971, he left no question about the potential of the motivational field. When he died of heart failure in 1989, soon after his sixty-eighth birthday, Nightingale had lived just long enough to see the motivational genre grow into a profitable business of publishers, organizations, and individuals. Within a decade of Nightingale's passing, the medium of records and cassette tapes that he knew gave way to CDs, DVDs, and, finally, digital downloads. Today whenever a psychology, self-help, or marketing lecture is clicked on, downloaded, or viewed through websites such as TED or BigThink, an echo is being heard from the day in 1956 when Earl Nightingale first recorded his "Strangest Secret."

"If You Want More Money . . ."

In the years following Nightingale, the positive-thinking philosophy completed its transformation into a methodology of winning. It abounded in both business and religious circles. Money and ethical issues were sometimes at stake. Some of the leading inspirational evangelists, and several longtime New Thought figures, prescribed tithing (the ancient practice of giving away 10 percent of one's income) as a means to wealth attraction.

As the practice frequently unfolded, tithes were supposed to be directed not to charities but to the institutions where a congregant was "spiritually fed"—often enough back to the prosperity ministries themselves.

"The purpose of it is to acknowledge that we know that God is our source," Unity prosperity minister Edwene Gaines said in 2002. "It is very important that the tithe go to where we are fed spiritually, not to charity."

The formula, as oft-stated by Christian evangelists and New-Thoughters alike, was that certain Scriptural verses promised riches to those who gave their 10 percent. One example was Malachi 3:10: "Bring the whole tithe into the storehouse, so that there may be food in My house, and test Me now in this, says the Lord of hosts, if I will not open for you the windows of heaven and pour out for you a blessing until it overflows."

The practice could be brutally utilitarian. Discussions abounded on whether a tithe was supposed to be based on net or gross income, or whether a person could tithe time rather than cash. (On the latter question, the prosperity minister Gaines once saucily told a workshop attendee: "If you tithe time what you'll get is all the time you need. Now, if you want more money in your life you got to tithe money. . . . Look for the loophole, honey, you're not gonna find it.")

Not all New Thoughters were quite so settled on the matter. One of the movement's most intellectually vibrant figures was an ex–Christian Scientist, Joel Goldsmith, who wrote, "One must not tithe for reward, for then it becomes a business proposition." In a departure from prosperity theologians, Goldsmith insisted that tithing to spiritual institutions was an archaic practice; he encouraged tithing to philanthropies and charities. But even Goldsmith's subtler interpretation rested on the premise that what was given in secret would be rewarded openly. No matter how tithing was framed, it proved difficult for congregants, of either New Thought or larger evangelical prosperity ministries, to avoid seeing tithing as a quid pro quo—a harnessing of spiritual laws where, if certain rules were followed, the house would always pay up.

Although tithing had Biblical roots, it was, until the early twentieth century, a fairly rarified practice in modern life. How did an ancient Biblical financial custom return to prominence on the modern scene? Tithing seems to have been reintroduced into the popular spiritual culture through New Thought, particularly Charles Fillmore's Unity ministry. Around 1905, discussions of tithing started to regularly appear in Fillmore's *Unity* journal. "It seems to me that tithing is a good thing to teach in regard to giving," wrote a reader in the issue of July 1905. "I have practiced it about three or four years, and have always something on hand to give. Also my income has increased." The next month a subscriber wrote enthusiastically of wanting to give "a tithe of the benefit I have received from Unity." It is significant that these exchanges occurred in 1905, which was one year before the Pentecostal movement is generally considered to have commenced with a series of revival meetings at the Azusa Street Mission in Los Angeles.

Early Pentecostal congregations emphasized the manifestation of miracles, spontaneous healings, and speaking in tongues. This modern embrace of "signs and wonders" cracked open the door for evangelical prosperity ministries of the 1970s, which variously endorsed tithing, prayer, and affirmation as means to wealth attraction. This approach proved massively popular. It is today estimated that of America's twelve largest churches, three are prosperity oriented: Joel Osteen's Lakewood Church in Houston; T.D. Jakes's Potter's House in Dallas; and Tommy Barnett's Phoenix First in Arizona. Some of the nation's most popular media ministers are also, in some measure, prosperity oriented, such as Kenneth Copeland, Eddie Long, Benny Hinn, Paul and Janice Crouch, and Joyce Meyer.

To be sure, many contemporary evangelical worshippers are critical of the prosperity gospel. And theological disputes persist among prosperity gospelers themselves. Evangelical critics of the prosperity gospel generally (and rightly) trace its roots to New Thought, which for them is cause for deep concern. New Thought, when it is heard-of at all in the evangelical culture, is considered a "quasi-Christian heresy," as Christian scholars David W. Jones and Russell S. Woodbridge put it in a critical history of the prosperity gospel. "Although the New Thought movement is unknown by name to most contemporary Christians," Jones and Woodbridge wrote, "the prosperity gospel consists largely of the ideas of the New Thought movement repackaged with new faces, new technology, new venues, and a slightly altered message."

Their analysis was astute. While today's prosperity megachurches are far bigger and better known than even the largest Unity or New Thought congregations, there is no question that New Thought provided the template for the prosperity gospel, often down to specific phraseology. Compare, for example, the words of Unity minister Edwene Gaines, from a talk she delivered in the 1980s before several hundred attendees at a Tucson Unity church, to sentiments heard in 2006 from Georgia-based prosperity minister Creflo Dollar, a popular prosperity gospeler whose television audiences number in the millions:

> GAINES: You are a child of God, now it's time to grow up. What do children of God do when they grow up? What do they become? What do children of cats, when they grow up, [become]? They become cats. What do children of God do, when they grow up? They become gods.

> DOLLAR: If cats get together, they produce what? [Congregation: "Cats!"] So if the Godhead says "Let us make man in our image," and everything produces after its own kind, then they produce what? [Congregation: "Gods!"] Gods. Little "g" gods. You're not human. Only human part of you is this flesh you're wearing.

Positive Heresy?

A large and popular evangelical movement called Word of Faith attracts particular controversy today among critics of the prosperity gospel. Rising to popularity in the late 1960s through the ministry of Kenneth E. Hagin, Word of Faith theology espouses "positive confession." Positive confession entails repeating, in affirmation style, certain Biblical passages for health, wealth, or the fulfillment of personal needs. Word of Faith ministers include some of the past century's best-known (and often most controversial) evangelists, including Jimmy Swaggart, Kenneth Copeland, and Jim and Tammy Faye Bakker.

The Word of Faith movement got its inception in the theology of E. W. Kenyon, a Massachusetts-born minister and writer who began his career in the late nineteenth century. A New Englander, Kenyon honed his style at the Emerson School of Oratory in Boston in 1892. The two-year Emerson School featured an immersive program of literature, writing, and oration. It was not connected to Ralph Waldo Emerson, but was founded by a Unitarian-Universalist minister, C. W. Emerson. The school was steeped in New Thought. One of E. W. Kenyon's instructors during his 1892–1893 academic term (the only one he attended) was Ralph Waldo Trine, the author of In Tune with the Infinite. Kenyon's fellow students included motivational hero Elbert Hubbard and his wife, Alice, a New-Thoughter and suffragist. Hubbard later returned as a faculty member. Another graduate with high pedigree in New Thought was philosopher and Quimby-chronicler Horatio Dresser. And a top instructor during Kenyon's academic year was Leland Powers, a Christian Scientist who went on to found the School of the Spoken Word, an oratory college that Science of Mind founder Ernest Holmes attended in 1908.

This was the atmosphere surrounding E. W. Kenyon. The Word of Faith pioneer later came to see New Thought as a heresy. In 1945 he characterized New Thought, Unity, and Christian Science as "libel upon the modern church"—yet he also insisted that the "amazing growth" of these metaphysical faiths posed a "challenge" to which Christianity had to answer. Hence, he ventured to establish his own "spiritual science," which emphasized healing and help from God. Still employing the classic New Thought formula, Kenyon urged followers to turn away from the evidence of their senses and affirm God's will that they be happy.

"Basically you are a spirit," he wrote in 1939, "and spirit registers Words just as a piece of blotting paper takes ink." There is no question that Kenyon's Word of Faith theology emerged from his exposure, and response, to the metaphysical currents he encountered at the Emerson School.

Some of Kenyon's ideological offspring are unabashed about their positive-thinking connections. Minister Kenneth Hagin Jr., son of the Word of Faith movement's pioneer Kenneth E. Hagin, wrote in 1984: "Somebody will argue, 'You're talking about positive thinking!' That's right! I am acquainted with the greatest Positive Thinker who ever was: God! The Bible says that he called those things that be as though they were . . ."

"Praise the Lord for This Car"

Where did Word of Faith evangelists get the idea that God is a "positive thinker" who wishes material happiness for man? Many Word of Faith devotees point to the Scriptural passage 3 John 2: "I wish above all things that thou mayest prosper and be in health, even as thy soul prospereth."

Some of the sharpest critics of Word of Faith theology came from Oral Roberts University, but minister Oral Roberts himself—a figure of almost unrivaled influence in evangelism in the latter twentieth century—pointed to his discovery of 3 John 2 as a turnaround in his religious life. That Biblical passage, he explained, led him to see God not as a punitive figure but as a source of joy and prosperity. Roberts's discovery opened the door to a new, positive-themed Christian expression in the second half of the twentieth century.

Roberts's transformation began when he was a twenty-nine-year-old pastor at a church in Enid, Oklahoma, in 1947. The young minister's life was one of financial embarrassment and dollar stretching. He often rode the bus to his classes because he could not afford gas. The family routinely had to remove items it could not afford from the shopping cart at the grocery checkout. Oral and his wife, Evelyn, struggled to make payments on a rundown car and a home filled with wornout furniture. With two children to support, Oral asked the church board to increase his fifty-five-dollar weekly salary. But, to his humiliation, the board responded with a demand for an itemized list of his expenses, down to how many haircuts he had a month (it was two). The young pastor was torn between a "feeling of destiny" and the depressing outer reality of living near the poverty line, as many southern preachers did. Oral grew depressed and took to praying late into the night.

One morning he rushed from the house to catch a bus and realized that he had forgotten his Bible. He went back inside and grabbed the book, which fell open to 3 John 2: "I wish above all things that thou mayest prosper." For Oral the words flicked on a light. "Evelyn," he told his wife, "we have been wrong. I haven't been preaching that God is good. And, Evelyn, if this verse is right, God is a good God."

His wife saw this as the point that "opened up his thinking."

Oral soon managed to buy a new car through the help of a local friend. Possessing a brand-new Buick was a signature moment for the family. Evelyn told her husband, "We have got to hold hands and praise the Lord for this car." Cynics might roll their eyes, but for the Roberts family the new automobile was a symbol of possibilities. And much else followed. Oral soon moved to a bigger congregation in Tulsa, Oklahoma, and he gained national notice for his healing crusades and a popular book, *If You Need Healing—Do These Things!* The years immediately ahead took him around the world as a revival speaker and healing crusader. His tent meetings attracted hundreds of thousands of people, some of whom would wait in long lines to be touched and prayed over for their illnesses. Many reported healings, though with little in the way of medical evaluation or follow-up.

Oral's meetings formed the basis for popular television programs that brought him into millions of households by the late 1950s, making him the best-known minister in the world next to Billy Graham. In 1963, a little more than fifteen years after his family had to scrape the bottom of his paycheck to pay the grocery bill, Roberts opened Oral Roberts University in Tulsa.

"I Don't Believe in the Judgmental Gospel"

Seen from a certain perspective, it was peculiar that Roberts latched on to 3 John 2 that morning in 1947. Read in context, the passage is simply a greeting that the apostle John used to open a letter to a friend. It is a salutation and not a doctrinal statement. But according to some interpretations of Scripture, each line is a God-given statement of Truth—and this was Roberts's approach.

For him the passage cracked open a new perspective on religion: God's role was not to punish but to heal. "I don't believe it is the will of God that man be sick," he told journalist Will Oursler in 1957. "It cannot be the will of God that man suffer. It cannot be the will of God that man endure poverty and despair."

Roberts insisted that Christian ministers focus not (or not exclusively) on a sin-and-salvation model of worship, but on a joyous, therapeutic type of worship that asserted: "In the Word of God you can find the answer to every problem." Roberts specifically distanced himself from the style of evangelist Billy Graham, in favor of an emphasis on forgiveness and joy. "I don't believe in the judgmental gospel that Billy preaches," he said in 1972. "I ran away from it as a boy. Billy meets the needs of a lot of people. . . . I reach other needs." Among those followers who had been raised in a punitive brand of worship, Roberts's message of "positive faith" arrived with the same kind of liberating shock that New Thought had delivered to an earlier generation.

While Roberts could never be described as anything like a religious liberal, many critics, disdainful of his gung-ho fund-raising methods and faith-healing revivals, failed to note the flexibility of his approach. In the area of faith-healing, where Roberts made his name in the 1940s and 1950s, he discouraged the worst excesses of the movement, encouraging followers never to eschew mainstream medical care and to follow up with doctors. Roberts acknowledged the psychological dimension of what happened during his tent revivals. Indeed, his notions about a collaborative relationship among religion, psychology, and medicine sometimes foreshadowed the tone of later advocates of body-mind health, such as Norman Cousins, Andrew Weil, and Jon Kabat-Zinn. In 1956, Roberts told a reporter visiting one of his healing crusades: "I hope God lets me live another 30 years, for I think by then we'll see an unbelievably close alliance between science and the kind of healing I encourage."

One prominent evangelical supporter noted Roberts's capacity to view religion "wholistically," using a variant of *holistic*—a term rarely heard in evangelical circles. "Gradually the Spirit began to show me," Roberts said in 1974, "that in the Bible healing is for the whole man. It's for the body, it's for the soul, it's for the mind, for finances. It's for any problem that needs to be healed."

Given Roberts's theological eclecticism and emphasis on buoyant faith, it is not surprising that the language of positive thinking permeated his books, sermons, and articles. One of his closest friends and confidants, North Carolina businessman S. Lee Braxton, was deeply attached to positive-thinking literature, which he began pressing upon Roberts as the minister was making his name in the late 1940s. Braxton identified Dale Carnegie's *How to Win Friends and Influence People* as "the book that really put me in business." Speaking at Braxton's funeral in 1982, Roberts noted that every year since 1949 he had reread one of the motivational books that Braxton had given him, *How I Raised Myself from Failure to Success in Selling* by Frank Bettger.

Typical passages from Roberts's writings came straight from the positive-thinking playbook: "Whatever you can conceive, and believe, you can do";* "Like Begets Like"; "Expect a Miracle"; "Change your outlook on life"; "God is your source"; "Give that it may be given to you"; and "I am in tune with God"—this last echoing Ralph Waldo Trine's *In Tune with the Infinite*. Reader testimonials in Roberts's *Abundant Life* magazine featured headlines such as "A Raise, Plus a Bonus"; "New Job as General Manager"; "A Bonus Surprise from Day to Day"; and "Sales Have Tripled."

Throughout the 1970s and 1980s the Roberts ministry placed considerable emphasis on prosperity—overshadowing the healing emphasis of earlier days. At times, Roberts's prosperity methods were indistinguishable from New Thought. In 1983, after a camp meeting with Word of Faith pioneer Kenneth E. Hagin, Roberts counseled followers to create a "Decree List" of desires. "By definition," he wrote, "DECREE means to

---

* Compare this to Napoleon Hill's statement "What the mind of man can conceive and believe, the mind of man can achieve . . ."

determine, to decide, or to MAKE UP YOUR MIND what you want God to do in your life, then set your heart upon it by your faith. . . . When you or I DECREE a thing according to God's word, we have God's AU-THORITY behind that DECREE." This was New Thought 101.

Journalists often focused on whether Roberts's first loyalty was to mammon. Roberts certainly enjoyed good restaurants and golf courses, and he had a large family home in Tulsa and a getaway house in California. But he opted to live out his final years in a fairly ordinary Orange County condo. Even during his peak years in the 1970s and 1980s his lifestyle was no more opulent than that of a bestselling author. He drove Cadillacs, not Lamborghinis. He went fishing but not yachting. He ate in good restaurants but didn't partner in any. His Oklahoma ranch was no bigger than those owned by other denizens of the Tulsa Chamber of Commerce. Roberts lived very comfortably but not extravagantly. His activities were far more austere than those of a rising generation of prosperity ministers.

Gaming the System

It is natural to assume that the massive prosperity ministries were built on cynicism alone. They were not. When looked at quickly, the prosperity ministries seem to be products of guile. When they are looked at closely, a more kaleidoscopic perspective emerges. To understand the American religious experience of the late twentieth century, it is necessary to grasp the coexistence of sincerity and chicanery that motivated some of its flashier figures.

When sexual and financial scandals toppled Jim Bakker's multimillion-dollar PTL ministry in 1987, Bakker—a far less serious figure theologically than Oral Roberts—explained his and wife Tammy Faye's opulent lifestyle: "We preach prosperity. We preach abundant life." He felt that in order to point the way toward a God-centered prosperity, he was right, indeed obligated, to display it—and blindly so. In 1989, Bakker was convicted of defrauding PTL donors, to whom he had promised lifetime hotel stays and time-shares in resorts that never got built. An appellate court, however, threw out Bakker's forty-five-year sentence in 1991, and he was eventually released to a halfway house after serving about five years. The appellate court ruled that the federal judge who had sentenced Bakker, Robert "Maximum Bob" Potter, had been improperly influenced by his own religious views, which resulted in his making a series of denigrating comments about Bakker from the bench.

Unknown to most of their detractors, the Bakkers eschewed Christian-right politics and maintained an ardently nondenominational ministry. They spoke frankly and sympathetically about AIDS before any other media ministers. Bakker's son, Jay, is today an evangelist known for his defense of gay marriage. For television viewers, Jim and Tammy Faye's shows were a kind of spiritual comfort food, featuring inspirational talks, dancing dogs, and wacky musical production numbers, with no doom-and-damnation podium pounding. To many PTL followers, Jim and Tammy Faye's descent made them seem less like a power-hungry Lord and Lady Macbeth than a beleaguered, fallen Lucy and Ricky of evangelism, unable to ethically manage and wield the religious empire that grew beneath them.

A harder breed of media evangelists arose in the early twenty-first century. They sidestepped scandal not so much because they were more virtuous than their predecessors, but because they possessed greater financial savvy and used take-no-prisoners legal strategies. The next generation of prosperity ministers so closely resembled lavishly paid CEOs, and frequently lived with such visible extravagance, that in 2007 Iowa senator Charles Grassley, a Republican and then–ranking member of the Senate Finance Committee, authorized an investigation into six of the most prominent tax-exempt media ministries. Grassley questioned whether the megachurches' fund-raising networks, highly compensated pastors, and myriad of eminently profitable business apparatuses violated their tax-exempt status as religious ministries.

Of the six megachurches investigated by Grassley's finance committee from late 2007 to early 2011, only two cooperated: Joyce Meyer Ministries, based in Missouri, and Benny Hinn Ministries, based in Texas. Leaders of the remaining four, who often refused the committee's most basic requests for information, were Kenneth and Gloria Copeland of Kenneth Copeland Ministries of Texas; Creflo and Taffi Dollar of World Changers Church International in Georgia; Randy and Paula White of Without Walls International Church of Florida; and Bishop Eddie Long of New Birth Missionary Baptist Church of Georgia.

The Joyce Meyer and Benny Hinn ministries vowed to practice better financial transparency, but the other four megachurches dismissed the committee's activities, calling its inquiries intrusive and violative of religious freedom. Senate investigators were left with little choice but to accept such stonewalling. Grassley's staffers acknowledged that they had neither time nor resources to issue and enforce subpoenas. What's more, many potential informants told the committee that they were too frightened to testify, fearing "retaliation by the churches," including harassing lawsuits.

In a disappointment to megachurch critics, Grassley's report, which appeared in January 2011, after more than three years of investigation, found no conclusive evidence of wrongdoing and proposed no new legislation related to church tax exemption, transparency, or financial disclosure. Yet despite the odds stacked against the finance committee's investigation, the report did call attention to a disturbing trend among tax-exempt megaministries: the creation of networks of IRS-shielded co-businesses operating under church umbrellas. These offshoot entities often lacked any clear connection to ministerial activities. They included private airports, aircraft leasing firms, recording companies, hotels, real-estate holdings, and fleets of vehicles. The four churches that had refused to cooperate with the committee were discovered to harbor "multiple for-profit and non-profit entities" and "multiple 'assumed' or 'doing business as' names were also used." Kenneth Copeland Ministries, for example, operated under "at least 21 'assumed names,'" which included record companies and recording studios. One minister who was not investigated by the committee, Star Scott of Calvary Temple in Sterling,

Virginia, explained that the hundreds of thousands of dollars' worth of automobiles that he and his wife used were part of a "racing ministry."

"This raises the question," the committee wrote, "of whether church status is being gamed to shield such activities of a tax-exempt entity from public scrutiny."

Ministers Eddie Long and Creflo Dollar, meanwhile, experienced separate legal struggles in early 2011 around the time the Grassley report came out. Reverend Long fended off court challenges by four young men who claimed the prosperity minister had coerced them into sexual relationships, charges the pastor vigorously denied. The cases were settled out of court. Reverend Dollar was arrested in summer 2012 following an argument with his fifteen-year-old daughter, who accused him of choking and beating her, claims that Dollar disputed.

At the time of the report's appearance in 2011, it seemed doubtful that the political culture within Congress would permit a more decisive legislative oversight of the megaministries. When challenged with calls for greater regulatory measures, the megachurches raised cries of religious persecution and used a network of magazines, television broadcasts, and social media to fend off calls for reform.

Critics believed that more oversight was needed not only to determine whether the megapulpits' finances fell within the boundaries of their tax-exempt status, but also whether their political activities adhered to the law. As part of their privileged IRS status, the megaministries, like all tax-exempt churches, are prohibited from electioneering and significant lobbying efforts. This was another requirement run through with leaks and loopholes. The 2012 presidential campaign witnessed the now-familiar ritual of millions of church "voter guides," generally prepared by conservative political action committees and foundations, being distributed throughout, and by, many of the megachurches.

As the twenty-first century opened, many of the nation's largest ministries conducted their financial and political affairs without transparency or federal tax obligations.

Pushing the Boundaries

Outside the domes of the megachurches and the pep-rally atmosphere of motivational seminars, some life coaches and positivity teachers drew connections between physical endurance and peak performance. Rather than use mental preparation to bolster physical stamina, as in athletic training, they reversed the equation: Some motivational coaches pre-scribed physical challenges to workshop attendees as a means to achieve mental breakthroughs. Such breakthroughs, the reasoning went, would build greater self-assurance and foster a willingness to venture boldly through life.

Done responsibly, the testing of physical boundaries could bring constructive results, as sometimes occurs in Outward Bound nature pro-grams. From the 1980s onward, several motivational instructors used fire-walking ceremonies as a confidence-building exercise. In such pro-grams, participants were trained to walk barefoot across hot coals. Oc-casional injuries occurred, usually minor burns and blisters.

In July 2012, the *San Jose Mercury News* reported that during a fire-walk event hosted by life coach Anthony Robbins, and attended by six thou-sand people, three participants went to the hospital for burns and a total of twenty-one were injured. A San Jose fire captain told the Associated Press that several attendees reported second- or third-degree burns. The *Mercury News* quoted a San Jose City College student who witnessed the fire walk saying that he heard "wails of pain, screams of agony" among participants.

The Robbins organization vociferously disputed the accounts. The Fox News morning show *Fox and Friends* issued an on-air correction of a segment that it had run on the event, in which it reported that "nearly two dozen" attendees were hospitalized following the fire walk. Fox's retraction stated that "none were hospitalized" and "a few of the six-thousand received minor burns akin to a sunburn, they received on-site medical attention, and continued to participate in the event." Regarding the reported "wails of pain," a writer in *The Huffington Post* stated, "Those who participated said the young man must not have realized that seminar participants are encouraged to yell and scream to psyche themselves up and they were not all screaming in physical pain."

The conflicting accounts indicated the tension of covering motivational teachers like Robbins. Journalists sometimes cast a jaundiced eye at the ivory-toothed, mountainous man who seemed to be selling miracles to stadium-sized audiences. This titan-of-the-positive did, in fact, proffer innovative programs to teach participants to linguistically and psychologically "model" the habits of highly successful figures through step-by-step protocols of communication, body language, and internal dialogues, sometimes called Neuro-Linguistic Programming. Robbins's insights about self-taught limitation, and the root motives that drive us toward success or failure, were shrewder and more complex than the ideas offered by many on the motivational circuit.

Tragedy in Sedona

The success of the 2006 book and movie The Secret increased the demand for motivational seminars and brought new stars to the field. Hungry to copycat Robbins and build empires of their own, a few life coaches devised incredibly busy appearance schedules and developed their own brand of over-the-top methods to lead weekend workshop attendees into "breakthroughs." In one horrendously tragic case, a motivational superstar showed no decency or judgment in how far he was willing to push his attendees.

James Ray, a bestselling author and former telemarketer and internal trainer with AT&T, conducted a brutal Arizona sweat lodge in fall 2009 that led to multiple injuries and the deaths of three participants: two from heat stroke and one from heat-related organ failure. Ray was convicted of three counts of negligent homicide in November 2011 and sentenced to two years in prison.

After initially rising to fame for his commentary in The Secret, and subsequent appearances on The Oprah Winfrey Show and Larry King Live, Ray drew growing audiences. Known for a frenetic events schedule, as well as a hard-driving presentation style, the former marketer crossed the nation delivering talks, seminars, and weekend and weeklong empowerment programs.

In October 2009, fifty-six participants joined him at a lodge in the Sedona desert for a weeklong "Spiritual Warrior" retreat. Ray's program for self-development was extreme: Even before the evening sweat-lodge ceremony—a sauna-like ritual adapted from Native American rites—most of his attendees had endured a night outside in the desert without food or water for thirty-six hours. The two-hour sweat lodge became a nightmarish ordeal as many participants in the darkened, broiling structure vomited, passed out, or struggled to assist others while Ray admonished them to stick it out for the sake of personal growth. Two people died at the scene and another later passed away in the hospital.

One of the most revealing aspects of the Ray episode was the apparent lack of acknowledgment with which he and his organization initially responded to the deaths. Ray left Arizona the morning after the deaths without speaking to the survivors or visiting those hospitalized. He did not reach out to victims' families until days later, after hosting another positive-thinking motivational seminar over the weekend.

From the start, Ray was a coarser breed of motivator. Pioneers such as Napoleon Hill and Norman Vincent Peale attracted millions of people with promises of self-development. But their methods were private, contemplative, and oriented toward personal illumination. Intense and public displays were never part of their program. Yet a handful of early-twenty-first-century motivational teachers, of whom Ray was the most extreme, used psychologically or physically grueling activities, often without the full foreknowledge of participants.

In one of the troubling aspects of intense motivational seminars, participants can experience a strong but subtle pull to "go along" with questionable exercises, especially under the urgings of workshop leaders, who typically label refusal to join in as precisely the kind of inner resistance that requires breaking down. The high fees that sometimes accompany such programs—Ray charged up to ten thousand dollars per person—also discourage participants from pulling out.

A Simple Man

Prosperity ministries and extreme motivational seminars created a chasm between the promise and the reality of positive thinking. The earlier ideals of the movement seemed at risk. Yet one of the most distinctive and skilled spiritual thinkers of the late twentieth century deftly avoided these pitfalls. He was a man who began his career in the tradition of the success gospel but eventually distanced himself from it. Leaving behind his old life, and with it the ethical and materialist dilemmas of positive thinking, he defined a wholly fresh concept of spiritual mind-power.

His name was Vernon Howard. While this spiritual writer and philosopher lacked fame or renown, he possessed an extraordinary, and probably singular, gift for distilling the complexities of the world's religious and ethical philosophies into aphoristic and deeply practical principles. Howard was the most remarkable figure to emerge from the modern mind-power movement; though as his outlook matured, it became impossible to pin any labels on him.

In the first leg of his writing career, from the late 1940s to the early 1960s, Howard produced books that could have come out of the conventional New Thought catalogue. They bore such titles as *Success Through the Magic of Personal Power; Time Power for Personal Success; Your Magic Power to Persuade and Command People;* and *Word Power: Talk Your Way to Life Leadership.* His oeuvre extended to works of popular reference, trivia, and children's nonfiction, such as *Lively Bible Quizzes* and *101 Funny Things to Make and Do.* To the outside observer, the Los Angeles–based author was just one more writer-for-hire, of the type found in any large city.

But in the mid-1960s, Howard's outlook underwent a remarkable maturation. His personal genesis began with a wish to escape from the cycles of euphoria and depression that characterize the life of an ambitious writer. "I started realizing the uselessness of the extraneous," he told the Los Angeles Times in 1978. "People could tell me I was a good writer and I realized all it did was make me hungry for more applause. And when that didn't come, I'd get hurt. I decided I had to find something without applause so I could live independently, without the approval of other people."

Howard found his own solution to this predicament. He left behind his career as a writer of success literature and resettled in out-of-the-way Boulder City, Nevada. "Not exactly a community noted for breeding literary mystics," observed the Las Vegas Review-Journal in a 1979 profile. In Boulder City, from the late 1960s until his death in 1992, Howard became a wholly new kind of spiritual thinker. He produced a remarkable range of pamphlets, essays, full-length books, and cable-televised talks in which he expounded with total clarity and directness on the need to abandon the fleeting rewards of outer life in exchange for an authentic and self-directed inner existence.

In a sense, Howard's teachings could be said to come down to the inner meaning of the parable of Jacob and Esau. Esau sells out his birthright for a bowl of porridge—not realizing that he has given up his life for a fleeting pleasure, which quickly gives way to pain and resentment. Howard urged people to see how we do this every moment of our existence. He encouraged listeners to exchange the baubles and trinkets of worldly achievement, and the depression that quickly follows, for the rewards of real Truth: a contented, flowing, inner state that is the birthright of all people.

Howard's psychology pivoted on two core ideas, which ran throughout his literature. They can be summarized this way:

1. *Humanity lives from a false nature.* What we call our personal will is no more than a fearful, self-promoting false "I." This counterfeit self chases after worldly approval and security, reacting with aggression one moment and servility the next. The false "I" craves self-importance and status, which, in turn, bind the individual to the

pursuit of money, careerism, and peer approval. For a
person to be truly happy, this false self must be shaken
off, like a hypnotic spell. In its place, the individual
will discover his True Nature, which emanates from a
Higher Will, or God.

2.   *Human behavior is characterized by hostility, corruption, and weakness.*
Friends, neighbors, lovers, coworkers, and family
members often manipulate or exploit us, causing agony
in our lives. "It's not negative to see how negative
people really are," Howard wrote. "It is a high form
of intelligent self-protection to see thru the human
masquerade." Howard was uncompromising on this
point. When someone makes a habit of diminishing
you, he taught, you must resolve inwardly—and, as soon
as you're able, outwardly—to remove yourself from
that person, without feeling constrained by convention,
apologetics, or hesitation. Once we see through human
destructiveness, we will attract relationships of a higher
nature.

Howard eventually attracted a circle of fifty or so students in the
Boulder City area. "We send our message out but we have no concern for
the results," he told a reporter. "What does the size of our audience have
to do with the truth?" He only occasionally ventured out of the Nevada
town to deliver talks in Southern California.

Howard did, however, reach a national audience through a prodi-
gious output of writings, tapes, and talks, which his students video-
taped and broadcast through the early medium of cable television. Many
of his presentations are today preserved on DVDs and the Internet. In
his lectures, Howard appeared exactly as he did in daily life: casually
dressed in a polo shirt or short-sleeved button-down, physically robust
though slightly paunchy. He looked like any ordinary, late-middle-aged
man—not quite professorial (his edges were too rough), more like an

avuncular gym teacher. But Howard's voice and gaze were those of a distinctively poised and purposeful individual: a simple man with a profound message—namely, that inner freedom awaits you at any moment you turn to it, provided you learn to mistrust the attachments of outer life.

In a carryover from years as a success writer, Howard gave his books sensationalistic titles, such as *The Mystic Path to Cosmic Power; Esoteric Mind Power; Secrets for Higher Success;* and *The Power of Your Supermind.* His ever-practical pamphlets—with titles such as *Your Power to Say No* and *50 Ways to Escape Cruel People*—were advertised in popular psychology magazines and in the grocery tabloid *The Weekly World News.* A typical ad for one of his pamphlets read: "**Worried?** *50 WAYS TO GET HELP FROM GOD.*" The ads were in no way cynical. Tucked amid competing advertisements for weight-loss programs and wrinkle creams, Howard's ads, like those of mail-order prophet Frank B. Robinson, reflected the dictum to *go out to the highways and hedges and bring them in.* Howard knew how to reach people in need.

In a mark of Howard's virtuosity, his writing could be picked up almost at random—any chapter, any page, any pamphlet or book—and the reader could fully enter into his philosophy. There were no prerequisites involved, no partially thought-through idea to be sat through. Howard's gift was to fully and continually illustrate and restate core truths in dramatically fresh ways, a talent possessed by Ralph Waldo Emerson, but very few contemporary writers.

Although Howard could not be plainly classified, his psychological insights coalesced with ideas found in the work of spiritual teacher Jiddu Krishnamurti and, at times, with the distinctly important twentieth-century spiritual philosopher G. I. Gurdjieff. But Howard's language and methods possessed a down-to-earth, hands-on immediacy that perhaps no other contemporary spiritual figure displayed. He insisted that a program of self-development had to manifest real change in the ordinary hours of a person's life. He was absolute on that point.

"Will you trust a religion or philosophy," Howard asked, "that does not produce a truly poised and decent human being?"

Prove It

Howard's question is one to which every spiritual system must ultimately submit. It has special poignancy for New Thought and positive thinking. Since positive thinking promises achievable, practical results, it cannot sidestep the demand: *prove it.*

This returns us to William James's philosophy of pragmatism. The only viable measure of a private belief system, James believed, is its *effect on conduct.* And that, finally, is the one meaningful assessment of the legacy and efficacy of positive thinking. If *it works,* it doesn't matter much what its detractors say. And if *it doesn't,* then the philosophy has no claim on sensitive people—like the misguided instrumentalities of "heroic" medicine, it belongs in books of social history and museum cases but not in the folds of daily life.

Most contemporary critics begin from the following perspective: *well, of course* positive thinking *doesn't* work; to suggest otherwise is akin to believing in unicorns. Granted, they say, a determinedly positive outlook may make you a nicer carpooler, but it has nothing to do with negotiating the real demands of life, and in many regards it blinds you to them.

Pragmatism, however, requires judging a personal system of conduct not by whether it squares with the general conception of what *ought* to work, but by whether it *does* work. Empiricism, in James's view, means measuring an idea without reference to how it stands or falls in comparison to widely held reasoning, but by what an individual can perceive of its nature, its consistency, and its effects. Pragmatism requires inspecting an ethical or religious idea by the *experience of its use,* including within oneself.

We will now submit positive thinking to that test.

chapter eight

does it work?

If a person says: I toiled and found nothing,
don't believe him.

—Talmud, Megillah 6b

From the earliest experiments of Phineas Quimby up through the popularity of *The Secret*, the movements of mind-power metaphysics have sought to explain evil, suffering, and illness as an illusion—as the result of an individual's inability to understand and experience the ultimate reality of the universe: a beneficent, creative intelligence whose divine inflow permeates all of life. Evil is said to appear like darkness in a room once the light is blocked out.

When life is viewed from this perspective, a person visits hardship, disease, or catastrophe upon himself through wrong thoughts and flawed self-conception. Sensitive people rightly object: How could such a notion possibly account for the victims of mass murder, infant mortality, and natural disaster? And, on an intimate level, what mature person has not witnessed a life extinguished, even in surroundings of hope and love? No movement can aspire to moral seriousness without convincingly resolving such questions.

This brings us, finally, to the positive-thinking movement's most serious and lingering dilemma: What are the ethics and moral credibility of a movement that considers the outer world nothing more than a reflection of an individual's private outlook?

An eccentric but surprisingly well-thought-out book from 1954, *Three Magic Words*, sought to take on this problem. In defending the perspectives of New Thought and Christian Science, writer U. S. Andersen argued: "Now it must be thoroughly understood that we are not denying the existence of evil; we are simply denying the *reality* of evil, naming it illusion as it surely is." Andersen made the allowance that sometimes we succumb to this illusion simply through the weight of conditioned thought, which gets "indelibly recorded" in the psyches of successive generations. "It is also true," he wrote, "that thought conceptions of other persons than ourselves, nay even every person who has ever lived, may show themselves in our experience." Hence, human consciousness is burdened by a kind of collective neurosis, which can block out the generative and positive flow of creative thought. Are we thus trapped in a world of illusory evil? No, Andersen insists: "For evil befalls the righteous and the unrighteous, *but it cannot visit him who sees and is convinced of nothing but good.*" Here we see the familiar belief that mental therapeutics—prayer, affirmations, visualizations, inspirational literature, and conversion experiences or moments of illumination—can reveal the true good within and all around us.

For all the limitations of his arguments—about which more will be heard—Andersen does as good a job as any twentieth-century thinker in attempting to defend the ideas of New Thought. And his perspective also highlights a key difference between various creative-thought movements and traditional mysticism. To understand this difference, and how it separates the mind-power culture from the mystical traditions, requires exploring the foundations of traditional mysticism. From this vantage point, we will be better able to confront the problems—and possibilities—of positive thinking.

The Snake in the Road

An identifiable mystical tradition appears within the teachings of all historic faiths, from Christianity to Sufism to Hinduism. This thread of mystical teaching has traditionally taught that human beings live in a state of ego illusion. In this state, we seek gratification in the form of power, flattery, toys, sex, and money—unconsciously using these things to prop up the needs and hungers of the ego. For most of us, most of the time, desire-fulfillment is our only experience of existence. Absent a connection to any sense of higher purpose, or to some greater principle of life, our pursuit of possessions and attachments, both directly and indirectly, forms our primary feeling of aliveness. The momentary thrill of attainment is also our chief means of avoiding the fear that bodily death spells our complete annihilation.

This critique of human life, as seen in comparable systems of mystical thought, seeks to explain our inability to loosen the bond of worldly attainments and to become aware of the greater truth of existence: Namely, that each individual is part of a larger whole and is a fragment of intelligent creation, or God. Only this awareness, so it is taught, can free us from both the repressed fear of death and the frantic consumption of daily life. Unaware of our true nature, however, we are stuck perpetually consuming—but never to satisfaction. Every gain, promotion, or advancement is a cause for further fear and craving because our attachments are always prone to slipping away. And, ultimately, at our life's end, they will slip away.

In terms of human neurosis, the mystical tradition describes our psychology with parables such as "The Snake in the Road," derived from a Vedic teaching but found in many faiths. It goes this way: A traveler is walking down a road and suddenly gets frightened by the sight of a snake up ahead. The traveler fears he's going to get bitten. But on closer inspection he sees that what he thought was a snake is only a harmless piece of rope. This is how the ego-driven man lives: constantly project-ing his fears, then experiencing temporary solace, only to reimagine another snake just ahead. The mystical tradition doesn't deny the reality of suffering: sometimes the snake is real. Rather, this tradition attempts to summon men and women to seek a state of awareness in which the barriers between the individual and whole, the perpetrator and the vic-tim, the giver and the taker, can be seen to fade. From this perspective, ultimate reality reveals that the barriers we see between "good" and "bad," or sickness and health, are themselves illusion. In all things, so the tradition teaches, man is at one with the whole, and everything fig-ures usefully and necessarily into the order of existence.

Let's not delude ourselves: At almost every moment of existence, this sense of oneness is impossibly distant, especially when we are fac-ing an immediate need. And yet this higher truth can also reveal itself in moments of transcendent joy, such as the birth of a child, as well as in moments of true crisis, such as when confronting the untimely death of a loved one. Such tragedies drive us to the limits of our conditioned responses to life, as well as to the limits of our belief in our ability to change conditions. In times of tragedy or joy, when our human will is suspended, and when grief does not crush us or euphoria sweep us away, a more expansive view can settle over us. Again, this experience of oneness can appear hopelessly far away. Yet its occurrence is long recognized not only in spiritual literature, but in the testimony of many modern individuals who experience such a state, albeit briefly, at times of acute need or intense joy.

The Christian Science and New Thought views share commonalities with the mystical tradition—but only up to a point. While Christian Science specifically denies the reality of illness, it also promises a *change in condition from illness*; or, as Christian Scientists put it, *a revelation of truth*.

Christian Science testifies that if you realize higher truth, in understanding the absolute permeation of all things by the beneficence of God, you will experience that goodness as freedom and true healing. In Christian Science this often involves sickness yielding to health; in New Thought it typically means poverty transforming to plenty. This *change in outer circumstance* is the central promise of the psycho-metaphysical philosophies. It is what distinguishes them from mysticism, Transcendentalism, and various strands of existential or meaning-based psychology.* The traditional mystical philosophies recognize the *problem of illusion*, but they also recognize the realness of suffering and evil—and they offer the same corrective: A higher or inner perspective that can dispel our conditioned ideas of separateness between the individual and the whole, and, ultimately, between deprivation and satisfaction.

Many acolytes of New Thought and other spiritual-therapeutic therapies would rush to signal their agreement with the mystical point of view. But do they really agree? They teach that evil is an illusion, but they nonetheless *seek a measurable change in outer conditions*. To call suffering an illusion, yet also demand that it bend to desired change, signals a core inconsistency in the mind-power perspective. Rather than seeing all of worldly clamor as an illusion, New Thought defines whatever is discomforting as illusory and its opposite as a reflection of higher truth. Hence, New Thought and the mind-power philosophies seek to rise above the world and consume its bounty at the same time. In a biting critique, historian Freeman Champney called New Thought a rationale of "transcend your cake and eat it too."

Matters get more troublesome when New Thought tries to explain chronic tragedies or catastrophes. In the twentieth century, some New Thought voices attempted to explain calamity by appending ideas of

---

* Apart from the belief in a change of conditions, the New Thought and Christian Science perspectives diverge. As noted earlier, Christian Science does not see the mind as an instrument of good but as a tool of illusion. New Thought, by contrast, views the mind as a divine and empowering agency. For the remainder of this chapter I focus chiefly on New Thought, which undergirds the positive-thinking culture.

karma onto the positive-thinking philosophy. Past-life sins, in this view, could explain why a person, or millions of people, experience painful lives or violent deaths. Such reasoning appeared in the late 1950s in the work of a widely read metaphysical writer, Gina Cerminara. Cerminara had previously done a great deal to popularize the work of the medical clairvoyant and psychic Edgar Cayce in her 1950 book, *Many Mansions*. In a later book, *The World Within*, Cerminara attempted to bring a karmic perspective to global suffering. "Present-day Negroes," she suggested in 1957, might understand the roots of their racial oppression if they

> can project themselves back into the past and in imagination see themselves to be brutal English slavetraders, arrogant Virginia slaveholders, or conscienceless Alabama auctioneers, smugly assured of their white supremacy—if they can make this imaginative leap, their own present situation may seem far more intelligible and far more bearable.

Her advice continued:

> Present-day Jews who feel that they are the victims of unjust prejudice should reflect that a long racial history of regarding themselves as a "chosen people," and of practicing racial exclusiveness and pride, cannot but lead to a situation where they themselves will be excluded.

Such arguments collapse under any degree of scrutiny. Spiritual insight arrives through *self-observation*—not in analyzing, or justifying, the suffering experienced by *others*. To judge others is to work without any self-verification, which is the one pragmatic tool of the spiritual search. The private person who can maturely and persuasively claim self-responsibility for *his own* suffering, or who can endure it as an inner obligation, shines a light for others. The person who justifies *someone else's* suffering, in this case through collective fault, only casts a stone.

In a sense, all of this ethical difficulty arises from the mind-power movement's tendency to see reality *as subject to a single law*—namely, the Law of Attraction, with its absolute powers of cause and effect.

Unlike the Transcendentalists, who studied the cycles of nature, the teachers of New Thought made no allowance for the inevitability of night following day. They made no room for the balance of life and death, illness and health that Emerson depicted in his essays, which many New Thoughters called their inspiration. (In actuality, references to Emerson did not appear in New Thought literature until the late 1880s.) Diverging from Transcendentalism, New Thought viewed life as subject to a single principle and ignored the prospect of multiple laws and forces. This limited New Thought's ability to respond to life's tragedies, complications, and reversals.

New Thought's incomplete perspective can be traced back to a theological error made at its founding. To unearth this error may point the way toward fixing it—and expanding the positive-thinking movement's capacity to address all aspects of the human experience.

Rule One

When early New-Thoughters embraced the principle of the Law of Attraction, they gave the mind-power culture its best-known phrase and most enduring concept. As noted earlier, the Law of Attraction began with medium Andrew Jackson Davis, who in 1855 used it to describe correspondences between the earth and the spirit world. In 1892 the term got remade in the work of journalist Prentice Mulford as a mental law of *like attracts like*. Generations later this principle re-emerged as the core concept of New Age spirituality, echoed in the oft-heard phrase: *There are no accidents*. The concept of "no accidents" holds that everything in life is purposeful, advancing, and reflective of an individual's needs.

In many ways, New Age spirituality is an update of New Thought. Throughout New Age culture—and especially within the popular literature of channeled spirituality—the most common message is of the mind's ability to shape and attract circumstance. In this view, all events are meaningful and arise from the inner requirements of the individual, whether for growth, learning, or fulfillment. Hence, the Law of Attraction has linked the culture of New Thought and New Age, from the nineteenth century to the current day.

But where did this "no accidents" idea come from?

The conviction that thought is an all-encompassing force, one that supersedes happenstance or randomness, got launched in the final book of Warren Felt Evans. It was a work called *Esoteric Christianity and Mental Therapeutics*, which the mental-healer published in 1886. By that point, Evans was the preeminent figure in the mind-power culture. He incorporated a wide array of sources into its theology, ranging from Swedenborg to Buddhism to the occult ideas of Theosophy, thus creating the spiritual openness for which New Thought became known.

In his final book, Evans declared: "In case of accidents, or chance occurrences, there is always the relation of cause and effect, for it is inconceivable that a thing should occur without a cause, and all causes are mental."

To support his point that "all causes are mental," Evans drew upon a book that also happened to be Swedenborg's final work, *The True Christian Religion*, which the seer published in 1771.* Evans enlisted the philosophical muscle of the Swedish mystic to validate his observation, quoting Swedenborg this way: "There is not anything in the mind, to which something in the body does not correspond; and this which corresponds may be called the embodying of that." Evans took this to mean that illness, or any condition in the world, stems from "the principle of thought."

But Evans did not properly capture, or contextualize, Swedenborg's full statement. The seer's complete sentence was of a different tenor (and far more discursive) than what Evans used. It went this way:

---

* Evans used an 1875 English translation.

> There is not anything in the mind, to which something in the body does not correspond; and this, which corresponds, may be called the embodying of that; wherefore charity and faith, whilst they are only in the mind, are not incorporated in man, and then they may be likened to an aërial man, who is called a spectre, such as *Fame* was painted by the ancients, with a laurel around the head, and a *cornucopia* in the hand.

What Swedenborg is saying is: Ethical thoughts without corresponding action make man's life a charade. The section of Swedenborg's book in which this passage appears makes no mention of bodily health or accidents; it deals specifically with questions of "Charity and Faith," and the need to act on one's highest ideals. "That Charity and Faith are only mental and perishable Things," Swedenborg wrote, "unless, when it can be done, they are determined to Works, and coëxist in them."

Swedenborg believed in correspondences between events on earth and events in the heavens; he likewise believed the mind, when properly used, possessed a profound creative faculty, which could place a person in touch with higher energies. But he never made a claim like the one that Evans describes, in which all events, tragic or cheerful, emanate from the mind alone.

Regardless, the metaphysical journalist Prentice Mulford wasted no time seizing upon this idea, and in the same year as Evans's book he wrote: "Success in any business or undertaking comes through the working of a law. It never comes by chance: in the operations of nature's laws, there is no such thing as chance or accident."

And there it was: *There is no such thing as chance or accident.* It was the premise of the Law of Attraction, a term Mulford resurrected a few years later, as well as the future credo of the New Age: *There are no accidents.* This perspective was rooted in Evans's misinterpretation of Swedenborg, and then got memorably reworked by the journalist Mulford.

The Law of Attraction ultimately burdened New Thought with a principle that was difficult to defend, and one that was never really constructed, in its foundational sources, to function as an overarching rule of life. The founders of New Thought evidently did not pause over Evans to ask: Isn't it possible that humanity exists under multiple laws and demands, including accidents? And that our lives may serve many imperatives, some of them inscrutable and even painful? Don't we, like all creatures, exist to fertilize, feed, and facilitate an unimaginably vast scale of creation, on which we have little perspective?

New Thought considered no such limits on the mind of man. The Idealist philosophers had long acknowledged the problem of the mind's limits, and they noted that the mind, when searching and conceiving, was finally limited to experiencing itself—that is, the mind's filtered view of reality rather than the ultimate nature of things. The influential twentieth-century spiritual philosopher G. I. Gurdjieff also acknowledged this problem, though in a different way. Gurdjieff saw man as capable of experiencing higher energies, but also as a being situated on a relatively low rung in the scale of creation, with a great chain of existence stretching above him in the cosmos, which man's thoughts and prayers could not reach.

New Thought's pioneers never pondered the potential limitation, or disadvantages, of man's place in creation. The British judge Thomas Troward, who formed a key influence on Ernest Holmes, surmised in a series of 1904 lectures that man was the pinnacle of evolutionary creation. As such, Troward reasoned, man possessed access to the "ultimate principle of intelligence," with which he served as a cocreator. The flaw in Troward's approach is that he did not question man's apex; he did not consider that a ladder of creation may extend far beyond man in an unimaginable cosmic scheme in which man plays no part. Troward and his closest followers did not consider the possibility that man possesses limited perspective, and is a being whose existence may be relative to some higher intelligence just as a plant is relative to man. There is no reason to believe that man shares in an ultimate intelligence. Man is neither all-seeing nor all-knowing; and his creative faculties, whatever their nature, cannot surpass his point of perspective.

Emerson actually sought to deal with this problem. He took account of both aspects of human existence—man's great potential and unthinkable smallness—in his 1860 essay, "Fate." Making the kind of pronouncement that later was selectively quoted by mind-power acolytes, Emerson wrote, "But the soul contains the event that shall befall it; for the event is only the actualization of its thoughts, and what we pray to ourselves for is always granted." Yet Emerson also insisted that man's creative faculties are not all that he lives under. He added that there existed just "one key, one solution to the mysteries of human condition." And that was to acknowledge that man exists under both self-direction and nature's will. And the will of nature contains purposes we cannot know, but can only bow to, and thus take our place in creation. "So when a man is victim of his fate," Emerson continued, ". . . he is to rally on his relation to the Universe, which his ruin benefits. Leaving the daemon who suffers, he is to take sides with the Deity who secures universal benefit by his pain."

Thinking Big

When confronted with questions of evil and suffering, New Thought, unable to fully account for tragedy and limitation in a self-created world, tended to slip into circular reasoning or contradiction. New Thought's popular minister and writer Joseph Murphy tried to confront the problem of suffering in his 1971 book *Psychic Perception*.

Murphy, in a similar vein to U. S. Andersen, described man as subject to the thoughts of a "world mind" or "race mind," which contained the substance of every thought—good or ill, nourishing or punishing—that every soul had ever conceived. Hence, an infant born ill could be a victim of this "world mind." To assume, as Murphy does, that every thought has a potential ripple effect—so that a person can be affected by something thought centuries earlier—places us at the mercy of a near-infinitude of influences and outcomes. This amounts to a tacit acknowledgment of randomness or accident, the very thing that Warren Felt Evans said didn't exist.

By the early twenty-first century, this hopeful, innovative movement of New Thought, which posited man as a being of ultimate self-destiny, seemed incapable of accounting for man in his varied roles and predicaments. In 2007, *The Secret*'s creator, Rhonda Byrne, who was the preeminent New Thought voice of the early twenty-first century, replied to a reporter's question about what caused the Holocaust by saying, "The law of attraction is absolute." Byrne continued: "In a large-scale tragedy, like 9/11, Hurricane Katrina, etc., we see that the law of attraction responds to people being at the wrong place at the wrong time because their dominant thoughts were on the same frequency of such events."

When facing ultimate moral questions, Byrne, like Cerminara more than a generation earlier, spoke of the experience of *others*, describing events that she had never personally encountered or reckoned with. Opinions, like philosophies, demand verification, either by logic or lived experience. Byrne's logic was akin to that of a person visiting a neighbor's house, whistling for a dog, receiving no response, and concluding that the neighbor has no dog. She took no account of possibilities outside of her purview.

"A Pathless Land"

This question of personal verification highlights one further challenge to New Thought. As noted earlier, the positive-thinking approach seeks measurable outcomes—in effect, the individual is promised, if I think *correctly I will escape, recover, receive*, and so on. This perspective can ultimately reduce the human search to desire-attainment. This is not to say that desires are wrong. Indeed, an individual's desires may point to profound and necessary things at certain stages of life.

But seeing a Law of Attraction as the governing principle of existence is potentially damaging because it limits self-discovery to what I might generally think my needs are, not what they may be in the light of the deepened question that mysticism encourages. The search for awareness is at risk when we are told precisely what our deliverance is supposed to look like: the fulfillment of what we want.

The twentieth-century spiritual teacher Jiddu Krishnamurti observed: "Truth is a pathless land." When the path is mapped, usually based upon our current mind's-eye image of where we want to be, the inner search and the unknown realizations that it may bring are proscribed. A narrowly conceived New Thought can slam closed the doors of perception that it was once envisioned to open.

The Beauty of the Good

Given the extent of New Thought's flaws, can anything of lasting value be attributed to this homegrown metaphysics, this audacious attempt by ordinary people to chart their own course to the Divine? The answer is yes. And here, we return to Ralph Waldo Emerson. Although he despised the pursuit of easy success and the shallowness of self-adulation, Emerson acknowledged—quite decisively—that *life favors enthusiasm*. He wrote in his essay "Success":

> Don't hang a dismal picture on the wall, and do not daub with sables and glooms in your conversation. Don't be a cynic and a disconsolate preacher. Don't bewail and bemoan. Omit the negative propositions. Nerve us with incessant affirmatives. Don't waste yourself in rejection, nor bark against the bad, but chant the beauty of the good.

When bound up in the expectancy of magical results, enthusiasm can degenerate into blindness and single-mindedness. It can inculcate a person to failure or foolishness. It has no ethical dimension. But what sensitive person has not felt and observed the impact of an attitude? Who could deny that thoughts of confident expectancy, or gloomy resignation, seem to influence the events of our lives? When not wildly over-stated, the claims of New Thought possess enough commonsense appeal and anecdotal evidence to attract any earnest listener. And there is more to it than that.

Carl Jung noted the role that enthusiasm can play in a thought system. Jung studied a series of experiments conducted by Duke University research psychologist J. B. Rhine in the 1930s to test for clairvoyant perception. Rhine's subjects consistently, and inexplicably, scored higher "hits" on a deck of cards early in sessions when excitement and expectancy ran high. As time passed, accurate hits would taper off, though they could spike again if the subject's interest was newly aroused. Thus, reasoned Jung:

> Lack of interest and boredom are negative factors; enthusiasm, positive expectation, hope, and belief in the possibility of ESP make for good results and seem to be the real conditions which determine whether there are going to be any results at all.

Jung's observations amount to more than they first appear. It is not always easy for twenty-first-century readers to appreciate the stature in which experimental psychologist Rhine and his ESP tests were once held. For about a generation, from the early 1930s through the 1960s, Rhine was one of the most talked about scientists in America, a subject of public fascination and scholarly respect. Years of mostly polemical and tautological criticism have quieted the renown once associated with his name. For intrepid readers, however, Rhine's 1934 monograph, *Extra-Sensory Perception*, will still prove an extraordinary journey into the statistical findings he amassed in his ESP experiments with so-called Zener cards. Zener cards are a deck of twenty-five cards with five symbolic images (such as a circle, a cross, squiggly lines), which Rhine employed in tens of thousands of trials to track the persistence of higher-than-average hits among various subjects. Rhine's statistics and the conditions of his testing have been subjected to probably more scrutiny than any other lab-based psychological study; they have never been overturned. But for the persistent controversy surrounding ESP in general, the Rhine experiments demonstrated, beyond evidentiary doubt, the occurrence of some kind of anomalous transfer of information in a laboratory setting. If ESP, or trans-physical data conveyance of some kind, does not exist, then the clinical model on which we base our data testing is itself flawed in some not yet understood way.

Rhine was so dedicated to eschewing any kind of sensationalism that he hesitated to draw conclusions from his own studies. In the British appendix to his classic 1934 work, Rhine, in the kind of quietly monumental communication that marked his style, did briefly remark on the effects of enthusiasm among subjects in his ESP lab:

> Since my greatest interest is in stimulating others to repeat some of these experiments, I should like to mention here what has seemed to me to be the most important condition for ESP. This is *a spontaneity of interest in doing it*. The fresh interest in the act itself, like that of a child in playing a new game, seems to me the most favorable circumstance. Add now . . . the freedom from distraction, the absence of disturbing skepticism, the feeling of confidence or, at least, of some hope, and I think many good subjects can be found in any community or circle.

In effect, not only was the researcher commenting on advantageous circumstances for the occurrence of ESP, but his remarks amounted to a capsule playbook in the circumstances that cultivate any human achievement.

Rhine and Jung made points that could aptly be applied to religious experience, as well. How often do people find the household faith of their childhood a bore, seeming to hold no mystery or promise? By comparison, other belief systems can appear electrifyingly fresh and portentous. Because of its promise of concrete results, New Thought and its offshoots can seem veritably magical to the newcomer. Such expectations are a precondition for producing objective changes in a person's outer life, at least temporarily.

Just Think About It

The methods of positive thinking can arouse hope because they are so enticingly simple. The key to New Thought, as it has been restated for decades, is that a person must "think from the end"—that is, think as if the goal he desires has *already* come to pass. *Imagine how it would it feel,* New Thought counsels, if you already possessed the job, mate, or healthiness that you crave. But here the movement's methods hit a peculiar bump.

Permeating the space in between the lines of New Thought doctrine was the assumption that an individual could enter into a feeling or emotive state more or less at will—and that the aggrieved or anxious individual could "change his thinking," in New Thought terms, and "change his life." In such instances New-Thoughters seemed to conflate thoughts with emotions. The failure to see that thoughts and emotions operate on different lines, and often in a fashion that is unnervingly ruptured from each other, is a blind spot found not only in New Thought but in many psychological traditions. And if a person comes to believe that he can *think* his way in or out of a feeling state, further difficulties can ensue. C. S. Lewis's character Screwtape put it this way:

> Keep them watching their own minds and trying to produce *feelings* there by action of their own wills. . . . Teach them to estimate the value of each prayer by success in producing the desired feeling; and never let them suspect how much success or failure of that kind depends on whether they are well or ill, fresh or tired, at the moment.

A British Methodist minister named Leslie D. Weatherhead looked for a way around this problem. Weatherhead was active in the Oxford

Group in the 1930s, and he wrote a series of penetrating psychological and spiritual works. He had a particular interest in using suggestions or affirmations to improve a person's sense of self-worth and to puncture limiting beliefs. In essence, Weatherhead was attempting to update the work of French therapist Emile Coué.

The minister understood that affirmations—such as "I am confident and poised"—could not penetrate the "critical apparatus" of the human mind, which he compared to "a policeman on traffic duty." Other physicians and therapists similarly noted the problem of affirmations lacking emotional persuasiveness. Some therapists insisted that affirmations had to be credible and achievable to get through to the subject; no reasonable person would believe exaggerated self-claims, a point that Coué had also made. While Weatherhead agreed with these critiques, he believed that the rational "traffic cop" could be eluded by two practices. The first was the act of repetition: "A policeman on duty who refuses, say, a cyclist, the first time, might ultimately let him into the town if he presented himself again and again," he wrote in 1951. Continuing the metaphor, Weatherhead took things a step further:

> I can imagine that a cyclist approaching a town might more easily elude the vigilance of a policeman if the attempt to do so were made in the half-light of early dawn or the dusk of evening. Here also the parable illumines a truth. The early morning, when we waken, and the evening, just as we drop off to sleep, are the best times for suggestions to be made to the mind.

As Weatherhead saw it, the hypnagogic state—that is, the drowsy state between wakefulness and sleep, generally experienced when a person is drifting off in the evening or coming to in the morning—is a period of unique psychological flexibility, when ordinary barriers are down. This is probably why people suffering from depression or anxiety report the early waking hours as the most difficult time of day—the rational defenses are slackened. If the individual could use the gentlest efforts to repeat affirmations, without rousing himself fully to a waking state, the new ideas could penetrate, Weatherhead reasoned.

Neville Goddard made a similar point about the malleability of the hypnagogic mind. So did the twentieth-century psychical researcher and scientist Charles Honorton, who used this observation as a basis for testing the potential for telepathy between individuals. Honorton believed that a hypnagogic state was, in effect, "prime time" for the reception of extrasensory communication.

In the early 1970s, Honorton and his collaborators embarked on a long-running series of psi experiments, known as the ganzfeld experiments (German for "whole field"). These trials were designed to induce a hypnagogic state in a "receiver." The subject was placed, seated or reclining, in a soft-lit or darkened room and was fitted with eye covers and earphones, to create a state of comfortable sensory deprivation or low-level stimulation (such as with a "white noise" machine). Seated in another room, a "sender" would attempt to telepathically convey an image to the receiver. After the sending period ended, the receiver was asked to select the correct image among four—three images were decoys, establishing a chance hit-rate of 25 percent. Experimenters found that receivers consistently made higher-than-chance selections of the correct "sent" image. Honorton collaborated with avowed skeptic and research psychologist Ray Hyman in reviewing the data from a wide range of ganzfeld experiments. The psychical researcher and the skeptic jointly wrote: "We agree that there is an overall significant effect in this data base that cannot be reasonably explained by selective reporting or multiple analysis." Honorton added, "Moreover, we agree that the significant outcomes have been produced by a number of different investigators."

Hyman insisted that none of this was proof of psi, though he later acknowledged that "contemporary ganzfeld experiments display methodological and statistical sophistication well above previous parapsychological research. Despite better controls and careful use of statistical inference, the investigators seem to be getting significant re- sults that do not appear to derive from the more obvious flaws of previ- ous research."

My references here do not rest upon sufficiently acknowledged modes of research to settle any arguments about the potentialities of the mind. But they suggest the unique suppleness and flexibility of the mind in the hypnagogic state. It is a period of distinct mental openness, and it presents the possibility for self-conditioning, and perhaps much more. The ganzfeld trials point to the continued validity of psi experiments, which today encompass a much wider range of procedures and meth- odologies. Such work, however, is historically funded at very low levels, making study a continual challenge

We will return to clinical studies of the mind and its abilities. But to get a more intimate look at the occurrence of exceptional mental states, and their potential, requires considering an individual's most private experiences, to which we now turn.

The Bucket List

In the first decade of this century, I spent several years within a spiritual group dedicated to the ideas of Russian philosopher G. I. Gurdjieff. I was under the guidance of a remarkable and very gifted teacher—a gruff, lovable man of razor-sharp intellect. He demanded the most from every- one around him, though no one so much as himself. He used to delight in giving my colleagues and me "impossible" tasks to perform. At every turn we found our mettle tested and our limits stretched.

One time in preparation for a winter camping trip, he instructed me to purchase some plastic buckets, for a choice purpose: to serve as chamber pots for those female campers who didn't want to venture out- side of their tents into the icy woods at night. The buckets, he directed me, with glee, must be heart-shaped and colored pink. Or, as a second- best option, he allowed, they could be red. I began searching—visiting hardware and bed-bath stores in New York City. No pink buckets could be found, and certainly no heart-shaped ones. I made calls, and checked still more stores. Aside from receiving some odd looks, I turned up nothing. I fell back on looking for red plastic buckets, of an ordinary shape— not too difficult a task, it seemed. But, once more, in the commercial capital of the nation, no one seemed to have red plastic buckets for sale. By this point my wife was losing patience with me. Why, she wondered, didn't I show the same zeal for ordinary household projects as I did for this task? After more days of searching, it was final: I could find no pink, no red, and certainly no heart-shaped buckets. I would have to call up my teacher and say, "I tried, but I failed."

This phone call was on my mind just before I embarked on an errand at a small neighborhood grocery store near my home on Manhattan's East Side. I stood outside the store with my cell phone in my hand, but something told me: just wait, don't make the call right now. I went inside the store and walked straight to the back, to the cold-foods section. And there, at the rear of this modest, around-the-corner store, stood a pile of fresh, shiny plastic buckets—not only pink but also heart-shaped. I couldn't believe it. I stopped a stock boy and asked, "What color are those buckets?" Fixing me with the nut-of-the-day look, he replied: Pink. They had just arrived in, he said.

I cannot assert that my tireless search somehow manifested the yearned-for buckets. But nor can I call the situation ordinary. It's the kind of incident that a person has to be *involved* in, with some skin in the game: a situation in which you endeavor past all conventional effort, to the point where giving up seems like the only reasonable option, and the experience of then suddenly accomplishing an aim, or in this case finding an unlikely item in the unlikeliest of places, carries an emotional charge that no actuarial table can fully capture.

Statistics are wonderful for measuring odds, but not for measuring the emotional gravity that one attaches to them. It can be argued that emotions are incidental to odds. But not entirely. An event is notable not solely for its odds (and these odds were slim) but for the *quality of the event's meaning* given the expectations and needs of the individual. And at such times, an act of positive persistence seems to net a result that goes beyond ordinary cause and effect: something *additional* seems to occur. Exceptional commitment appears to summon an exceptional factor, neither fully expected nor describable.

It is also possible to observe a contrary case—in which panic, impatience, or anxiety conspires to overturn all reasonable, positive odds, and foments a negative outcome. I purposely used a simple example above not to highlight life's most dramatic stakes but to illustrate something about the nature of an outlook within the confines of everyday life. But we can also consider graver circumstances, on which a person's life depends.

"Bill Wanted It with His Whole Soul"

In 1934, Ebby Thacher introduced a hospitalized and desperate Bill Wilson to the principle that alcoholism required a spiritual solution. Bill was able to stay sober by embracing the ideas that Ebby brought to him, including principles from the Oxford Group, Carl Jung, and William James. Bill used these philosophies, and the experience of his own spiritual awakening, to lay the basis for Alcoholics Anonymous.

Yet, tragically, Ebby Thacher, the man who ignited Bill Wilson's interest in spiritual self-help, soon relapsed into drunkenness. Ebby spent much of his remaining life in a battle with alcohol, often ill and destitute. When Ebby died in 1966, he was sober but living as a dependent at a recovery center in upstate New York. Bill regularly sent him checks to keep him going. Not that Bill's legs were always strong. Although he remained sober until his death, Bill continually struggled with depression and chain-smoking. But he did attain his life's goal. Until his death in 1971, he never drank again.

Why did one man remain sober and another fall down?

Bill's wife, Lois, in a passage from her memoir, *Lois Remembers*, explained, in an understated manner, the difference she saw between the two men. In so doing, Lois also illuminated a mystery, maybe even the mystery, of human nature:

> After those first two years . . . why did Ebby get drunk? It was he who gave Bill the philosophy that kept him sober. Why didn't it keep Ebby sober? He was sincere, I'm sure. Perhaps it was a difference in the degree of wanting sobriety. Bill wanted it with his whole soul. Ebby may have wanted it simply to keep out of trouble.

Bill wanted it with his whole soul. Could that be the key? Within the parameters of physical possibilities, you receive what you "want with your whole soul"—whether inner truth, a personal accomplishment, relationships, whatever it is. Excluding some great countervailing force, and for either ill or good, the one thing that you want above all else is *what you get.*

In 1964, the spiritual teacher Jiddu Krishnamurti conducted a series of dialogues with a group of young students in India. The teacher spoke of the pull of conformity and the need to develop a sense of inner freedom. A boy asked him: "How can we put into practice what you are telling us?" Krishnamurti replied that if we want something badly enough, we know exactly what to do. "When you meet a cobra on the road," the teacher said, "you don't ask 'What am I to do?' You understand very well the danger of a cobra and you stay away from it." Krishnamurti noted:

> You hear something which you think is right and you want to carry it out in your everyday life; so there is a gap between what you think and what you do, is there not? You think one thing, and you are doing something else. But you want to put into practice what you think, so there is this gap between action and thought; and then you ask how to bridge the gap, how to link your thinking to your action.
>
> Now, when you want to do something very much, you do

it, don't you? When you want to go and play cricket, or do some other thing in which you are really interested, you find ways and means of doing it; you never ask how to put it into practice. You do it because you are eager, because your whole being, your mind and heart are in it.

Whether the answer to a personal crisis, the attainment of a desire, or the wish for some kind of inner awareness, the only aim that ever gets reached is the one that we want with everything in us. But what if someone doesn't possess a single soul truth? This may be the meaning behind Revelation 3:16, which condemns those who are lukewarm: "So then because thou art lukewarm, and neither cold nor hot, I will spit thee out of my mouth." The hesitators, the undecided, those who commit to no path—they receive nothing. Life permits us no halfway measures.

In that sense, too, the positive-thinking approach places a demand on us, one that we may think we've risen to but have never really tried. And that is: *To come to terms with precisely what we want.* When we organize our thoughts in a certain way—with a fearless maturity and honesty—we may be surprised to discover what our desires really are. A person who thinks of himself as "spiritual" may discover a deep wish for worldly attainment; someone who has labored to support the work of others, or of family members, may find that he has deeply unsettled yearnings of his own for self-expression; a person who is very public or extroverted may discover that he really wants to be alone.

This is where the list-building exercises from a book such as R. H. Jarrett's *It Works* can yield surprising results. Taking a mature and sustained inventory of desires can open us up rather than limit us. It's not enough to tell ourselves that we know what we want, but to really dwell on it in a concentrated way. *Such an inquiry will almost always produce unexpected insights.*

As the story of Bill Wilson and Ebby Thacher suggests, the true yearnings of our soul are not only the best predictor of where we'll go in life, but the primary means of getting us there.

The Four Schools

People approach positive thinking because of an unmet need. They want to get somewhere in life; they're looking to solve a problem or find personal peace. To meet a person's most deeply felt wishes, the different groups and individuals that make up the positive-thinking movement variously rely on psychological techniques, metaphysical beliefs, behavioral conditioning, and sometimes on the cultivation of meaning and purpose.

To consider which of these approaches works best, and at what cost or benefit, it is helpful to break down and critique what I see as the four primary schools of positive thinking. They are:

1. The Magical Thinking or Divine Thought School
2. The Conditioning or Reprogramming School
3. The Conversion School
4. The Meaning-Based School

We will now evaluate each.

1. The Magical Thinking or Divine Thought School

This is the most widespread form of the mind-power philosophy, encompassing the outlook of figures such as Norman Vincent Peale, Joseph Murphy, Ernest Holmes, and Wallace D. Wattles. It informs the outlook of *The Secret*'s Rhonda Byrne. The Magical Thinking perspective sees the individual as a kind of holy channel for a higher power. It could also be called the Law of Attraction School. It is the least "provable" approach, yet the most popular and enduring.

Each of the aforementioned thinkers professed a different version of the philosophy—Peale was a conservative Christian who used Scripture to support his ideas about "prayer power"; Murphy was a New Age mystic who told of an all-powerful subconscious mind that represented an inner God; Wattles, Holmes, and Byrne adhered to an occult science that considers man a transmitter of an infinite power, or a "thinking stuff," as Wattles put it. Each denizen of this approach, whatever his or her individual wrinkle, sees the mind as a vessel and ignition engine constantly out-picturing all of our thoughts into reality. Seen from their perspective, the mind, with proper awareness, can function as a tool to dispatch every right desire.

This school's ethical framework is poorly developed, though Peale and Holmes did hew to Scriptural ethics, and other practitioners spoke of karmic reciprocity. Ultimately, this approach amounts to an intensely personal theology. And as rationalist philosopher David Hume wrote of Christianity: "Mere reason is insufficient to convince us of its veracity."

That said, the power of such faith in the life of an individual should not be discounted. Every religion has its allegories—whether it's Moses parting the Red Sea or Muhammad ascending to heaven on a winged horse. Some believers see such things as literally true, but for many they are symbolic. The notion of an *attitude as a literal force* may be seen as the central allegory of the New Age.

"No scientist can prove that our thoughts create our reality," life coach Anthony Robbins writes. "But it's a useful lie. It's an empowering belief. That's why I choose to believe in it."

I believe that no act of self-deception can be useful. But Robbins does get at a certain point: That faith in the force of one's mind, whether definitively provable, can serve as a mechanism for a greater, and deeply affecting, psychological truth. This is explored directly below.

2. The Conditioning or Reprogramming School

This school represents the reconditioning approach of figures such as the Reverend Leslie Weatherhead, French psychologist Emile Coué, and an American cosmetic surgeon and motivational writer named Maxwell Maltz. It is worth noting the case of Maltz, whose 1960 book, *Psycho-Cybernetics*, was a motivational landmark.

As a reconstructive surgeon, Maltz discovered that many of his patients—from burn victims to people with deformities to nonimpaired individuals desirous of a change in appearance—did, in fact, experience improved self-esteem following surgery. But he also noticed that some manifestly did not. He questioned why. Maltz came to believe that man is a creature of conditioning. Maltz saw the mind as a homing device that seeks out and works to manifest the subconscious images that we constantly and unknowingly send it. The pictures of the mind *cannot remake reality*, he wrote, but they can lead to and shape outcomes in remarkable ways. Recondition the mind, Maltz reasoned, and you can objectively alter your life.

Maltz's philosophy is a good overall summary of this school, which sees the mind as a complex, conditioned machine capable of reprogramming. In this view, *conditioning is destiny*. The Conditioning School prescribes affirmations, visualizations, behavior modeling, and guided meditations to reprogram our self-image, and thus improve our functioning. Many inquirers who attempt this approach are surprised by the rigor demanded from such programs—at least an hour a day of visualizations and guided meditations can be required in Maltz's program, for example.

Significantly, the Conditioning School sought to jettison the religio-mystical qualities of the Magical Thinking School and reconfigure New Thought as a secular, success-based psychology that could be used for business, relationships, athletics, and general happiness. In so doing, it popularized the field of business motivation and laid some of the groundwork for the general field of positive psychology. This approach also foresaw recent advances in neuroscience, in particular the concept that the electro-neural responses of the brain are self-reprogrammable, in a process that has been called "neuroplasticity." (Neuroplasticity is examined later in this chapter.)

The Conditioning School has a weakness similar to that of the Magical Thought School: it offers little in the way of ethical development; the aims of reconditioning are often careerist or success based. But as a motivational psychology it has undeniable validity.

3. The Conversion School

Philosopher William James and psychologist Carl Jung shared a key idea: that a conversion experience, or religious awakening, could objectively alter the circumstances of a person's life.

This approach was echoed in the narratives of Helen Wilmans and Psychiana's Frank B. Robinson, both of whom described their arrival at the positive-thinking philosophy through a kind of religious awakening. Alcoholics Anonymous cofounder Bill Wilson described a similar experience—though with different ends—which led him to found a faith-based approach to addiction recovery. As related earlier, Jung told Wilson that his method for defeating alcoholism was *spiritus contra spiritum*—"Higher Spirit over lower spirits" (or alcohol). It was a confirmation of what Wilson and others had experienced, and this outlook is at the heart of Alcoholics Anonymous and all of the offshoot twelve-step programs.

The Conversion School sees man as a psycho-spiritual being who is capable of experiencing dramatic, visible life changes through a consuming experience of faith, which reorders a person's priorities and perspective. "Conversion," wrote Bill Wilson, "does alter motivation, and does semi-automatically enable a person to be and to do the formerly impossible."

Conversion experiences, while obviously not limited to the positive-thinking movement, help explain New Thought's ability to attract newcomers, some of whom earnestly testify to personal breakthroughs upon discovering its ideas. For individuals who have been raised within uninspiring or punitive religious backgrounds, the self-affirming beliefs of mind-power can generate tremendous enthusiasm and reorientation. The problem is in sustaining that experience. For individuals with a defined and well-ordered aim, such as staying sober, support groups such as AA do provide a sustaining structure. But most people discover positive-thinking philosophy through books, such as *The Secret* or *The Power of Your Subconscious Mind*. And their initial excitement—along with the self-validation they may experience—is not generally sustainable. Hence, positive-thinking bestsellers and seminars can attract droves of excited newcomers—but the movement is like a great revolving door through which the curious quickly come and go (another issue to which we will return).

The conversion effect seems most likely to succeed when: (a) it is combined with a support structure, such as AA meetings or church services, and (b) it focuses a person's energies on solving a specific and well-defined problem. The closest thing to a blueprint for conversion is found in the first three of AA's twelve steps, as noted in Chapter 5.

There are, of course, certain forms of conversion that go beyond the needs of addiction recovery or crisis intervention—and that lead to a sustainable and dramatically reorganized sense of existence and personal worth, to which we now turn.

4. The Meaning-Based School

This approach is found within the spiritual ideas of Rabbi Joshua Loth Liebman and the existential philosophy of psychologists such as Erich Fromm and Viktor E. Frankl. Frankl—writing after he survived Auschwitz—drew upon his wartime experiences to reach stark conclusions about the depths of human indecency, but also about the very real possibilities of an inner grace appearing from within a person even under the most horrific conditions.

Frankl and his contemporaries saw man as a being of great potential—but one who is trapped in a state of psychical slumber. In a crisis, Frankl reasoned, man can awaken to his higher self. The key is to locate some meaning in life, to find personal terms in which suffering or travails amount to some worth in the world; this revelation can dramatically alter a person's viewpoint and provide new possibilities.

In his 1946 book *Man's Search for Meaning*, Frankl used the analogy of an exhausted mountaineer who finds renewed stamina upon spotting the mountain peak. Even though the climber has not reached the peak (and, in some cases, may never), its sight alone changes his outlook and freshens his energies. Whether the peak is self-understanding, self-rescue from destructive behavior, or the personal embodying of a higher principle—if it is morally persuasive and sustainable, the effect is the same: the individual, like the mountaineer, can experience extraordinary new perspective and will for living. The essential point of the Meaning-Based School is that a higher perspective can rescue a person from an existence of aimlessness and undefined anxiety.

Another spiritual thinker who promulgated this view was Vernon Howard. As noted earlier, Howard's career as a spiritual teacher and writer began loosely in the New Thought tradition. But the books he wrote in his spiritual maturity, from the mid-1960s until his death in 1992, represented works of extraordinary independence and insight. While unknown within most circles of psychology and spirituality, Howard provided actual, concrete methods for self-development, areas where writers like Liebman and Frankl were weaker.

It could be objected that the Meaning-Based School is not a mind-power or positive-thinking philosophy at all. Yet this outlook positioned the agency of the mind as a misunderstood and extremely potent instrument, and through the mind's proper use and powers of perception a person's way of life could be radically altered, even if outer circumstances remained static. This is probably the most morally and spiritually convincing philosophy to emerge from the mind-power tradition.

"Positive-Thinking B.S."

For all these different approaches, and for all of their influence across varying fields, the positive-thinking philosophy is taken seriously almost nowhere in mainstream culture today. Even some of the most famous exponents of motivational thought seem to flee from the association. Without irony, life coach Anthony Robbins insisted on television in 2010 that his motivational advice wasn't "positive-thinking B.S."

The poor reputation of positive thinking and New Thought is not necessarily due to its perceived lapses in realism. Every religious movement begins with supernatural claims, and if any faith were evaluated solely in terms of demonstrable, quantifiable facts, none would pass. Movements of a similar vintage to New Thought, such as Mormonism and Seventh-day Adventism, have gained acceptance.

Rather, New Thought's historical dilemma, as previously explored, is its insistence on embracing a single, all-encompassing theory of life, which is to say, the Law of Attraction. This is what keeps New Thought's claims from attaining greater acknowledgment, and perpetuates its inability to come to terms with evil and other crises. The idea of a mental super-law binds New Thought to a paradigm of extremist self-responsibility, which cannot be defended to its limits.

While the mind *does* possess influences that are not yet fully understood, and that are palpably felt by many people, the wish to depict the universe as the ultimate result of mentality contradicts our overwhelming experience of living under mechanics, chance, and physical limitations. As the body of Christ was pierced on the cross, there is no spiritual, ethical, or physical imperative, in religious literature or in the experience of daily existence, to suggest that even the self-aware person, mystic, or saint is immune from such effects.

Until this fatal mistake—this reliance on a single metaphysical law of cause and effect—is corrected, the positive-thinking movement and its offshoots will continue to seem theologically and ethically unserious. While its literature may survive, and even thrive, there are already signs that the movement is unable to maintain a flourishing and long-term congregational culture.

The late twentieth and early twenty-first centuries have witnessed shrinking congregations within Christian Science, as well as stagnant or declining attendance at most New Thought churches. While Mary Baker Eddy prohibited the release of membership numbers, it is possible today to enter a beautifully maintained Christian Science church on a Sunday morning, or during a weekday service, and find just a handful of congregants. I've personally been to a Sunday service in a magnificent domed church on New York's Park Avenue and encountered no more than twenty worshippers, several of them elderly. At a weekday service in a cavernous, cathedral-sized church in midtown Manhattan—this being lunchtime and, hence, a naturally smaller gathering—I counted no more than six people in the pews. These numbers may not typify what is found at a major Boston or California congregation, but they were at two of New York City's most visible Christian Science churches.

This trend can also be seen in the institutional New Thought world. At the time of Ernest Holmes's death in 1960, formal membership in his Science of Mind churches stood at more than 100,000. A 2001 study found about 55,000 active congregants within the two main Holmes ministries. (Notably, though, Holmes's magazine, *Science of Mind*, continued to be read beyond the membership base, at a circulation of about 80,000.) This drop in institutional membership appeared in the total number of churches, as well. A 1991 study found about 175 active churches within the United Church of Religious Science (UCRS), the larger of the two ministries based in Holmes's ideas. Twenty years later, my best estimate of the number of congregations with regular services and facility space, based on published and online directories, showed about 155 active UCRS churches in the United States and Canada.* This decline occurred even as *The Secret* and its many offshoots exploded.

Modern Mental Healing

But what if New Thought can break away from this one-law-above-all approach? If affirmative thought can be understood as one ray of light, one vital method and outlook, within life's greatly deep forest of forces and causes, the positive-thinking paradigm may experience a new form of relevance and reinvention in the early twenty-first century. Indeed, the philosophy's core ideas are already echoed within many precincts of contemporary science and medicine.

In 2007, nearly half of medical doctors polled in a Chicago survey

---

* UCRS has since merged with Religious Science International, the other major Holmes ministry, to form United Centers for Spiritual Living.

revealed that they routinely and knowingly prescribed medications to their patients that they considered ineffective, or in dosages that were too low to produce any real effect. Their aim was to create a placebo response. For more than fifty years, double-blind studies have shown consistent results from the placebo response. Today, a steady spike of placebo responses in control groups perplexes researchers for pharmaceutical companies. In tests of new antidepressants, for example, the placebo effect is often found to match or exceed the efficacy of trial medications. The placebo effect has also been repeatedly prevalent in recent studies of medications for pain relief, anxiety, sexual dysfunction, and the tremors associated with Parkinson's disease.

The placebo response seems to operate on factors including positive anticipation, empathy of the caregiver, and support-group dynamics, such as experiencing and discussing the positive benefits of a treatment with fellow patients. These traits mirror the methods of early mental healing and New Thought. Researchers who are studying the mechanics of the placebo response obviously share none of the spiritual assumptions of the mental-healing traditions; yet the placebo phenomenon is, in effect, the mind-cure of our era.

Some medical authorities might privately nod in sympathy with the defense of Mesmer by Charles d'Eslon, the late-eighteenth-century Paris physician: "It may indeed be entirely imagination. And if it is? Then imagination is a force as potent as it is little understood. Let us work with this mysterious imagination, let us use it to cure, let us learn more about it." Or, as it was put to Benjamin Franklin's committee by a patient of Mesmer's: "If it is to an illusion that I owe the health which I believe that I enjoy, I humbly beg the scholars who are seeing so clearly, not to destroy it; let them enlighten the universe, but let them leave me to my error; and let them allow to my simplicity, to my weakness, and to my ignorance, the use of an invisible force, which does not exist, but which heals me."

Many physicians counter that misleading a patient, as in the Chicago study, has no place in ethical medicine. They make a vital point.

But through further study, physicians and researchers may discover new ways to transparently replicate the settings and circumstances that produce the placebo response. A 2010 study by Ted J. Kaptchuk and fellow researchers at Harvard's Program in Placebo Studies and the Therapeutic Encounter produced remarkable findings in this very area: Patients reported relief *even when they knew they were receiving a placebo pill.* Researchers informed eighty sufferers of irritable bowel syndrome that some would be receiving a placebo while others would be in a no-treatment control group. Fifty-nine percent of sufferers who took the "honest placebo" reported "adequate relief" (compared to 35 percent in the control group). It marks one of the first pieces of modern clinical data that reveals the powers of the mind to give physical relief even when a "sugar pill" is transparently administered.

Why do people respond to a substance they know is inert? It may be that these results reflect the public's general acceptance and acknowledgment of a placebo response. People generally *believe* in the efficacy of placebos, even when transparently administered. They have often heard or read about them in popular sources, such as *Reader's Digest.* They already possess *confidence* that a placebo can work. What seems to be required in order to harness that faith is a setting in which this perspective is validated and formalized—which naturally arises from the environs of a formal clinical study, where patients are led to trust that they are involved in something therapeutically sound, responsibly administered, and proffered in an atmosphere of hopeful expectancy.

In his Duke University experiments of the 1930s, psychical researcher J. B. Rhine noted the same dynamic: A supportive, validating atmosphere consistently appeared to "spike" responses above chance in his card-guessing experiments. A similar environment prevails in the structure of twelve-step meetings, where addicts often credit their success to peer support and empathy.

A related area for additional study is hospital care. For decades, patients have complained about the serious discomfort and demoralizing qualities of hospital settings. Further research may uncover a relationship between recovery and the nature of hospital surroundings—specifically, whether the rate and pace of wellness may improve according to a patient's privacy, physical comfort, mood, and rapport with caregivers.

Clinicians have found that treating patients as mature, capable partners, and sharing vital information with them, can make a difference in their recovery from functional diseases such as migraines, stomach and bowel disorders, and chronic back pain. Physician John Sarno called it "knowledge therapy." A professor of clinical rehabilitation medicine at NYU School of Medicine, Sarno has treated thousands of patients for neck, back, or shoulder pain—and he found that the vast majority of such patients had also previously experienced persistent headaches, heartburn, and stomach disorders. Yet few of them showed any structural abnormalities. Sarno hypothesized that their maladies were related to stress and tension. He found that if back pain sufferers understood how muscular tension arose from stressful emotive states, they could experience relief. The very act of sharing this information, in a constructive and accurate manner, appeared to have a therapeutic benefit. Sarno wrote in his book *Mind Over Back Pain*:

> What I discovered was that faith or belief in a concept could have a powerful, permanent therapeutic effect if it *was based on accurate information*. When patients were taught the facts of tension mitosis syndrome [his term for tension-based back pain] they were able to develop confidence in the diagnosis; it made sense to them; they believed it at a *conscious* level. In a sense, I made my patients partners in the diagnostic process. "This is how it works," I said. "Do you agree?" I found that patients who were able to say "yes" to that question got better—*without* a recurrence of their pain.

Frontiers of the Mind

The mind-power thesis takes on a different type of relevance within the most extraordinary and contentious field of physics: quantum mechanics. Contemporary physics journals discuss what is called the "quantum measurement problem." Many people have heard of some version of it. In essence, more than eighty years of laboratory experiments show that atomic-scale particles appear in a given place only when a measurement is made.

Astonishing as it sounds—and physicists themselves have debated the data for generations—quantum theory holds that *no measurement means no precise and localized object*, at least on the atomic scale. Put differently, a subatomic particle literally occupies an infinite number of places (a state called "superposition") until observation manifests it in one place. In quantum mechanics, a decision to look or not look actually determines what will be there. In this sense, an observer's consciousness determines objective reality on a subatomic level. Some physicists would dispute that characterization. Critics sometimes argue that certain particles are too small to measure; hence any attempt at measurement inevitably affects what is seen. But there exists a whole class of "interaction-free measurement" quantum experiments that don't involve detectors at all. Such experiments have repeatedly shown that a subatomic object literally exists in more than one place at once until a measurement determines its final resting place.

How is this actually provable? In the parlance of quantum physics, an atomic-scale particle is said to exist in a wave-state, which means that the location of the particle in space-time is known only probabilistically; it has no properties in this state, just potentialities. When particles or waves—typically in the form of a beam of photons or electrons—are directed or aimed at a target system, such as a double-slit, scientists have found that their pattern or path will actually change, or "collapse," depending upon the presence or measurement choices of an observer. Hence, a wave pattern will shift, or collapse, into a particle pattern. A ray of light, for example, will display the properties either of a wave or of distinct particles, depending upon the activity of the observer. It is not light alone that behaves this way. Classical quantum experiments show that if you project an atom at a pair of boxes, *interference patterns prove that the atom was at one point in both boxes.* The particle existed as a wave, and became localized in one box only *after* someone looked. In this sense, an atom can be observed shifting from a *potential* to an *actual thing.* The outcome depends on whether someone is watching. Contrary to all reason, quantum theory holds that reality is a duality. Opposing outcomes simultaneously exist.

The situation gets even stranger when dealing with the thought experiment known as "Schrodinger's cat." The twentieth-century physicist Erwin Schrodinger was frustrated with the evident absurdity of quantum theory, which showed objects simultaneously appearing in more than one place at a time. Such an outlook, he felt, violated all commonly observed physical laws. In 1935, Schrodinger sought to highlight this predicament through a purposely absurdist thought experiment, which he intended to force quantum physicists to follow their data to its ultimate degree. Schrodinger may have succeeded too well, as his model, rather than exposing quantum physics' apparent impossibilities, became a rallying point for the field's most audacious theorizing.

Schrodinger reasoned that quantum data dictates that a sentient being, such as a cat, can be simultaneously alive and dead. A variant of the "Schrodinger's cat" experiment could be put this way: Let's say a cat is placed into one of a pair of boxes. Along with the cat is what Schrodinger called a "diabolical device." The device, if exposed to an atom, releases a deadly poison. An observer then fires an atom at the boxes. The observer subsequently uses some form of measurement to check on which box the atom is in: the empty one, or the one with the cat and the poisoning device. When the observer goes to check, the wave function of the atom—i.e., the state in which it exists in both boxes—collapses into a particle function—i.e., the state in which it is localized to one box. Once the observer takes his measurement, convention says that the cat will be discovered to be dead or alive. But Schrodinger reasoned that quantum physics describes an outcome in which the cat is *both* dead and alive. This is because the atom, in its wave function, was, at one time, in either box, and either outcome is real.

Of course, all lived experience tells us that if the atom went into the empty box, the cat is alive, and if it went into the box with the cat and the poisoning device, the cat is dead. But Schrodinger, aiming to highlight the frustrations of quantum theory, argued that if the observations of quantum mechanics experiments are right (and for decades they have not been in dispute), you would have to allow for each outcome.

To take it even further, a cohort of quantum physicists in the 1950s theorized that if an observer waited some significant length of time, say, eight hours, before checking on the dead-alive cat, he would discover one cat that was dead for eight hours and another that was alive for eight hours (and now hungry). In this line of reasoning, conscious observation effectively manifested the localized atom, the dead cat, the living cat—and *also manifested the past*, i.e., created a history for both a dead cat and a living one. Both outcomes are true.

Absurd? Impossible? Yes to that, say quantum physicists—but decades of quantum experiments make this model—in which a creature can be dead/alive—into an impossible reality: an unbelievable yet entirely tenable, even necessary, state of nature. Schrodinger's thought experiment forced a consideration of the meaning of quantum mechanics (though not many physicists pay attention to the radical implications).

It must be emphasized, of course, that classical quantum data is derived strictly from events on an atomic scale. We are only at the beginning of testing the "superposition" function in the everyday macroscopic world in which we live, where Newton's laws still reign. Laws, however, demand consistency. So, why is there an apparent divide in our view of reality, in which one set of rules governs the events of the micro world and another set governs the macro world? It may be due to the limits of our observation in the macro world. Some twenty-first-century quantum physicists call this phenomenon "information leakage." The theory of "information leakage" holds that the apparent impossibilities of quantum activity exist all around us. They govern reality. However, when we step away from whatever instrument we are using to measure micro particles, and begin looking at things in larger frames and forms, we see less and less of what is really going on. We experience a "leakage" of data. William James alluded to a similar dynamic in his 1902 Gifford Lectures: "We learn most about a thing when we view it under a microscope, as it were, or in its most exaggerated form. This is as true of religious phenomena as of any other kind of fact."

Some quantum physicists are attempting to deal with this predicament by replicating "superposition" experiments on a larger scale, using molecules rather than atoms. Some are attempting to devise experiments with macro-sized objects, such as proteins. Only future experiments will determine whether the implications of "leakage" keep us from seeing reality. For now, however, decades of quantum data make it defensible to conclude that observation done on the subatomic scale: (1) shapes the nature of outcomes, (2) determines the presence or absence of a localized object, and (3) possibly devises multiple pasts and presents. This last point is sometimes called the "many-worlds interpretation," in the words of physicist Hugh Everett. This theory of "many worlds" raises the prospect of an infinite number of realities and states of being, each depending upon our choices.

The concept of multiple worlds and outcomes finds its closest New Thought analog in the ideas of Neville Goddard, who reasoned that our thoughts create an infinitude of realities and outcomes. Neville argued that everything we see and experience, including one another, is the product of what happens in our own individual dream of reality. Through a combination of emotional conviction and mental images, Neville believed, each person imagines his own world into being—all people and events are rooted in us, as we are ultimately rooted in God. When a person awakens to his true self, Neville argued, he will, in fact, discover himself to be a slumbering branch of the Creator clothed in human form, and at the helm of infinite possibilities.

Most quantum physicists wouldn't be caught dead/alive as

Schrodinger's cat reading an occult philosopher such as Neville. Indeed, many physicists reject the notion of interpreting the larger implications of quantum data at all. "Shut up and calculate!" is the battle cry popularized by physicist N. David Mermin. The role of physics, critics insist, is to *measure things*—not, in Einstein's phrase, to lift "the veil that shrouds the Old One." Leave that to gurus and philosophers, but, for heaven's sake, critics argue, keep it out of the physics lab. Others adopt the opposite position: If physics isn't for explaining reality, then what *is* it for?

The latter principle may carry the day. A rising generation of physicists, educated in the 1960s and '70s and open to questions of consciousness, is currently reaching positions of leadership in physics departments (and gaining authority in areas of grant making and funding). This cohort was educated in a world populated by Zen and motorcycle maintenance, psychedelic experimentation, and *Star Trek*; they tend to be open to philosophical questions and meta-analysis. As scientists they are every bit as rigorous as the past generation of classical empiricists. Hence, we could be on the brink of a renaissance of inquiry into the most remarkable scientific issue since Newton codified classical mechanics. As more data is known, purveyors of quantum physics and metaphysics may be headed for a new and serious conversation.

But the pitfalls are too important not to consider before waltzing off into the world of "both/and" realities. To the frustration of scientists, spiritual seekers often prove overeager to seize upon the implications of quantum data, declaring that we now have *proof* that the universe is the result of our minds. The correlation between the events of the micro world and those of the daily life that we see and feel is far from clear. Spiritual seekers should resist the temptation to cherry-pick from data that seems to confirm their most deeply cherished ideas. Likewise, physicists should be patient with lay seekers who want to ponder the possibilities of quantum physics. If the right balance can be struck, serious and thoughtful people from both worlds, science and spirituality, have something to talk over.

Changing the Brain

Since the 1990s, an intriguing courtship has emerged between certain branches of quantum theorizing and psychology. Neuroscientists and research psychiatrists, notably Jeffrey M. Schwartz, M.D., of UCLA, have been studying what has been termed neuroplasticity. Brain scans show that patients with obsessive-compulsive disorder (OCD) who repeatedly and effectively redirect their thoughts from intrusive or ritualistic impulses not only alleviate symptoms, but over time can actually change their brain biology by "rewiring" neural pathways.

The necessary formula is this: When an obsessive thought or ritual begins to take hold, the individual immediately redirects his thinking to something else that is pleasurable and diverting, such as listening to music, watching a favorite TV show, or performing a desirable physical activity. After a time, researchers find, the repeated diversions actually create new nerve-cell structures in the brain, which replace the electro-neural pathways associated with OCD.

"I propose," Schwartz writes, "that the time has come for science to confront serious implications of the fact that directed, willed mental activity can clearly and systematically alter brain function; that the exertion of willful effort generates a *physical force* that has the power to change how the brain works and even its physical structure."

Schwartz linked his UCLA findings to developments in quantum physics. "The implications of direct neuroplasticity combined with quantum physics," he wrote in his 2002 book *The Mind and the Brain*, "cast new light on the question of humanity's place, and role, in nature." The co-emergence of the two fields, he argued, "suggests that the natural world evolves through an interplay between two causal processes."

Hence, if our thought process can alter the pathways through which electrical impulses travel in the brain, and permanently change behaviors that are produced, then brain biology can be understood as the *product of thought*, as much as the other way around. This process, Schwartz claims, "allows human thoughts to make a difference in the evolution of physical events." And the method at the back of it, he writes, "is what I call directed mental force."

Brain imaging and several years of clinical study support the findings of neuroplasticity. Yet the same insight existed instinctively—and with virtually the same methods and exercises—in early New Thought. Between 1909 and 1911, minister and philosopher John Herman Randall issued a series of pamphlets that explored the ideas of positive thinking and the new mental therapeutics. He collected them in his 1911 book, *A New Philosophy of Life*, in which he described an intriguing method to escape nagging thoughts. Randall called it *substitution*. He wrote:

> Divert your mind from the discordant thought by thinking in other channels. Do not wait a moment, when the wrong thought gets into your mind, but turn to the magazine or the book, and read until your mind is filled with other thoughts. Or, take up some task that calls for all your energy, and forces you to concentrate your mental activities along other lines. It may be a little difficult at first, but I want to tell you, on the experience of multitudes of men and women [that this approach] if persevered in, will succeed in every life.

Randall's technique and terminology foreshadowed the precise method of neuroplasticity as it relates to OCD.* People fail to devise constructive new habits, Randall wrote, "because they are not persistent and patient enough in forming the new brain centres from whence must be permanently expressed the new life, that may in very truth be born in them . . ." And elsewhere: "Our thinking must be turned into other channels than those which we know will lead to the worrisome thoughts"—the remedy being to "substitute some new line of thought," anything that gets us out of "narrow restricted grooves." Randall's in-

---

* In 1904 the Nobel-winning Spanish neuro-anatomist Santiago Ramón y Cajal also had the insight that thoughts repeated by "mental practice" would reinforce neural pathways, though the brain imaging that would prove his point did not yet exist.

sights anticipated the language and findings of twenty-first-century neuroplasticity.

The Positive-Thinking Revolution

This brings us, finally, to a convergence among the questions and possibilities probed by the contemporary psychiatric researcher, the earnest New-Thoughter, and the broad-minded quantum theorist. If overstatement or conclusion-leaping can be avoided, the questions that surround today's studies of physical reality and the uses of the mind can be understood as extraordinary and profoundly challenging—both to students of physics and metaphysics, and for the same reasons.

In 2009, I attended a presentation on the "quantum measurement problem" delivered by scientist Dean Radin before an audience of scientists, social thinkers, and scholars of religion. I asked Radin to address the 800-pound gorilla in the room: If observation and perspective alter material on a micro level, in the world of waves and particles, might that say something about the legitimacy of the New Thought or mind-power thesis? "It's not complete bullshit," Radin replied. "There may be an inkling of something to it." Another physicist and longtime military researcher was also present. "As the resident skeptic," he said, "I concur."

Boston University geologist Robert M. Schoch has an expression: "Something only has to be a little bit true to change everything." Is New Thought "a little bit true"? The experiences of the past 150 years suggest as much. Yes, positive thinking does work—but it works amid a variety of different forces: accidental, biological, natural, and psychological. We live under the accidents of fortune, illness, forces of nature, traumas of the past, and on the waves of relationships with others, who may possess conflicting needs and aims. These are lawful facts of life. But the mind also wields a shade of influence—it is an influence that we don't fully understand, but one that is accorded steadily greater credibility by generations of study in medicine, psychology, biology, and the physical sciences. Historically, the powers of attitude, observation, and outlook become ever greater-seeming, never more-proscribed.

In medicine, the positive-thinking movement, long before any other thought school, anticipated our still-expanding conception of how a patient's mind can be used to manage illness and discomfort. In psychology, positive thinkers foresaw the potential for behavior modification, auto-suggestion, hypnotherapy, and reconditioning as a means to relieving dysfunction. In the emergent field of neuroplasticity, in which thoughts are seen to alter aspects of brain biology, the protocols prescribed to patients echo methods that positive thinkers devised over a century ago. And, finally, before the foundations of quantum mechanics were laid in the early twentieth century, the positive-thinking movement struggled to express a ragged, rough-hewn instinct for one of the remarkable challenges being considered in some of today's quantum physics labs: Namely, if the presence of an observer not only affects the thing being observed, but actually localizes an object or brings it to its resting place when an observation or measurement is made, then what is the nature of the mind and observation, and what is meant by creation itself?

On a personal scale, at those moments when the mind and emotions are at one—at such times it may be better to speak of a psyche than a mind—the experience of generations of self-aware individuals testifies that our focus adds *something extra* to our experience. This is not strictly a matter of rewiring the brain or making suggestions to the subconscious. "Psi studies," Radin related to me, "go one step further and suggest that all this positive thinking also tweaks the world at large in small but measurable ways we still don't understand."

Returning to Krishnamurti's dialogues with Indian youths, the spiritual teacher responded this way to a student who feared being thrown out of his home if he violated his father's wishes and pursued an engineering career:

> If you persist in wanting to be an engineer even though your
> father turns you out of the house, do you mean to say that

you won't find ways and means to study engineering? You will beg, go to friends. Sir, life is very strange. The moment you are very clear about what you want to do, things happen. Life comes to your aid—a friend, a relation, a teacher, a grandmother, somebody helps you. But if you are afraid to try because your father may turn you out, then you are lost. Life never comes to the aid of those who merely yield to some demand out of fear. But if you say, "This is what I really want to do and I am going to pursue it," then you will find that something miraculous takes place.

Yet the exertions of the psyche and the determinations of the soul cannot be seen in isolation from the forces around us. When we suffer—as we inevitably will, probably in a fifty-fifty mixture with our joys over the course of a lifetime—we can aspire not to glibly affirm away our suffering, which can lead to desperation and frustration, but rather to see ourselves as *thinkers* who have charge over a certain range of circumstances, which may variously loop and weave within and without our control. From such a state, we can face life finally and fully *as ourselves*, possessed of soul desires that will, if persisted in and within natural parameters, be reflected in the folds of our experience.

The act of questioning, probing, and affirming the fullness of our possibilities can avert the psychological pain of feeling that we haven't faced life as we should, which is actually the chief cause of shame and anger. The wish to authentically search for the self and its true aims is, perhaps, the greatest form of mental affirmation to which a person can aspire, *and the one that brings the most help.*

The pioneers of the positive-thinking movement, acting with deep practical intent, probed the possibilities and capacities of our psyches earlier than any scientists, theologians, or psychologists of the modern industrialized age. The founders of New Thought and affirmative thinking created a fresh means of viewing life, one that was rough and incomplete, rife with mistakes and dead ends, but also filled with possibility and practical application. These pioneers, whose work commenced only in the latter half of the nineteenth century, began an extraordinary conversation and experiment about the power of thought to shape the experience of the individual. There exists an authentic and efficacious beginning in their ideas, which remain relatively new. In that sense, the positive-thinking movement created the genuine and still-unfolding Reformation of the modern search for meaning for which William James had hoped.

Notes on Sources

These notes are intended to supplement attributions that appear in individual chapters. When a source is already cited within a chapter, it is not generally repeated here.

CHAPTER ONE:
TO WISH UPON A STAR

Emerson is quoted from his 1870 essay "Success." The Talmudic precept is from *Pirkei Avot* ("Ethics of the Fathers"), chapter 1:15.

William James used the term "the religion of healthy-mindedness" in *The Varieties of Religious Experience* (Longmans, Green & Co., 1902). In his memoir *Manifest Victory* (Harper & Brothers, 1941, 1947), religious scholar J. R. Moseley recalls James's conviction that New Thought "constituted, together with Christian Science, a spiritual movement as significant for our day as the Reformation was for its time." James referred to "a wave of religious activity" in his essay "The Energies of Men," *Philosophical Review*, January 1907.

Thomas Jefferson's statement about Unitarianism is from his letter of June 26, 1822, to Dr. Benjamin Waterhouse. Mark Twain's explorations of Christian Science date back to *Cosmopolitan* magazine of October 1899 and appeared in their fullest form in his book *Christian Science* (Harper & Brothers, 1907).

My reference to the work of Barbara Ehrenreich is from her book

Bright-Sided: How Positive Thinking Is Undermining America (Metropolitan Books, 2009). Richard Hofstadter's observations are from his *Anti-Intellectualism in American Life* (Alfred A. Knopf, 1962, 1963). The X song "I Must Not Think Bad Thoughts" appeared on the band's 1983 album, *More Fun in the New World*.

The quoted correspondence is from Christy Croft, written to me in an e-mail of March 5, 2012. I am grateful for her permission to quote from it, as well as for her broader insights into the ethical issues of positive thinking.

Gary Ward Materra is quoted from his dissertation, *Women in Early New Thought: Lives and Theology in Transition, From the Civil War to World War I* (Department of Religious Studies, UC Santa Barbara, 1997).

CHAPTER TWO:
POSITIVE NATION

Historian John K. Simmons highlighted the positive-thinking roots of popular advertising slogans in his "Christian Science and American Culture," *America's Alternative Religions* edited by Timothy Miller (State University of New York Press, 1995).

George Berkeley's passages are from his 1710 work *Principles of Human Knowledge* (Penguin Classics, 1988, 2004).

On the excesses of heroic medicine, and related topics in early American medicine, I have benefited from Wakoh Shannon Hickey's dissertation, *Mind Cure, Meditation, and Medicine: Hidden Histories of Mental Healing in the United States* (Department of Religion, Duke University, 2008). Also helpful on the issues of nineteenth-century American medicine are Materra (1997); *Other Healers: Unorthodox Medicine in America* edited by Norman Gevitz (Johns Hopkins University Press, 1988); and *Nature Cures: The History of Alternative Medicine in America* by James C. Whorton, Ph.D. (Oxford University Press, 2002), from which Benjamin Rush is quoted.

Of the many volumes that survey Phineas Quimby's life and writing, a uniquely helpful resource is Ronald A. Hughes's *Phineas Parkhurst Quimby: His Complete Writings and Beyond* (Phineas Parkhurst Quimby Resource Center, 2009); Hughes's collection identifies errors that have persisted in earlier collections. Also valuable is *The Complete Collected Works of Dr. Phineas Parkhurst Quimby* edited by Rev. Lux Newman and the Phineas Parkhurst Quimby Philosophical Society (Seed of Life Publishing, 2008, 2012). Quimby's recovery story is drawn from "My Conversion," January 1863, as published in *Phineas Parkhurst Quimby: The Complete Writings*, vol. 3, edited by Ervin Seale (DeVorss, 1988). Details on Quimby's life are also from a biographical treatment written by Quimby's son George and published in the March 1888 edition of *The New England Magazine*, as reprinted in the Belfast (ME) *Republican Journal* of January 10, 1889. Other aspects of Quimby's early career are drawn from commentary by Hughes (2009) and Seale (1988); *The Quimby Manuscripts* edited by Horatio Dresser (Thomas Y. Crowell, 1921, 2nd edition); and *The Philosophy of P. P. Quimby* by Annetta G. Dresser (Geo. H. Ellis, 1895).

A great deal has been written about Quimby in surveys of American religion and psychology, much of it drawn from the early work of Dresser and George Quimby; as covered elsewhere in these notes and in footnotes in the narrative, I have, wherever possible, corroborated early biographical information with period newspaper coverage and studies of the mental-healing and New Thought cultures, including the volumes *Spirits in Rebellion: The Rise and Development of New Thought* by Charles Braden (Southern Methodist University Press, 1963, 1987); *Each Mind a Kingdom: American Women, Sexual Purity, and the New Thought Movement, 1875–1920* by Beryl Satter (University of California Press, 1999); *History and Philosophy of Metaphysical Movements in America* by J. Stillson Judah (Westminster Press, 1967); and Hickey's above-referenced 2008 Duke dissertation. Also helpful are Robert Peel's seminal study, *Mary Baker Eddy: The Years of Trial* (Holt, Rinehart and Winston, 1971), and *Mind Cure in New England: From the Civil War to World War I* by Gail Thain Parker (University Press of New England, 1973). An important adjunct to these works is Donald Meyer's *The Positive Thinkers* (Wesleyan University Press, 1965, 1980, 1988), which provides a rigorous historical overview of the movement from a dissenting and critical perspective. For a thoughtful contemporary critique see Oliver

Burkeman's *The Antidote: Happiness for People Who Can't Stand Positive Thinking* (Faber & Faber, 2012).

The literature on Mesmerism is vast. The most valuable volumes in assembling this account were *The Discovery of the Unconscious: The History and Evolution of Dynamic Psychiatry* by Henri F. Ellenberger (Basic Books, 1970); *From Mesmer to Freud: Magnetic Sleep and the Roots of Psychoanalytic Healing* by Adam Crabtree (Yale University Press, 1993); *Abnormal Hypnotic Phenomena*, vols. 1–4, edited by Eric J. Dingwall (J. & A. Churchill/ Barnes & Noble, 1968); *A History of Hypnotism* by Alan Gauld (Cambridge University Press, 1992); *The Covert Enlightenment: Eighteenth-Century Counterculture and Its Aftermath* by Alfred J. Gabay (Swedenborg Foundation Publishers, 2005); *Franz Anton Mesmer: A History of Mesmerism* by Margaret Goldsmith (Doubleday, 1934); *Franz Anton Mesmer: Between God and the Devil* by James Wyckoff (Prentice-Hall, 1975); and *The Wizard from Vienna: Franz Anton Mesmer* by Vincent Buranelli (Coward, McCann & Geoghegan, 1975).

Mesmer himself wrote relatively little. His native language was German, and his public writings were in French and, less often, in Latin. A rare and valuable collection of Mesmer's written work is *Mesmerism: A Translation of the Original Scientific and Medical Writings of F. A. Mesmer* translated and compiled by George Bloch, Ph.D., introduced by E. R. Hilgard, Ph.D. (Walter Kaufman, 1980). Where I quote Mesmer, I used the Bloch collection, Ellenberger (1970), and Goldsmith (1934).

On the Franklin report, I have benefited from "Mesmerism and Revolutionary America" by Helmut Hirsch, *American-German Review,* October 1943, and *Mesmerism and the End of the Enlightenment in France* by Robert Darnton (Harvard University Press, 1968), which has valuable details on political attitudes toward Mesmerism. Also helpful were Anne Harrington's *The Cure Within: A History of Mind-Body Medicine* (Norton, 2008), and a translation of the commission's report by Charles and Danielle Salas published with an introduction by Michael Shermer as "Testing the Claims of Mesmer" in *Skeptic Magazine,* vol. 4, no. 3 (1996). Puységur's credo ("I believe in the existence within myself") is from Ellenberger (1970). Sources on the decline of Mesmerism in Europe include Darnton (1968), Gauld (1992), Ellenberger (1970), and Dingwall (1968).

On the careers of Charles Poyen and Robert J. Collyer, I am indebted to exchanges with historian Keith McNeil, who provided citations and transcriptions of the Belfast (ME) *Republican Journal* articles noted in the chapter. Where Poyen is quoted, it is from his memoir, *Progress of Animal Magnetism in New England* (Weeks, Jordan & Co., 1837). Sources on Poyen's life include "Charles Poyen Brings Mesmerism to America" by Eric R. Carlson, *Journal of the History of Medicine and Allied Sciences*, vol. 15, 1960; "How Southern New England Became Magnetic North" by Sheila O'Brien Quinn, *History of Psychology*, August 2007; and *The Heyday of Spiritualism* by Slater Brown (Hawthorn Books, 1970). The reference to Poyen being mistaken for an ex-slave is from *The Mad Forties* by Grace Adams and Edward Hutter (Harper & Brothers, 1942). On Robert H. Collyer's life I benefited from his book *Psychography* (Redding & Co., 1843), his memoir, *Lights and Shadows of American Life* (Brainard & Co., 1838, 1843), Dingwall (1968), and Gauld (1992).

The dates that Quimby encountered Poyen and Collyer can be elusive. Varying accounts, often published many years after the events in question, place Quimby at Mesmerist demonstrations in Maine in the years 1836 and 1838. It is well established that Charles Poyen made a presentation in Bangor in 1836, and Quimby, writing in his notes, places himself there. Less clear are references to an 1838 demonstration. Quimby's son and executor, George, writing in a biographical article about his father in the *New England Magazine* in 1888, placed Quimby at a Belfast demonstration "about the year 1838"—a date that historians frequently repeat. This may have resulted from a slip in George's memory (he was writing around fifty years after the fact). The next publicly noted demonstration of Mesmerism in Maine occurred in fall 1841, when the Belfast *Republican Journal* recorded visits from Robert H. Collyer in both September and October. Collyer also cited 1841 as the year he began his presentations. Quimby's notes recollect his seeing both Poyen and Collyer. Hence, Quimby witnessed the demonstrations of each man, respectively, in 1836 and 1841. The 1838 date, though widely repeated, appears in no public record.

No precise records show when Quimby and Lucius Burkmar started working together, but the intrepid researchers Ervin Seale and his collaborator Erroll Stafford Collie, in *Phineas Parkhurst Quimby: The Complete Writings*, vol. 1 (1988), turned up letters of introduction that show the two men traveling together by early November 1843. Horatio Dresser in *The Quimby Manuscripts* (1921) reprints an article from the *Bangor Democrat* (ME) in April 1843, that shows Quimby and Lucius, age seventeen, giving a demonstration, along with Lucius's twenty-three-year-old brother, Henry. It is not fully clear when Quimby stopped working with Lucius, but Seale's annotations indicate 1847. Lucius's extant journal writings about his experiences with Quimby conclude in 1845.

Quimby's quote "disease is in his belief" is from Dresser (1921). His reference to the cure being "not in the medicine" is from his letter to the *Portland Daily Advertiser* (ME), published February 14, 1862. His statement "why cannot I cure myself" appears in *Phineas Parkhurst Quimby: Revealer of Spiritual Healing to this Age* by Ann Ballew Hawkins (DeVorss, 1951) and in "True Origin of Christian Science," an unsigned article in the *New York Times*, July 10, 1904. Neither Hawkins nor the *Times* article have proven wholly reliable sources for quoted material, but the statement is closely echoed in Dresser's *The Quimby Manuscripts*. Quimby's statement "all science is a part of God" is from *The Complete Collected Works of Dr. Phineas Parkhurst Quimby* (2008, 2012). Quimby's statements on "false beliefs" and "our happiness" are from Dresser (1921). Arthur Vergara's "New Thought's Unfounded Foundation," *Creative Thought*, July 2011, directed me to Quimby's early use of the term "unconscious." For a full view of Quimby's use of the term, see Hughes (2009) and *The Complete Collected Works of Dr. Phineas Parkhurst Quimby* (2008, 2012).

Quimby's cure of the mayor of Bath, Maine, is from "Mary Baker G. Eddy," part 2, by Georgine Milmine, *McClure's Magazine*, February 1907. The Milmine series of articles is controversial; if approached cautiously it can provide useful historical portraiture. For the series background, see Gillian Gill's indispensable *Mary Baker Eddy* (Perseus/Radcliffe Biography Series, 1998). Quimby's reported cure of the woman who was unable to speak is from a transcribed letter of April 29, 1862, in the *Portland Daily Advertiser*, found in the archives of the Mary Baker Eddy Library for the Betterment of Humanity, Boston. Quimby's large number of patients is reported in "Warren Felt Evans, M.D.," by William J. Leonard, *Practical Ideals*, vol. 10, no. 2, September–October 1905. The article on his patients coming from "the four winds of heaven" is quoted from Dresser (1921).

The neighbor's recollection of Quimby in Belfast is from a testimonial dated January 14, 1907, by Charles C. Sargent, in the archives of the Mary Baker Eddy Library. Quimby's unsuccessful treatment was reported in a letter dated April 10, 1907, by Lydia P. French, also in the Mary Baker Eddy Library archives. These passages are quoted courtesy of the Mary Baker Eddy Library.

A rare biographical record of Warren Felt Evans appears in an early-twentieth-century series of articles by William J. Leonard in the journal *Practical Ideals*, starting with "The Pioneer Apostle of Mental Science," in vol. 6, no. 1, July–August 1903, and continuing with "Warren Felt Evans, M.D.," published in three parts: in vol. 10, no. 2, September–October 1905; vol. 10, no. 3, November 1905; and vol. 10, no. 4, December 1905. Unless otherwise indicated, Evans is quoted, as are his journal passages, from this series. Also helpful is the article "Warren F. Evans" by Robert Allen Campbell, *The Christian Metaphysician*, November 1888. I am grateful to historian Keith McNeil for providing these rare articles.

Swedenborg is quoted on the mind and body from his 1771 book, *The True Christian Religion*, English translation published by J. B. Lippincott, 1875. See Chapter 8 of this book for the full rendering of Swedenborg's statement. Evans's quote about the preexistence of disease is from his book *The Primitive Mind-Cure* (H. H. Carter & Co., 1885). Julius Dresser's 1876 recollection is from his pamphlet, *The True History of Mental Science* (1887).

On the life and career of Mary Baker Eddy key books include Gill

(1998); Satter (1999); *The Emergence of Christian Science in American Life* by Stephen Gottschalk (University of California Press, 1973); Robert Peel's three-volume biography, *Mary Baker Eddy*, published by Holt, Rinehart and Winston: *The Years of Discovery* (1966), *The Years of Trial* (1971), and *The Years of Authority* (1977); and Peel's *Christian Science: Its Encounter with American Culture* (Holt, 1958). Peel and Gottschalk were each affiliated with the Christian Science church, but their scholarship has proven independent-minded and impeccable. For an overview, I also benefited from the exhibits and resources at the Longyear Museum in Chestnut Hill, Massachusetts. Eddy is quoted about her father from her *Retrospection and Introspection* (1891, 1892, First Church of Christ, Scientist)

The Eddy-Dresser correspondence of 1866 appears in Peel (1966) and Gill (1998). Eddy's handwritten note is preserved in the archives of the Mary Baker Eddy Library.

Eddy's statement on evil is from her *Message to the Mother Church*, June 1901 (Rumford Press, 1902). Her reference to "material medicines" is from her *Miscellaneous Writings* (1896). Eddy's tribute to Quimby ("who healed with the truth that Christ taught") appeared in the *Lynn Weekly Reporter* (MA), February 14, 1866. Eddy's statement on "Quimbyism" is from Peel's *The Years of Discovery* (1966), which is also the source for Eddy's correspondence calling Evans a "half scientist."

Details on the Dresser family can be found in C. Alan Anderson's doctoral thesis, *Horatio Dresser and the Philosophy of New Thought* (Department of Philosophy, Boston University, 1963). Anderson provides rare and important source material on the life of Horatio Dresser, whom he depicts, with persuasiveness, as a notable philosopher. For Horatio Dresser's analysis of New Thought and related movements, see his essay collection, *Voices of Freedom* (G. P. Putnam's Sons, 1899). Anderson himself was an impassioned and thoughtful scholar of New Thought; he passed away in 2012. His essays on the history of New Thought can be found at www.NewEveryMoment.com.

The career of Edward J. Arens is considered in J. Gordon Melton's important article "The Case of Edward J. Arens and the Distortion of the History of New Thought," *Journal for the Society of the Study of Metaphysical Religion* (hereafter cited as JSSMR), Spring 1996. The *Journal for the Society of the Study of Metaphysical Religion* was the sole scholarly journal dedicated to the study of New Thought. Its twenty volumes, published from spring 1995 to fall 2004, gathered some of the finest historical study and criticism of this metaphysical movement, whose impact and history have generally been underappreciated in academia. The journal's tenure was too short and its availability today is unfortunately limited. I am very grateful to its founding editor, Dell deChant, for lending me his very rare complete set.

Andrew Jackson Davis's reference to a "Divine Positive Mind" is from his 1847 book, *The Principles of Nature, Her Divine Revelations, and a Voice to Mankind*, a massive and sprawling channeled work that briefly gained considerable popularity.

Eddy's charge of "ignorant Mesmerist" typifies the byzantine polemics of this debate. Historian Horatio Dresser repeated this charge—e.g., in the journals *The Arena* of May 1899 and *Unity* of March 1906, and again in his 1919 book *A History of the New Thought Movement*. Eddy used the phrase once in a private letter to Unitarian minister James Henry Wiggin on January 15, 1886. It is not clear whether Dresser would have seen this letter. Likewise, important historical works, such as Charles Braden's *Spirits in Rebellion*, suggest that Eddy called Quimby a "mere Mesmerist." The sources again are unclear.

Eddy is further quoted on Quimby from her self-published pamphlets *Historical Sketch of Metaphysical Healing* (1885) and *Historical Sketch of Christian Science Mind-Healing* (1890).

Horatio Dresser's handwritten letters of February 3, 1900, to Mary Baker Eddy, and January 15 and February 3, 1900, to Judge Hanna, are in the archive of the Mary Baker Eddy Library. They are quoted courtesy of the Mary Baker Eddy Library.

George Quimby's guardedness about his father's manuscripts is depicted in "The Story of the Real Mrs. Eddy," *Human Life*, April 1907, one article of a thirteen-part series that Sibyl Wilbur wrote on Eddy for *Human Life* magazine from December 1906 to December 1907. Horatio Dresser also alludes to his long efforts to gain access to Quimby's writings in *The Quimby Manuscripts* (1921). Valuable details about this appear in Gill (1998).

Eddy's quote "I re-arranged a few" is from her *Mind-Healing: Historical Sketch* (1888). George Quimby's observation about Eddy sitting with Quimby is from Dresser's *The Quimby Manuscripts* (1921). The *New York Times* published its unsigned assessment of Eddy as "True Origin of Christian Science," July 10, 1904. My conclusion about the article mislabeling Eddy's preface as Quimby's own is from a comparison of transcribed manuscripts in the Mary Baker Eddy Library to the *New York Times* analysis. Specifically, a transcription of a Quimby manuscript acquired by the archive in 1941 shows the preface with the tagline "Mary M. Glover," the name Eddy used in 1868. Gillian Gill (1998) notes: "It is also accepted by all that by 1868 Mrs. Glover had appended to this text a signed preface of her own . . ."

CHAPTER THREE:
"TO REDEEM DEFEAT BY NEW THOUGHT"

Any study of Emma Curtis Hopkins must begin, as mine did, with J. Gordon Melton's seminal article, "New Thought's Hidden History: Emma Curtis Hopkins, Forgotten Founder," JSSMR, Spring 1995. (For alternate viewpoints see "Quimby as Founder of New Thought" by C. Alan Anderson, JSSMR, Spring 1997, Arthur Vergara's "New Thought's Accidental Acquisition," *Creative Mind*, June 2011, and "New Thought's Unfounded Foundation," *Creative Mind*, July 2011.) Also important are Satter (1998); Gill (1998); Braden (1963, 1987); Materra (1997); Peel (1971); Gottschalk (1973); and *Emma Curtis Hopkins: Forgotten Founder of New Thought* by Gail M. Harley (Syracuse University Press, 2002). Harley is particularly strong on Hopkins's final years. On the social atmosphere of Hopkins's career see "Christian Science and the Nineteenth Century Women's Movement" by Gage William Chapel, JSSMR, Spring 2000.

Hopkins's report of a "late serious illness" is from a letter of December 12, 1883, quoted from Harley (2002). Hopkins's letter of January 14, 1884, is from Peel (1971). Hopkins's letters of August 16, 1884, and her undated letter ("I received a peremptory message") are from Harley (2002). Her letter of November 4, 1885, is from Peel (1971). Gottschalk (1973) called my attention to Hopkins's article "God's Omnipresence," which appeared in The Journal of Christian Science, April 1884.

Materra is quoted from his 1997 dissertation, Women in Early New Thought. The numbers of female Christian Science practitioners are from Rolling Away the Stone: Mary Baker Eddy's Challenge to Materialism by Stephen Gottschalk (Indiana University Press, 2006, 2011).

Hopkins's attacks on A. J. Swarts are reported in Peel (1971), Braden (1963, 1987), and Harley (2002). Hopkins and Swarts are announced as joint editors of Mental Science Magazine and Mind Cure Journal in the March 18, 1886, issue of The Index: A Weekly Paper, a progressive journal connected with the Unitarian-Universalist movement.

For information on Hopkins's husband and son I drew on Harley (2002), New Hampshire Death and Burial Records, and the 1906 Manchester (NH) City Directory.

On Hopkins's spiritual outlook and her relationship with Mary H. Plunkett I benefited from Gill (1998), Harley (2002), Satter (1999), Peel (1971), and Gottschalk (1973). Hopkins is quoted from her Class Lessons 1888 compiled and edited by Elizabeth C. Bogart (DeVorss, 1977). Hopkins's final letter to Eddy on Christmas of 1886 is from Peel (1971).

I am indebted to Charles Braden's Christian Science Today: Power, Policy, Practice (Southern Methodist University Press, 1958) for directing me to Eddy's rule-tightening after Hopkins's departure. Eddy is quoted from there and from the April 1888 Christian Science Journal.

The testimonial of Hopkins's student ("her instruction not only gives understanding") appears in Braden (1963, 1987), who is quoting an unsigned 1889 article in the Fillmores' first journal, Modern Thought; the writer may be Charles Fillmore. The other student tribute ("her brilliance of mind and spirit") appeared in Unity in 1925 and is quoted from the foreword to a reissue of Hopkins's Scientific Christian Mental Practice (1888), as published in 1958 by the High Watch Fellowship, an organization founded by Hopkins's sister, Estelle Carpenter. In 1940 High

Watch Farm became an addiction-recovery retreat center based on the principles of Alcoholics Anonymous, which it remains today.

Margery Fox is quoted from Materra (1997). Chapel is quoted from "Christian Science and the Nineteenth Century Women's Movement" (JSSMR, Spring 2000). Also very helpful on nineteenth-century medicine and women is Ann Braude's groundbreaking study, *Radical Spirits: Spiritualism and Women's Rights in Nineteenth-Century America* (Indiana University Press, 1989, 2001), from which Braude is quoted. The quotations from Hopkins's seminary graduation appeared in Melton's article "New Thought's Hidden History" (1995). Melton is quoted on the numbers of Hopkins's female students from *Perspectives on the New Age* edited by James R. Lewis and J. Gordon Melton (State University of New York Press, 1992).

Emerson published his essay "Success" in 1870 in his collection *Society and Solitude*. The essay actually had its earliest roots in an address called "The Spirit of the Times," which Emerson began delivering in the late 1840s. He revised it in the early 1850s into a talk called "The Law of Success"; by the end of the decade, Emerson settled on the simple title "Success."

I am grateful to historian Keith McNeil for providing me with a very rare copy of William Henry Holcombe's pamphlet, *Condensed Thoughts About Christian Science* (Purdy Publishing, 1887).

The Hartford New Thought Convention is referenced in Judah (1967) and Braden (1963, 1987) and is covered in the April 1899 issue of *Mind* magazine. The Boston convention is noted in the aforementioned books and in Dresser (1919). The 1899 Boston proceedings were published by the International Metaphysical League, with the asterisk and note next to Charles Fillmore's name. The relationship between Fillmore and the International New Thought Alliance, and Fillmore's writing on the matter, are noted in *The Household of Faith: The Story of Unity* by James Dillet Freeman (Unity School of Christianity, 1951) and *The Unity Movement: Its Evolution and Spiritual Teachings* by Neal Vahle (Templeton Foundation Press, 2002).

Hopkins's 1919 correspondence of September 16 and November 20 was addressed to New York socialite and arts patron Mabel Dodge Luhan;

it is quoted from Harley (2002). Ella Wheeler Wilcox is quoted from her book *The Heart of the New Thought* (Psychic Research Company, 1902).

CHAPTER FOUR:
FROM POVERTY TO POWER

Court trials involving Christian Science treatments began to uptick in 1888. A judicious consideration of this period is found in Charles Braden's *Christian Science Today* (1958).

William James's quote about "fanatics and one-sided geniuses" is from *William James: In the Maelstrom of the American Modernism* by Robert D. Richardson (Houghton Mifflin, 2006). James's statement about an "impediment in the minds of people" is from *Genuine Reality: A Life of William James* by Linda Simon (University of Chicago Press, 1998). His letter about "fondness or non-fondness for mind-curers" is from *The Works of William James: Essays, Comments, and Reviews* edited by Frederick H. Burkhardt, Fredson Bowers, and Ignas K. Skrupskelis (Harvard University Press, 1987). James's letters to the *Boston Evening Transcript* of 1894 and his legislative address of 1898 appear in *The Works of William James* (1987). The passage deriding James's support for "quackery" originally ran in the *Philadelphia Medical Journal* and was reprinted in the *Boston Medical and Surgical Journal* of March 17, 1898. On the events before the committee, I benefited from the following: *William James: His Life and Thought* by Gerald E. Myers (Yale University Press, 1987); "'The Facts Are Patent and Startling': WJ and Mental Healing," parts 1 and 2, by John T. Matteson, *Streams of William James*, Spring and Summer 2002; *Pox: An American History* by Michael Willrich (Penguin Press, 2011); and coverage in the *Boston Globe* of March 3, 1898, which includes an illustration of crowds gathered outside the packed committee room.

On the proliferation of licensing laws in the 1890s, I benefited from *American Medicine in Transition, 1840–1910* by John S. Haller Jr. (University of Illinois Press, 1981). Sources on the improvement of medical care include "Richard Cabot: Medical Reformer During the Progressive Era" by T. Andrew Dodds, *Annals of Internal Medicine*, September 1, 1993; *The Social*

Transformation of American Medicine by Paul Starr (Basic Books, 1984); and *Medical Licensing in America, 1650–1965* by Richard Harrison Shryock (Johns Hopkins Press, 1967), from which I drew upon the survey of Tennessee doctors.

Charles Thomas Hallinan is quoted from "My 'New-Thought' Boyhood," *The Living Age*, March 5, 1921.

On the life of Frances Lord, I benefited from Kathi Kern's study *Mrs. Stanton's Bible* (Cornell University Press, 2001), which fills in several historical gaps and thoughtfully analyzes the intermingling of the suffragist and New Thought movements. I also benefited from an article on Lord in *The Women's Suffrage Movement: A Reference Guide, 1866–1928* by Elizabeth Crawford (University College of London Press, 1999). Also helpful were Satter (1999) and Gail M. Harley's article on Emma Curtis Hopkins in *Women Building Chicago, 1790–1990: A Biographical Dictionary* edited by Rima Lunin Schultz and Adele Hast (Indiana University Press, 2001). Stanton is quoted from Kern (2001) and from Stanton's biography, *Eighty Years and More, 1815–1897: Reminiscences of Elizabeth Cady Stanton* (European Publishing Company, 1898). On the life of Lord, I also benefited from Deirdre Mitchell's paper, "New Thinking, New Thought, New Age: The Theology and Influence of Emma Curtis Hopkins (1849–1925)," *Counterpoints: The Flinders University Online Journal of Interdisciplinary Conference Papers* (July 2002).

Prentice Mulford originally published his series of essays as "The White Cross Library"; he wrote them from 1886 until his death in 1891. Publisher F. J. Needham collected the essays as *Your Forces, And How to Use Them*, issued in six volumes from 1890 to 1892 (the last volume appeared posthumously). *Your Forces, And How to Use Them* comprises 74 essays; in later editions the publisher removed from volume 3 a verse work, "Voice of the Mountain," and added to each of the volumes a short prefatory work, "God" (which appears to have been written by Mulford but it is unclear). Mulford's initial use of the phrase "thoughts are things" is from his 1886 essay "You Travel When You Sleep," which opens volume 1 of *Your Forces*.

On the life of Prentice Mulford, I benefited from the essay "About

Prentice Mulford," which appeared in the last volume of *Your Forces*; it combined Mulford's autobiographical reflections with the biographical notes of others. Of further help was "Passing of Prentice Mulford" by Charles Warren Stoddard, *National Magazine*, September 1906, from which Mulford's journal passages are quoted. Also helpful was the same author's article "Prentice Mulford, the New Gospeler," from the *National Magazine* of April 1905, which is quoted regarding Mulford's Thoreau-like traits. For Mulford's own recollection of the period I quote from his autobiographical essay in *Your Forces*. On Mulford's New Jersey experiences, I quote from his memoir *The Swamp Angel* (F. J. Needham, 1888), which Mulford wrote as his equivalent of *Walden*. Mulford's quotes on Spiritualism are from "The Invisible in Our Midst," a series of sketches for *The Golden Era*, written from December 1869 to March 1870; they are reprinted in the rare *Prentice Mulford's California Sketches*, edited and with an introduction by Franklin Walker (Book Club of California, 1935). On Mulford's interest in Spiritualism I greatly benefited from Walker's *San Francisco's Literary Frontier* (Alfred A. Knopf, 1939). I am grateful for Enoch Anderson's foreword to a reissue of Mulford's 1889 *Life by Land and Sea* (Santa Ana River Press, 2004), a memoir of his whaling and mining years; Anderson provides an excellent overview of Mulford's San Francisco days and early life. Also helpful is a section on Mulford in *The American Idea of Success* by Richard M. Huber (Pushcart Press, 1971, 1987). William James's letter on Mulford is from Myers (1987). The *New York Times* reported Mulford's death in "It Was Prentice Mulford: Sheepshead Bay's Mystery Was Solved Yesterday," June 1, 1891.

Helen Wilmans recounted her personal story in her books, *A Search for Freedom* (Freedom Publishing Company, 1898) and *The Conquest of Poverty* (International Scientific Association, 1899); she is quoted from these sources. On Wilmans's life I benefited from the work of Satter (1999) and Materra (1997); I quote Wilmans's letter of August 31, 1907, from the latter's work. Other sources include coverage of the Wilmans court cases in Dresser (1919); in the articles "A Blow to Mental Science: Post Office Will Hold All Mail of a Florida Healer, Under the Fraud Order,"

New York Times, October 6, 1901, and "Helen Wilmans, the Conqueror," by Frederic W. Burry, The Balance, January 1908; and in Wilmans's personal statement of defense, "My Soul's Belief," The Balance, May 1907.

Key sources on James Allen are "James Allen: A Memoir" by Lily L. Allen, The Epoch, February–March 1912 (this was the magazine that the Allens originally published as The Light of Reason); and James Allen & Lily L. Allen: An Illustrated Biography, by John Woodcock (Sun Publishing, 2007), a valuable codex to Allen's life. William Allen ("I'll make a scholar out of you") is quoted from The Epoch (1912). Allen's quote "The man who says, 'My religion is true'" is from his posthumous 1912 work Light on Life's Difficulties. Lily Allen's statement "He never wrote theories" is from her introduction to Allen's posthumous 1913 work, Foundation Stones to Happiness and Success. Allen's statement "thoroughness is genius" is from his 1904 Byways of Blessedness. The quote from the Ilfracombe Chronicle obituary is from Woodcock (2007). Dale Carnegie is quoted from How to Stop Worrying and Start Living (Simon & Schuster, 1944). Bob Smith's interest in As a Man Thinketh is noted in Dr. Bob and His Library by Dick B. (Paradise Research Publications, 1992, 1994, 1998). For Marcus Garvey's interest in New Thought see my Occult America (2009). Michael Jackson's comment is from "Radnor Family Had Inside Look at Michael Jackson" by Patti Mengers, Delaware County Daily Times (PA), June 28, 2009. Curtis Martin's reference to Allen appeared in "Hobbled Martin Practices and Is Probable for Patriots," by Gerald Eskenazi, New York Times, September 14, 2002. Stedman Graham is quoted from "Stedman Graham Tells How to Achieve Personal Freedom" by Shannon Barbour, New Pittsburgh Courier, June 12, 1999.

A work as famous as As a Man Thinketh would seem to have an easily verifiable date of first publication, but sources conflict. Various records use the years 1902 or 1904. I have cited 1903, which represents the earliest verifiable year of publication based on records from the James Allen Archive at the Ilfracombe Library in Devon, England. Savoy Publishing Company of London issued it that year. Another historical complexity in Allen's life is the precise date when his father, William, reached New York. Lily Allen pegged William's arrival, and subsequent murder, to when James was age fifteen, which he turned on November 28, 1879. Passenger ship records show two men named William Allen reaching New York from the United Kingdom in that year: one, age forty, arrived from Liverpool on April 28, and another, age forty-seven, arrived from ports in Scotland and Ireland on November 1. The latter arrival better fits the time frame that Lily provided. The matter of exactly when William arrived requires further historical research.

Wallace D. Wattles's *The Science of Getting Rich* appeared at number one on the *BusinessWeek* paperback bestseller list on September 10, 2007. Sources on Wallace D. Wattles include these articles from the *Fort Wayne Sentinel*: "Leaves the Methodists," June 27, 1900; "News Paragraphs," June 13, 1908; "Totals on District Vote," November 15, 1908; "Trouble at Elwood," July 12, 1909; and "Indiana Socialist Dies," February 8, 2011. "Hoosier Writer Is Dead" appeared in the *Indianapolis Star*, February 9, 1911. His daughter, Florence Wattles, appears in "Says Even Dead Voted in Recent Elwood Election," January 29, 1911, *Indianapolis Star* (from which she is quoted), and "Woman Socialist Speaks to Kendallville Audience," July 12, 1911, *Fort Wayne Journal-Gazette*. Eugene V. Debs is quoted from *The Other American: The Life of Michael Harrington* by Maurice Isserman (Public Affairs, 2000).

Sources on Elizabeth Towne include "The Literature of 'New Thoughters,'" by Frances Maule Björkman, *The World's Work*, January 1910, from which I quote Towne's reply to "A Weakling"; also "Elizabeth Towne: Pioneering Woman in Publishing and Politics" by Tzivia Gover, *Historical Journal of Massachusetts*, vol. 37, Spring 2009; *Genealogical and Personal Memoirs Relating to the Families of the State of Massachusetts*, vol. 3, edited by William Richard Cutter and William Frederick Adams (Lewis Historical Publishing Company, 1910); "Elizabeth Towne, Author, Leader in Religion, Dies" by the Associated Press, *North Adams Transcript*, June 1, 1960; *Experiences in Self-Healing* by Elizabeth Towne (Elizabeth Towne Publishing Company, 1905); and Materra (1997); Satter (1999); and Parker (1973).

On the topic of New Thought and Marcus Garvey I am indebted to the work of UCLA historian Robert A. Hill. Hill has painstakingly assembled and annotated the invaluable *Marcus Garvey and Universal Negro Improvement Association Papers* for the University of California Press. Volumes 1 (1983) and 7 (1990), in particular, trace Garvey's connections to New Thought. Hill's volume with Barbara Bair, *Marcus Garvey Life and Lessons* (University of California Press, 1987), is also of great value. As noted above, I further consider Garvey and New Thought in *Occult America* (2009).

Rev. Al Sharpton is quoted from the *New York Times* feature column Sunday Routine: "Al Sharpton: The Wake-Up Is a Victory" by David M. Halbfinger, March 6, 2011.

The most complete study of Father Divine's connection to New Thought is Ronald Moran White's master's thesis, "New Thought Influences on Father Divine" (Department of Religion, Miami University, Oxford, Ohio, 1980). Jill Watts's biography, *God, Harlem U.S.A.: The Father Divine Story* (University of California Press, 1992) is invaluable as a measured and reliable overview of Father Divine's life. Also helpful are accounts of Father Divine in *These Also Believe: A Study of Modern American Cults and Minority Religious Movements* by Charles Braden (Macmillan, 1949), and *They Have Found a Faith* by Marcus Bach (Bobbs-Merrill, 1946). Braden and Bach, two of the twentieth century's most thoughtful observers of nontraditional religions, were among the very few journalists who grasped Father Divine's ties to New Thought. Father Divine is quoted ("this table is but the outer expression") from White (1980). For further information on Baird T. Spalding see my *Occult America* (2009). Of Walter C. Lanyon's many books, those most directly influenced by Father Divine are *It Is Wonderful* (E. K. Reader, 1931), *The Eyes of the Blind* (L. N. Fowler, 1932; Inspiration House, 1959), and *Behold the Man* (L. N. Fowler, 1933). Union Life Ministries reissued several of Lanyon's books in 1977, including *The Eyes of the Blind*. A "publisher's preface" replaces Lanyon's original forewords to the 1931 and 1959 editions, in which Lanyon acknowledged the influence of Father Divine and attributed italicized portions of the book to him. The elimination of those forewords obfuscates a critical link in New Thought history. The anti-Bilbo hymn appears in Braden

(1949). Robert Collier's statement "Mind is God" is from his *The Secret of Gold* (1927).

Louis Schneider and Sanford M. Dornbusch are quoted from their book, *Popular Religion: Inspirational Books in America* (University of Chicago Press, 1958). Actor Sherman Hemsley is profiled in "Don't Ask How He Lives or What He Believes In" by Dwight Whitney, *TV Guide*, February 6, 1982. For additional background on *The Kybalion* see my *Occult America* (2009) and *The Kybalion: The Definitive Edition* by William Walker Atkinson writing as Three Initiates, edited and introduced by Philip Deslippe (Tarcher/Penguin, 2008).

CHAPTER FIVE:
HAPPY WARRIORS

Horatio Dresser is quoted from his *A History of the New Thought Movement* (Thomas Y. Crowell, 1919). William James is quoted from his lecture and essay "The Gospel of Relaxation," first published in *Talks to Teachers on Psychology: And to Students on Some of Life's Ideals* (Henry Holt and Co., 1899). Emma Curtis Hopkins is quoted from her *Class Lessons 1888* (1977). Quimby is quoted from *The Quimby Manuscripts* (1921). Wilcox is quoted from her *The Heart of the New Thought* (1902). For Protestant attitudes toward spiritual healing see "Medicine and Christianity in the Modern World" by Ronald L. Numbers and Ronald C. Sawyer from *Health/Medicine and the Faith Traditions* edited by Martin E. Marty and Kenneth L. Vaux (Fortress Press, 1982).

On the career of Richard C. Cabot, I benefited from Ian S. Evison's doctoral dissertation, *Pragmatism and Idealism in the Professions: The Case of Richard Clarke Cabot* (University of Chicago Divinity School, 1995). In an age when academic specialization has sequestered too much scholarship behind inscrutable terminology and ever-narrowing topic areas (trends that Cabot himself foresaw), Evison's study is a marvel of clarity across a wide breadth of subjects. Also of significant help were "The Conceptual Underpinnings of Social Work in Health Care" by Sarah Gehlert from *Handbook of Health Social Work* edited by Sarah Gehlert and Teri Arthur Browne (John Wiley & Sons, 2006); "The Emmanuel Movement, 1906–1929," by John Gardner Greene, *New England Quarterly*, September 1934; " 'A Bold Plunge into the Sea of Values'; The Career of Dr. Richard Cabot" by Laurie O'Brien, *New England Quarterly*, vol. 58, no. 4, December 1985; "Richard Cabot: Medical Reformer During the Progressive Era" by T. Andrew Dodds, M.D., M.P.H., *Annals of Internal Medicine*, September 1, 1993; and "Clinical Pastoral Education" by Rodney J. R. Stokoe, *Nova Scotia Medical Bulletin*, vol. 53, 1974. William James's statement on the "cash-value" of an idea is from his "Philosophical Conceptions and Practical Results," *University Chronicle*, vol. 1, no. 4, September 1898. James's article is the text of a talk he delivered on August 28, 1898, at the Philosophical Union of UC Berkeley, where he outlined his philosophy of pragmatism; the event is worthy of a book in itself. Cabot's statement on "a thousand pities" is from Evison (1995). Cabot's statements on "moral or spiritual" diseases, and his passage on "functional" versus "organic" disease, are from his *Psychotherapy and Its Relation to Religion* (Moffat, Yard & Company, 1908). Cabot's book was one of a series of titles on medicine and religion published as a project of the Emmanuel Movement. Ted Kaptchuk is quoted from "Why Placebos Work Wonders" by Shirley S. Wang, *Wall Street Journal*, January 3, 2012. Charles Dean Young is quoted from his article "The Emmanuel Movement," *Boston Medical and Surgical Journal*, February 18, 1909. Both Freud and William James are quoted from Nathan G. Hale's *Freud and the Americans* (Oxford University Press, 1971). Peter D. Kramer is quoted from his *Freud: Inventor of the Modern Mind* (HarperCollins, 2006). On Cabot's advocacy of pastoral clinical training I benefited from Stokoe (1974) and from the outstanding dissertation *From Jewish Science to Rabbinical Counseling: The Evaluation of the Relationship Between Religion and Health by the American Reform Rabbinate, 1916–1954*, by Rebecca Trachtenberg Alpert (Department of Philosophy, Temple University, 1978). Carl J. Scherzer is quoted from his article, "The Emmanuel Movement," *Pastoral Psychology*, vol. 2, no. 11, February 1951. The survey of healing practices among

Protestant ministers is detailed in Charles S. Braden's "Study of Spiritual Healing in the Churches," *Pastoral Psychology*, May 1954.

For a movement so relatively small, Jewish Science has inspired a secondary literature of considerable quality. Of great help was Rebecca Trachtenberg Alpert's previously cited doctoral thesis (1978). Equally indispensable was *From Christian Science to Jewish Science: Spiritual Healing and American Jews* by Ellen M. Umansky (Oxford University Press, 2005); Umansky dedicates significant study to the career of Tehilla Lichtenstein, a key figure in the history of Jewish Science, whose life I am limited by space from exploring further here. Also of help were "Unity in Zion: A Survey of American Jewish Metaphysical Movements" by Richard L. Hoch, JSSMR, Fall 1995; and "Christian Science and the Jews" by John J. Appel, *Jewish Social Studies*, April 1969. Rabbi Maurice H. Harris is quoted from *Central Conference of American Rabbis Yearbook 1927*, vol. 37, edited by Rabbi Isaac E, Marcuson (CCAR, 1927). Rabbi Alfred Geiger Moses published two versions of his *Jewish Science*, the first in 1916 and a longer revision in 1920, from which I quote. The 1925 resolution on the founding of the Witt committee and the comments of Rabbi Philip Waterman are from Alpert (1978). Rabbi Louis Witt's committee report and personal testimony of June 26, 1927, are quoted from the *Central Conference of American Rabbis Yearbook* (1927), as cited above. For purposes of clarity, I made a few minor punctuation changes to the transcript of Witt's talk. On the progress of pastoral training, I am again indebted to Alpert (1978), who is quoted from her thesis. Also helpful are the historical notes of Rev. Robert Leas at the website of the Association for Clinical Pastoral Education (www.acpe.edu/cpehistory.htm). My references to pastoral counseling among military chaplains are from *A History of Pastoral Care in America* by E. Brooks Holifield (Wipf & Stock, 1983).

A vast amount of literature exists on the founding of Alcoholics Anonymous. It is a tribute to the integrity that Bill Wilson brought to AA that the "approved literature" issued by the AA General Service Conference, rather than having the intellectual vacuity of most official publications, is surprisingly open about Wilson and Smith's spiritual experiments, including their forays into Spiritualism, séances, mysticism, and Bill's experiments with LSD. In her biography, *My Name Is Bill* (Washington Square Press, 2004), Susan Cheever ably notes elements of Bill's life that are not included in the official literature, such as his struggles with depression and marital fidelity.

Important AA-approved literature includes *Pass It On: The Story of Bill Wilson and How the AA Message Reached the World* (Alcoholics Anonymous World Services, 1984), and *Dr. Bob and the Good Oldtimers* (Alcoholics Anonymous World Services, 1980). Also helpful is the pamphlet "Three Talks to Medical Societies" by Bill W. (Alcoholics Anonymous World Services, undated), from which I quote Bill on his awakening experience from a 1958 address to the New York Medical Society on Alcoholism. This talk also contains Bill's remark that he "devoured" the work of William James. Bill referred to James as an AA founder in *Bill W.: My First 40 Years* (Hazelden, 2000). Bill's reference to Jung's influence is from his letter of January 23, 1961. I have benefited from Lois Wilson's recollections in *Lois Remembers* (Al-Anon Family Group Headquarters, 1979), which is helpful on the Wilsons' split with the Oxford Group. Lois also notes that Emma Curtis Hopkins's family farm, High Watch, became an AA-based treatment center in 1940, a topic that deserves more attention than I am able to give it here. Also helpful on Lois's upbringing in the Swedenborgian Church is *Wings & Roots: The New Age and Emanuel Swedenborg in Dialog* by Wilma Wake (J. Appleseed & Co., 1999), from which Lois is quoted.

The Oxford Group and, more particularly, Frank Buchman remain a source of controversy. An important critique of Buchman and Oxford appears in Tom Driberg's *The Mystery of Moral Re-Armament* (Secker and Warburg, 1964), which reprinted the 1936 *New York World-Telegram* piece containing Buchman's infamous quotes. Important as his book was, Driberg, a British Labour MP, was deeply critical of the Oxford Movement. Any writer or researcher approaching Buchman's life and Oxford's influence on AA must cast a broader net. The works of Dick B., a contemporary historian who has doggedly catalogued the spiritual roots of AA, are a helpful window on Oxford's influence and its innovative spiritual program. Dick B.'s works include Dr. Bob and His Library (Paradise Research Publications, 1992, 1994, 1998); The Books Early AAs Read for Spiritual Growth (Paradise Research Publications, 1993, 1998); and the comprehensive Turning Point: A History of Early AA's Spiritual Roots and Successes (Paradise Research Publications, 1997), from which I quote Bill Wilson's recollections of the encounter between Rowland Hazard and Carl Jung. Also helpful on the Oxford Group is Charles Braden's These Also Believe (1949).

Additional sources on the history of AA include New Wine: The Spiritual Roots of the Twelve Step Miracle by Mel B. (Hazelden, 1991); Not-God: A History of Alcoholics Anonymous by Ernest Kurtz (Hazelden, 1979, 1991); AA: The Way It Began by Bill Pittman (Glen Abbey Books, 1988); AA's Godparents: Carl Jung, Emmet Fox, Jack Alexander by Igor I. Sikorsky Jr. (CompCare Publishers, 1990); and Ebby: The Man Who Sponsored Bill W. by Mel B. (Hazelden, 1998). I benefited from the reissued 1939 first edition of Alcoholics Anonymous, published by Anonymous Press, and the fourth edition of the "Big Book" published by AA.

Except where noted, Glenn Clark is quoted from his autobiography, A Man's Reach (Macalester Park Publishing Company), originally issued in 1949 and published posthumously with an epilogue by Marcia Brown in 1977. Charles Braden's Spirits in Rebellion (1963, 1987) considers the careers of Clark and F. L. Rawson. Bob Smith's affinity for Clark and Camps Farthest Out appears in Dr. Bob and His Library (1992, 1994, 1998). Clark's comments on Mussolini and appeasement are from his essay "Let Us Fight Hitler with Power," Clear Horizons, September 1940. Also helpful is J. Gordon Melton's article on Clark from Religious Leaders of America, second edition, edited by Melton (Gale Group, 1999).

Sources on Ernest Holmes include Neal Vahle's important biography Open at the Top (Open View Press, 1991); Ernest Holmes: His Life Times by Fenwicke Holmes (Dodd, Mead, 1970); In His Company: Ernest Holmes Remembered by Marilyn Leo (M Leo Presents, 2006); Gordon Melton's biographical article in Religious Leaders of America (1999); and Ernest Holmes: The First Religious Scientist by James Reid (Science of Mind Publications, undated). For an

overview of Holmes's religious development, see Arthur Vergara's series of historical articles published in the Cornerstone column of the
2011 and 2012 issues of *Creative Mind* magazine. On Fenwicke Holmes's
securities scandal see these *New York Times* articles: "Pastor Fights Suit to
Stop Stock Sale," May 3, 1929; "Pastor Fights Ward Move," May 9, 1929;
"Fenwicke Holmes Subpoena Vacated," May 15, 1929; "Court Finds Pastor Sold Bogus Stock," July 4, 1929; "Stock Fraud Bureau Finds W. H.
Holmes," July 11, 1929; "Minister's Tactics in Stock Deal Told," February
1, 1930; "F. L. Holmes Church Loses 4 Trustees," February 6, 1930; "Pas-
tor Is Indicted in Sale of Stock," March 19, 1930; "F. L. Holmes Leaves
Church Pending Trial," March 24, 1930; "F. L. Holmes Case May 28,"
May 13, 1930. Also on Fenwicke Holmes see "Pastor Grilled About His
Stock Sales to Flock," *Chicago Daily Tribune*, February 1, 1930. *High and Low
Financiers*, cited in the chapter, was published by Bobbs-Merrill in 1932.
Joseph Campbell's recollection is from *A Fire in the Mind: The Life of Joseph
Campbell* by Stephen and Robin Larsen (Doubleday, 1991). For a further
perspective on Fenwicke see Jesse G. Jennings's article "Finding Fen-
wicke," *Science of Mind*, August 2008, and Jennings's introduction to *The
Science of Mind: The Definitive Edition* (Tarcher/Penguin, 2010). For Barry Zito's
and Yolanda King's interest in Ernest Holmes see my interviews with
them in, respectively, the September 2003 and April 2005 issues of *Science
of Mind*.

The phrases noted from Christian D. Larson's work appear in *The Ideal
Made Real* (Progress Company, 1909), with the exception of "be all that
you can be," which is found in *Your Forces and How to Use Them* (Progress
Company, 1910). Sources on Larson's background and career include the
transcript of a 1940 interview/oral history that Larson gave to Maude
Allison Lathem—a literary collaborator to Ernest Holmes—as part of an
"Extension Course in the Science of Mind" offered by Holmes's Institute
of Religious Science. Also helpful are two highly engaging profiles: "The
Living Legacy of Christian D. Larson" by Mark Gilbert, *Science of Mind*,
October 2011, and "*The Pathway of Roses* and Christian D. Larson's Jour-
ney in New Thought" by Jessica Hatchigan, which appeared in *Science*

of *Mind*, April 2005, and was reprinted in a reissue of Larson's *The Path-way of Roses* the same year by DeVorss. Also see "The Literature of 'New Thoughters,'" by Frances Maule Björkman, *The World's Work*, January 1910. Progress Company's involuntary bankruptcy is reported in "Progress Company in Bankruptcy," *The Inland Printer* (Chicago), September 1911. In her history paper, Lathem reports that "the plant burned to the ground"; in the same oral history Larson described relocating to Los Angeles in August 1911. Also in that interview Larson identified the circulation of his magazine as 250,000—a remarkable figure but one that squares with the overall finances of his company. Sorting through Larson's trail of copyright registrations and re-registrations entailed reviewing U.S. copyright data, library catalogue entries, publishing trade notices, and various editions of his books. In July 1912, *The Editor*, a literary trade journal, noted that Larson was restarting *Eternal Progress*; that article also reported his essay contest. Fenwicke Holmes discussed Larson's influence in his *Ernest Holmes* (1970). For further background on Larson's "Optimist Creed" (originally published as "Promise Yourself") see my discussion with journalist David Crumm at http://www.readthespirit.com/explore/2012/6/28/christian-larson-meet-the-ultimate-pioneering-optimist.html; and the Larson anthology *The Optimist Creed* (Tarcher/Penguin, 2011).

Virtually no biographical literature exists on Roy Herbert Jarrett. My account is assembled from sources including U.S. Census data for 1880, 1900, 1910, 1920, and 1930; Los Angeles County birth and death records; Indiana state marriage records for 1900 and 1905; *Rochester Chamber of Commerce Directory* (1900–1901); U.S. copyright records and copyright data from various editions of *It Works* and *The Meaning of the Mark*; and Beverly Hills, California, real-estate records and listings. Jarrett published *It Works* independently in 1926 under the Larger Life Library; in about 1948 the book was licensed to the Los Angeles–based publisher Scrivener & Co.; and by 1978 it was published by the California press DeVorss, which retains the license today. These dates are sometimes difficult to pin down, as DeVorss also distributed the work at various points and records overlap among the various publishers. Sales estimates are based on information that Scrivener and DeVorss periodically provided to the book trade, along with an estimate of more recent sales through BookScan. Jarrett published *The Meaning of the Mark* in 1931 under his Larger Life Library; those rights, too, passed to Scrivener for a time beginning around 1948. Jarrett is reported joining the Jewell F. Stevens Company in the trade journal *Printers' Ink*, May 14, 1931. For information on the American Multigraph Company I drew upon company brochures and users' bulletins from 1919; "Multigraph Hundred Pointers Hold Big Convention," *Office Appliances*, September 1922; "District Meeting for Multigraph," *Office Appliances*, May 1927; and "Graphic Merger," *Time*, November 24, 1930, from which Tim Thrift is quoted. Jarrett's cause of death appears on his death certificate, dated August 28, 1937.

Emile Coué is quoted on will and imagination from his book *Self Mastery Through Conscious Autosuggestion* (Malkan Publishing Co., 1922). Coué is quoted in Chicago from "Coué Proves Theory Worth," *Los Angeles Times*, February 7, 1923 (I altered the article's amusing use of the phonetic "ze" for "the" in its attempt to capture Coué's French accent). Additional articles on Coué's first American tour (he returned briefly in 1924) include "Crowd in Orchestra Hall Cheers Coué as His First Attempt in Chicago to Effect Cure Seems a Success," *Chicago Daily Tribune*, February 7, 1923; "Youth's Tremors Quieted by Coué," *New York Times*, January 14, 1923; and "Emile Coué Dead, a Mental Healer," *New York Times*, July 3, 1926. For an engaging look back at Coué's Chicago visit see "Emile Coué: Chicago's Miracle Man" by John R. Schmidt at www.wbez.org/blog/john -r-schmidt/2012-02-06/emile-Coué-chicagos-miracle-man-95980. The headline from Marcus Garvey's *Negro World* appeared September 15, 1923, and the editorial quote is from February 10, 1923—for both references I am indebted to Robert A. Hill's *Marcus Garvey and Universal Negro Improvement Association Papers*, vol. 10 (University of California Press, 2006). Coué is quoted on his American audiences from *My Method, Including American Impressions* (Doubleday, Page & Company, 1923). Additional sources on Coué include *The Scientific Explanation of Mind Healing* by Albert Amao, Ph.D.

(Quest, 2014); *The Practice of Autosuggestion* by C. Harry Brooks (Dodd, Mead and Company, 1922); "Bypassing the Will: The Automatization of Affirmations" by Delroy L. Paulhus from *The Handbook of Mental Control* edited by Daniel M. Wegner and James W. Pennebaker (Prentice Hall, 1993); *Suggestion and Autosuggestion* by Charles Baudouin (George Allen & Unwin, 1920); "Emile Coué's Method of 'Conscious Autosuggestion'" by Donald Robertson, 2006-2009, posted at the website of the UK College of Hypnosis and Hypnotherapy (http://ukhypnosis.word press.com/2009/06/17/emile-coues-method-of-%E2%80%9Cconscious -autosuggestion%E2%80%9D/); and Huber's *The American Idea of Success* (1971, 1987).

Frank B. Robinson is quoted on his money-back guarantee from "'Money-Back' Religion," UPI, March 30, 1936. Robinson is quoted on his awakening experience from *The Strange Autobiography of Frank B. Robinson* (Psychiana, 1941); also helpful on Robinson's conversion is *They Have Found a Faith* by Marcus Bach (Bobbs-Merrill, 1946). Robinson is quoted on "the creative God-law" from his lesson plans, with thanks to John Black at www.johnblack.com/Psychiana/lessons.html. Robinson's call for "a workable, useable God" is from Bach (1946). Robinson's plan to help Finland is from "Idaho Publisher Offers Finns Plan to Beat Reds," UPI, December 3, 1939. On Robinson's finances and the Holmes-Robinson collaborations, I benefited from a wide range of Psychiana papers, correspondence, and transcripts of the Holmes-Robinson speaking appearances, archived at the University of Idaho Library Special Collections. I have written more extensively about Robinson's financial affairs in *Occult America* (2009). Marcus Bach's eulogy is from his "Life and Death of Psychiana," *Christian Century*, January 2, 1957. Other key works on Robinson include *These Also Believe* by Charles S. Braden (Macmillan, 1949); the pamphlet "Psychiana: The Psychological Religion" by Keith P. Petersen (Latah County Historical Society, 1991); and Bach's *Strange Sects and Curious Cults* (Dodd, Mead, 1961). Key articles include "Psychiana—The New Religion" by Clifford M. Drury, *The Presbyterian Banner*, August 3, 1933; "Moscow, Idaho, Once Home to a Booming Religion Known as Psychiana" by Rich Roesler, [Spokane] *Spokesman-Review*, September 3, 1996; "Money-Back Religion," *Time*, January 17, 1938; "Death of Psychiana," *Newsweek*, March 24, 1952; "Mail-Order Messiah" by Fred Colvig, *Sunday Oregonian*, December 26, 1937; and "A Visit to the Man Who Talked with God" by Herman Edwards, *Sunday Oregonian*, December 24, 1939.

On the career of the Fillmores, I have benefited from *Charles Fillmore* by Hugh D'Andrade (Harper & Row, 1974); James W. Teener's doctoral dissertation, *Unity School of Christianity* (University of Chicago Divinity School, 1939); *The Unity Movement* by Neal Vahle; and *The Household of Faith* by James Dillet Freeman (Unity School of Christianity, 1951). Charles Fillmore is quoted on his "chronic pains" from D'Andrade, and on *"Pure Mind Healing"* from Freeman. Sidney Sheldon's recollections are from an undated interview at www.harpercollins.com/author/authorExtra.aspx?authorID=18495&isbn13=9780060559342&displayType=bookinterview. Marcus Bach is quoted from his book *Report to Protestants* (Bobbs-Merrill, 1948).

Sources on the life of Neville Goddard include Israel Regardie's profile from *The Romance of Metaphysics* (Aries Press, 1946); Samuel Bousky's taped recollections (undated) in the collection of the Association for Research and Enlightenment, Virginia Beach, Virginia; "Lecturer Presents Bible in New Light" by George L. Beronius, *Los Angeles Times*, July 7, 1951; Margaret Broome's biographical chapter in her superb anthology of Neville's work, *The Miracle of Imagination* (Canterbury House, 1990); Neville student Freedom Barry's recollections at www.Lifeslight.org; and Neville's stage lectures, which he delivered from the early 1930s until his death in 1972. Hundreds of Neville's lectures are preserved on audio files and in transcripts, both privately held and posted online. Broome has collected several in her valuable anthologies, including the one mentioned above, and *Immortal Man* (DeVorss, 1999) and *The Magic of Imagination* (Canterbury House, 1992). Neville's story of exiting the army is from a lecture of February 26, 1958. The U.S. Army Human Resources Command provided me with Neville's existing service records. The only document remaining is his final pay statement, which shows his enlistment from November 1942 to March 1943 with the 490th Armored FA Battalion at

Camp Polk, Louisiana. Records from the U.S. National Archives and Records Administration show Neville's date of enlistment as November 11, 1942. A spokesman for the Army Human Resources Command, Ray Gall, is quoted on the fire from an e-mail of January 11, 2010. The New Yorker profile that shows Neville back on the lecture circuit is "A Blue Flame on the Forehead" by Robert M. Coates, September 11, 1943. Jimmie Fidler's syndicated column is from May 4, 1955. Neville's account of his initial meeting with Abdullah is from a lecture of October 23, 1967, and his story of returning to Barbados is from a lecture of 1948 (date unknown). Margaret Runyan Castaneda is quoted from her book, A Magical Journey with Carlos Castaneda (iUniverse.com, 2001); an earlier version appeared in 1996 from Millennia Press (Canada). Her recollections also appear in "My Husband Carlos Castaneda" by Margaret Runyan Castaneda as told to Wanda Sue Parrott, Fate magazine, February 1975 (that account has some differences from her book, possibly to protect the privacy of intimates). Journalist Mike Sager also tells Runyan's story in his entrancing "The Teachings of Don Carlos" from Scary Monsters and Super Freaks (Thunder's Mouth Press, 2003). Bernard Cantin is quoted from his book, Joseph Murphy se raconte à Bernard Cantin [Joseph Murphy Speaks to Bernard Cantin], published in 1987 by Quebec's Éditions Un Monde Différent. It is a rare and valuable window into Murphy's career.

Alan Watts initially suggested to me that Arnold Josiah Ford may have been Neville's Abdullah; I am grateful to him for this original insight. My sources on Ford include U.S. Census data for 1920 and 1930, along with the written sources "Arnold Josiah Ford" by Sholomo B. Levy from African American Lives edited by Henry Louis Gates Jr. and Evelyn Brooks Higginbotham (Oxford University Press, 2004); Garveyism as a Religious Movement by Randall K. Burkett (Scarecrow Press, 1978); and The Black Jews of Harlem by Howard Brotz (Schocken Books, 1964, 1970). The latter two historians are quoted from their respective books. Jill Watts is quoted on Ethiopianism from her God, Harlem U.S.A. (1992). Sources differ on when Ford departed for Ethiopia; some place his departure in 1930, but a New York Times article—"Harlem Church Group Restrained by Court,"

December 9, 1930—clearly shows Ford in New York by the end of that year. A 2008 article in *Tadias*, an excellent online journal of Ethiopian and African-American affairs, dates Ford's departure to 1931, following Selassie's land grant. See "African American and Ethiopian Relations" by Tseday Alehegn, August 10, 2008. At present, 1931 is the most persuasive date of Ford's departure.

Ernest Holmes's meeting with Einstein is recounted in Fenwicke Holmes's biography *Ernest Holmes* (1970). The reemergence of the placebo question during World War II is noted in *The Anti-Depressant Era* by David Healy (Harvard University Press, 1997), and *The Psychopharmacologists II*, interviews by David Healy (Lippincott-Raven Publishers, 1998).

CHAPTER SIX:
THE AMERICAN CREED

Napoleon Hill's "I gave a beggar a dime" remark is from his original eight-volume set of *The Law of Success*, published in 1928. Elbert Hubbard is quoted from his 1914 essay, "A Peace Picnic," reprinted in *Selected Writings of Elbert Hubbard* (Wm. H. Wise & Co., 1922). Hill's reference to "the richest man" is from his book *The Master Key to Riches* (Willing Publishing Company, 1945). Carnegie is quoted on Swedenborg from *Autobiography of Andrew Carnegie* (Houghton, Mifflin & Co., 1920). Carnegie is quoted on the "law of competition" from his essay "The Gospel of Wealth" as reprinted in *The "Gospel of Wealth" Essays and Other Writings* edited with an introduction by David Nasaw (Penguin Classics, 2006); I benefited from Nasaw's insightful introduction. The story of Hill covering up the bellhop's death is from *A Lifetime of Riches: The Biography of Napoleon Hill* by Michael J. Ritt Jr. and Kirk Landers (Dutton, 1995). The book is basically an authorized biography; it is to the authors' credit that the episode is included.

Sources on Dale Carnegie include "How to Win Friends and Influence People: Dale Carnegie and the Problem of Sincerity" by Gail Thain Parker, *American Quarterly*, Winter 1977; "He Sells Hope" by Margaret Case Harriman, *Saturday Evening Post*, August 14, 1937; "If You Want to Gather

Honey" by Peter Baida, *American Heritage Magazine*, February/March 1985; and "Dale Carnegie, Author, Is Dead," *New York Times*, November 2, 1955. For the earlier spelling of Carnegie's name, see *The Art of Public Speaking* by J. Berg Esenwein and Dale Carnagey (Home Correspondence School, 1915). On the publishing collaboration between Dale Carnegie and Leon Shimkin, I drew upon the commemorative booklet *Simon & Schuster: Our First Fifty Years, 1924–1974* (Simon & Schuster, 1973); *You're Too Kind: A Brief History of Flattery* by Richard Stengel (Simon & Schuster, 2000); *Dale Carnegie: The Man Who Influenced Millions* by Giles Kemp and Edward Claflin (St. Martin's Press, 1989); and "Leon Shimkin: The Businessman as Publisher" by John Tebbel, *Saturday Review*, September 10, 1966. Stengel (2000) related the account of the title change; a differing version appears in the memoir of Carnegie's fellow Missourian writer Homer Croy, *Country Cured* (Harper & Brothers, 1943), which reports Carnegie making the change over the phone with a Simon & Schuster art director. However, Stengel's account is more fully consistent with Shimkin's role in shaping the book. The "subtle cynicism" of Carnegie's approach is noted in "Miscellaneous Brief Reviews," *New York Times*, February 14, 1937.

Rabbi Joshua Loth Liebman is quoted from his *Peace of Mind* (Simon & Schuster, 1946), unless otherwise noted. Liebman's record on the bestseller list is from the reference book *The #1 New York Times Bestseller* by John Bear (Ten Speed Press, 1992). Liebman's earlier book title is referenced in Rebecca Trachtenberg Alpert's invaluable *From Jewish Science to Rabbinical Counseling* (1978). Fulton Sheen is quoted from Andrew R. Heinze's insightful article, "Peace of Mind (1946): Judaism and the Therapeutic Polemics of Postwar America," *Religion and American Culture*, vol. 1. no. 1, 2002. Ellen M. Umansky's *From Christian Science to Jewish Science* (2005) is also vitally helpful on Liebman's career.

For background on the life and career of Norman Vincent Peale I benefited from discussions with Rick Hamlin, the executive editor of the magazine Peale founded, *Guideposts*, conducted on August 18, 2011, and with Peale's successor at Marble Collegiate Church, Rev. Arthur Caliandro, conducted on August 23, 2011. Caliandro, a minister of great substance and sensitivity, passed away on December 30, 2012. The conclusions reached in the chapter are strictly my own. I am also grateful to Sally Rhine Feather and Susan Freeman for providing me with key primary documents from the Duke University Libraries Special Collection of Parapsychology Laboratory Records, 1893–1984, which includes correspondence between psychical researcher J. B. Rhine and both Peale and Blanton (material I hope to more fully explore in another volume), as well as early promotional literature from the Religio-Psychiatric Clinic. Peale's record on the bestseller list is from Bear (1992). Peale's reference to "scientist of the spiritual life" is from *A Guide to Confident Living* (Prentice-Hall, 1948). Blanton's statement on the transformative powers of the unconscious is from his and Peale's coauthored book (in which he and Peale wrote alternate chapters), *Faith Is the Answer: A Psychiatrist and a Pastor Discuss Your Problems* (Abingdon-Cokesbury Press, 1940). The numbers of clients at the clinic are from Carol V. R. George's indispensable biography, *God's Salesman: Norman Vincent Peale and the Power of Positive Thinking* (Oxford University Press, 1993). Peale's quotes on Ernest Holmes are from "The Pathway to Positive Thinking: Recollections by Dr. Norman Vincent Peale" by Elaine St. Johns, *Science of Mind*, June 1987. I further explore the Holmes-Peale relationship in my *Occult America* (2009) and in "The Mystic and the Minister," *Science of Mind*, October 2010. The intersections between Peale and Florence Scovel Shinn are explored in "Peale's Secret Source" by George D. Exoo and John Gregory Tweed, *Lutheran Quarterly*, Summer 1995. Peale's father is quoted from *The Tough-Minded Optimist* by Norman Vincent Peale (Prentice-Hall, 1961). The rescinded invitation to Dale Carnegie is noted by George (1993). The corporate subscriptions to *Guideposts* are noted in *The American Myth of Success: From Horatio Alger to Norman Vincent Peale* by Richard Weiss (University of Illinois Press, 1969), an important study on the shaping of a success mind-set in America.

Peale's reference to a "sinister shadow" is from George (1993). The Citizens for Religious Freedom statement is from "Protestant Groups' Statements," *New York Times*, September 8, 1960. Peale's reference to a "philosophical" discussion is from George. Peale's reference to "the general subject of religious freedom" is from his memoir, The True Joy of Positive Living (Ballantine, 1984). His statement "I never been too bright" and the congregation's reaction are from "Minister Backed by Congregation" by Homer Bigart, New York Times, September 19, 1960. Peale's 1960 comments "I don't care a bit" and "Protestant America got its death blow" appear in George, who provides an extremely valuable record of this period. Peale's statement "as time passes men's ideas change" is from a letter of February 5, 1936, to congregant Edward M. Porter. Porter's grandson, James Porter, shared this correspondence and other valuable material from his family's attendance at Marble Collegiate.

George Santayana is quoted from his memorial to William James in Santayana's Character and Opinion in the United States (Charles Scribner's Sons, 1920). Peale's friendship with Tehilla Lichtenstein is noted by Umansky (2005). Peale's quote "you couldn't get me near a politician" is from "Norman Vincent Peale: The High Priest of Positive Thinking Is Undiminished by Age, Untouched by Self-Doubt," by D. Keith Mano, People, April 12, 1982. Peale's assessment of New Thought is from a 1989 interview with George (1993). An overall help in grasping Peale's career, and an important critique of it, is Donald Meyer's The Positive Thinkers (1965, 1980, 1988).

Gerald Ford's evaluation of Reagan is from Governor Reagan: His Rise to Power by Lou Cannon (Public Affairs, 2003). Newsweek's assessment of Reagan was "What Would Reagan Really Do?" by Andrew Romano, July 19, 2010. Reagan's statements about his acting career are from Cannon (2003). Eden Gray's (1901–1999) recollections of Reagan were related to me by documentarian William Kennedy, who knew Gray, in an interview of January 27, 2011. Reagan's quotes about Jeane Dixon and his musings on the qualities of Aquarians appeared in a syndicated article by freelance journalist Angela Fox Dunn; the version I used is "Reagan: A Personal Profile," Spokesman-Review (Spokane, WA), July 20, 1980.

Reagan's childhood recollections are from his memoir, Where's the Rest of Me? coauthored with Richard G. Hubler (Duell, Sloan and Pearce, 1965). Lou Cannon calls Nelle a "determined improver" in his Reagan (Putnam,

1982). Dunn (1980) says Nelle "encouraged positive thinking." Nelle's poem is quoted from Bob Colacello's *Ronnie and Nancy: Their Path to the White House* (Warner, 2004). Colacello's account is one of the most insightful chronicles of Reagan's rise. Lou Cannon is quoted ("within the Reagan household") from his *Governor Reagan* (2003). The reference to a "class of destiny" is from Cannon's *Reagan* (1982).

D. D. Palmer's reference to "the spiritual world" is from his posthumous book *The Chiropractor* (Press of Beacon Light Printing Company, 1914). B. J. Palmer's reference to the serpent, and other details of his garden, are from his massive volume (one of several he produced), *The Bigness of the Fellow Within* (Palmer College of Chiropractic, 1949). Reagan recalled the college walls having slogans in his memoir (1965). B.J.'s "THINK! SPEAK!" appeared in his grandson David D. Palmer's book, *The Palmers* (Bowden Bros., 1977). B.J.'s reference to "INNATE" is from *Reagan's America: Innocents at Home* by Garry Wills (Doubleday, 1986).

Parts of my section on Reagan and Manly P. Hall previously appeared in my "Reagan and the Occult," *Washington Post*, April 30, 2010. Edmund Morris is quoted from his important and often-misunderstood biography of Reagan, *Dutch* (Random House, 1999). That book and Morris's "Portrait of the President as a Young Man," *New York Times*, April 2, 2006, expanded my understanding of Reagan's spiritual life. Also helpful in that regard were conversations with documentarian Stephen K. Bannon. Manly P. Hall's earliest writing on the "unknown speaker" appeared in his journal *Horizon*, February 1943, which served as a precursor to his 1944 account in *The Secret Destiny of America* (Philosophical Research Society). For more on Hall's career, see my *Occult America* (2009).

Reagan's statements about cancer are from "The Presidency: A Conversation with Ronald Reagan" by Hugh Sidey, *Time*, August 25, 1985. I am indebted to Cannon's *Governor Reagan* (2003) for directing me to that passage. Reagan's references to World War I are from Cannon (2003). For Reagan's affinity for science fiction see *Way Out There in the Blue: Reagan, Star Wars, and the End of the Cold War* by Frances FitzGerald (Simon & Schuster, 2000). Lucille Ball's recollection of Reagan's UFO account is from *Lucy in* the *Afternoon: An Intimate Memoir of Lucille Ball* by Jim Brochu (William Morrow & Co., 1990). Senator Charles Schumer is quoted from "The Senator and the Street" by Jeffrey Toobin, *The New Yorker*, August 2, 2010. Quimby's quote on "man's happiness" is from *The Quimby Manuscripts* (1921).

CHAPTER SEVEN:
THE SPIRIT OF SUCCESS

For a helpful digest of current prosperity-themed ministers and life coaches see John S. Haller Jr.'s *The History of New Thought* (Swedenborg Foundation Press, 2012). On the controversies surrounding Robert H. Schuller's Crystal Cathedral, sources include the following articles from the *New York Times*: "Opening of Crystal Cathedral Is a Feast for the Eyes and Ears" by Robert Lindsey, May 15, 1980; "Founder Retires from Megachurch" by Associated Press, July 11, 2010; "Dispute over Succession Clouds Megachurch" by Laurie Goodstein, October 23, 2010; "Ailing Megachurch Selling Its Property" by Ian Lovett, May 27, 2011; "Crystal Cathedral's Founder Quits Its Board" by Associated Press, March 10, 2012; and "Founding Family Decides to Leave Crystal Cathedral" by Ian Lovett, March 11, 2012. From *USA Today*, see "Catholic Diocese Buys Crystal Cathedral for $57M" by Douglas Stanglin, November 18, 2011. On the development of Schuller's career see "Mountains into Gold Mines: Robert Schuller's Gospel of Success" by Dennis N. Voskuil, *The Reformed Journal*, May 1981.

Earl Nightingale's comment "I started looking for security" is from "Success at 35: Retirement at $30,000 a Year" by Frank Hughes, *Chicago Daily Tribune*, March 29, 1956. Nightingale's business activities at WGN and his recruitment of insurance salesmen are recounted by Francis J. Budinger, the former president of Franklin Life Insurance Company, in "Francis J. Budinger Memoir" (1980), an oral-history interview conducted by Josephine Saner, Special Collections department, Norris L. Brookens Library, University of Illinois at Springfield. Nightingale's pitch ("if you, my listener") is recalled from memory by Budinger. Nightingale also described some of these activities in his book *Earl Nightingale's Greatest*

Discovery (Dodd, Mead & Company, 1987). Additional sources on the life of Nightingale include Nightingale's 1957 original professional recording of *The Strangest Secret* (Earl Nightingale Recordings); an updated version of *The Strangest Secret*, published in book form by Nightingale-Conant in 1998; Earl Nightingale's 1960 abridgment and recording of Napoleon Hill's *Think and Grow Rich* (Success Motivation Institute); *Learning to Fly as a Nightingale: A Motivational Love Story* by Diana Nightingale (Keys Company, 1997); "Radio, TV Broadcaster Earl Nightingale, 68," *Chicago Tribune*, March 29, 1989; "Earl Nightingale, the Millionaire Who Retired, Was Not and Did Not," by Clarence Petersen, *Chicago Tribune*, February 8, 1970; "Bob Proctor from 'The Secret' Shares His Insights on Learning, Creating Prosperity and the Law of Attraction" by Allison Kugel, www.pr.com, April 2, 2007; and "Lloyd Conant of Motivational-Record Firm," *Chicago Tribune*, April 4, 1986.

Edwene Gaines's quote about charity is from "Talking Prosperity: An Interview with Edwene Gaines" by Joel Fotinos, *Science of Mind*, December 2002. Her comment to a workshop attendee is from "Prosperity Plus," an audio recording of an engaging presentation Gaines delivered at Unity of Tucson in Tucson, Arizona. Joel Goldsmith is quoted from *Invisible Supply: Finding the Gifts of Spirit Within* (HarperOne, 1983, 1992, 1994). The proportion of America's largest churches oriented toward prosperity is from "Did Christianity Cause the Crash?" by Hanna Rosin, *The Atlantic*, December 2009. Gaines's statement "you are a child of God" is from "Prosperity Plus." Creflo Dollar's juxtaposed statement is from "Suffer the Children," a 2006 documentary on the Word of Faith movement, as transcribed at http://ivarfjeld.wordpress.com/category/benny-hinn-2/.

David W. Jones and Russell S. Woodbridge are quoted from their cogent book, *Health, Wealth & Happiness: Has the Prosperity Gospel Overshadowed the Gospel of Christ?* (Kregel Publications, 2011). The New Thought background of the Emerson School of Oratory is meticulously traced in Kevin Scott Smith's master's thesis, "Mind, Might, and Mastery: Human Potential in Metaphysical Religion and E. W. Kenyon" (Liberty University Graduate School of Religion, 1995). Of the many books, articles, and polemics written about the Word of Faith movement, Smith's analysis stands out for its historical scholarship and measured thought. Kenyon's quotes about "libel upon the modern church" are from *A Different Gospel: Biblical and Historical Insights into the Word of Faith Movement* by D. R. McConnell (Hendrickson Publishers, 1988, 1995, 2000). "Basically you are a spirit" is from Kenyon's sermon notes reproduced in *E. W. Kenyon and the Postbellum Pursuit of Peace, Power, and Plenty* by Dale H. Simmons (Scarecrow Press, 1997). Kenneth Hagin Jr. is quoted from *The Seduction of Christianity* by Dave Hunt and T. A. McMahon (Harvest House Publishers, 1985).

In documenting the career of Oral Roberts, enough cannot be said to the credit of journalist David Edwin Harrell Jr., author of *Oral Roberts: An American Life* (Harper & Row, 1985) and *All Things Are Possible: The Healing and Charismatic Revivals in Modern America* (Indiana University Press, 1975). Harrell's biography of Roberts, in particular, is a model of objective sympathy in mining the life story of the controversial (and often misunderstood) evangelical leader. Except where otherwise noted, quotes from Roberts are from Harrell's volumes. Roberts's remarks to Will Oursler are from Oursler's *The Healing Power of Faith: Exploring the World of Spiritual Healing* (Hawthorn Books, 1957; Berkley, 1991). For a sampling of the positive-thinking phraseology found in Roberts's work, see his books *If You Need Healing—Do These Things!* (Healing Waters Revival Ministry, 1947); *Miracle of Seed Faith* (Oral Roberts, 1970); *The Miracle Book* (Pinoak Publications, 1972); *A Daily Guide to Miracles* (Pinoak Publications, 1975); and *Don't Give Up!* (Oral Roberts Evangelistic Assn., 1980). The Napoleon Hill quote ("what the mind of man can conceive") is from *Success Through a Positive Mental Attitude* by Napoleon Hill and W. Clement Stone (Prentice-Hall, 1960, 1977).

On Jim Bakker's sentencing see the *New York Times* editorial "Jim Bakker's Startling Sentence," October 29, 1989. The appellate ruling is from "New Hearing for Jim Bakker Is Postponed" by Associated Press, *New York Times*, May 30, 1991. Also see "Jim Bakker Freed from Jail to Stay in a Halfway House," *New York Times*, July 2, 1994. I have quoted Bakker and Star Scott, as well as Senate committee informants' fears of "retaliation" by megachurches, from "Review of Media-Based Ministries," a report prepared by Senate Finance Committee staff members Theresa Pattara and Sean Barnett, and presented to Iowa senator Charles Grassley, January 6, 2011. On the resolution of the civil suits against Eddie Long see "Sex Lawsuit Involving U.S. Pastor Resolved, Lawyer Says," MSNBC.com, May 27, 2011. On Creflo Dollar's arrest see "Police: Creflo Dollar Choked, Slapped Daughter," by Christian Boone and Shelia M. Poole, Atlanta Journal-Constitution, June 9, 2012.

The San Jose Mercury News covered the Robbins fire walk in "21 People Treated for Burns After Firewalk at Tony Robbins Appearance" by Eric Kurhi and Mark Gomez, July 20, 2012. On August 8, 2012, Fox and Friends host Steve Doocy made an on-air correction of the show's July 23, 2012 depiction of the fire walk. An additional assessment of the fire walk appeared in "A Self-Improvement Quest That Led to Burned Feet" by Carol Pogash, New York Times, July 22, 2012, in which a fire department official reports several attendees seeking medical attention. The news coverage of the event is critiqued in "Tony Robbins Sets the Record Straight About Fire Walk 'Controversy'" by Marianne Schnall, Huffington Post, July 31, 2012. For an example of Robbins's program of success modeling, see his book Unlimited Power (Simon & Schuster, 1986).

For background on James Ray, see "Sweat-Lodge Trial: James Arthur Ray Often Misused Teachings, Critics Say" by Bob Ortega, Arizona Republic, April 10, 2011; "At the Temple of James Arthur Ray" by Christopher Goodwin, The Guardian, July 8, 2011; "Suicide at James Ray Event Raises New Questions," www.ABC15.com, March 18, 2010; "From Transcendence to Terror" by Tanya Castaneda, San Diego Union Tribune, October 22, 2009; "Families of Sweat Lodge Victims Detail Emotions," Associated Press, Wall Street Journal, June 28, 2011; and my "When Spirituality Kills," Wall Street Journal, July 8, 2011.

Vernon Howard is quoted ("it's not negative") from his pamphlet Be Safe in a Dangerous World (New Life Foundation, 1981). Howard's statement "I started realizing the uselessness" is from "He's on the Highway to Higher Truths" by Anne LaRiviere, January 1978, Los Angeles Times. The observation about Boulder City is from "Not All Mystical Sages Are Big Stars" by Ed Vogel, July 21, 1979, *Las Vegas Review-Journal*, which is also the source for Howard's quote "we send our message out." Other helpful articles include "Searching for the Mystic Path with Boulder City's Cosmic Master" by Eleanor Links Hoover, March 1979, *Human Behavior Magazine*; "New Age Prophet Offers Mystic Road Map to Inner Bliss" by Steve Chawkins, May 5, 1988, *Los Angeles Times*; and "New Life Foundation Founder Howard Dies of Natural Causes" by Carri Geer, September 3, 1992, *Las Vegas Review-Journal*. Howard's statement "will you trust a religion" is from *1500 Ways to Escape the Human Jungle* (New Life Foundation, 1978). Howard's books, pamphlets, and audio and video recordings are published today by the New Life Foundation (www.anewlife.org), which puts out a regular newsletter, and by the Eagle Literary Foundation (www.lifewithvernonhoward.com), which maintains a helpful online archive of articles and printed material relating to Howard's life.

CHAPTER EIGHT:
DOES IT WORK?

U. S. Andersen was the pen name of Uell Stanley Andersen, a retired pro football player, novelist, and metaphysical writer. Andersen's *Three Magic Words* first appeared in 1954 under the title *The Key to Power and Personal Peace*, as published by Hermitage House (a New York press that had incidentally issued L. Ron Hubbard's first edition of *Dianetics* four years prior). Andersen's book was republished in 1956 under its current title by Thomas Nelson & Sons, and later by the Wilshire Book Company. In its retitled version, *Three Magic Words* gained wide popularity.

Freeman Champney is quoted from his biography, *Art and Glory: The Story of Elbert Hubbard* (Crown, 1968). In fairness to Gina Cerminara, she also wrote critically of the excesses of New Thought in her *Insights for the Age of Aquarius* (Quest, 1973).

The translation of Swedenborg from which Warren Felt Evans is quoting is *The True Christian Religion* (J. B. Lippincott, 1875). Prentice

Mulford is quoted from his pamphlet "The Law of Success," which he wrote in 1886; it later became one of the early chapters in his compilation *Your Forces, And How to Use Them*, vol. 1 (1890).

Thomas Troward is quoted from his 1904 lectures, later expanded in 1909, and published as *The Edinburgh Lectures on Mental Science*; the edition I am using was published as *The Edinburgh and Doré Letures on Mental Science* (DeVorss, 1989).

Rhonda Byrne is quoted from an interview with Associated Press reporter Tara Burghart, which AP published June 24, 2007. Krishnamurti's statement "truth is a pathless land" was delivered in a talk of August 2, 1929, in which he dissolved the spiritual organization that had been organized around him. It is reprinted in *Total Freedom* (HarperSanFrancisco, 1996).

Carl Jung is quoted from his 1952 essay *Synchronicity* (Princeton University Press, 1960, 1969, 1973). J. B. Rhine's 1934 *Extra-Sensory Perception* is published, with its English prefaces and appendices, by Branden Publishing Company (1997). A more recent assessment of Rhine's experiments and career appear in Stacy Horn's superb study, *Unbelievable: Investigations into Ghosts, Poltergeists, Telepathy, and Other Unseen Phenomena, from the Duke Parapsychological Laboratory* (HarperCollins, 2009).

C. S. Lewis is quoted from *The Screwtape Letters* (HarperOne, 1942, 1996). Leslie D. Weatherhead is quoted from *Psychology, Religion, and Healing* (Abingdon-Cokesbury Press, 1951).

For a summary of Charles Honorton's ganzfeld experiments see *An Introduction to Parapsychology*, 5th edition, by Harvey J. Irwin and Caroline A. Watt (Garfield, 2007). Charles Honorton and Ray Hyman are quoted from "A Joint Communiqué: The Psi Ganzfeld Controversy" by Ray Hyman and Charles Honorton, *Journal of Parapsychology*, vol. 50, December 1986. Honorton, who died in 1992, is separately quoted from his posthumously published article, "Rhetoric over Substance: The Impoverished State of Skepticism," *Journal of Parapsychology*, vol. 57, June 1993. Hyman is quoted from his article, "Evaluation of a Program on Anomalous Mental Phenomena," *Journal of Scientific Exploration*, vol. 10, no. 1, 1996. Also useful on the ganzfeld controversy is Jessica Utts's 1991 article, "Replication and Meta-Analysis in Parapsychology," as reprinted in *The Parapsychology Revolution: A Concise Anthology of Paranormal and Psychical Research* edited by Robert M. Schoch, Ph.D., and Logan Yonavjak (Tarcher/Penguin, 2007). A volume that predates the ganzfeld debates but helpfully frames psychical questions is Arthur Koestler's *The Roots of Coincidence* (Random House, 1972).

Lois Wilson is quoted from *Lois Remembers* (Al-Anon Family Group Headquarters, 1979). Jiddu Krishnamurti is quoted from *Think on These Things* (Harper & Row, 1964).

David Hume is quoted from his 1758 "Of Miracles" from *An Enquiry Concerning Human Understanding*. Anthony Robbins is quoted from *Unlimited Power* (1986).

Maxwell Maltz's *Psycho-Cybernetics* was published by Prentice-Hall in 1960, and reprinted that year by the enterprising publisher Melvin Powers at his Wilshire Book Company, where it found its major success. Powers, who also republished the work of U. S. Andersen, had an eagle eye for mind-power classics that had been neglected or overlooked in earlier editions.

Bill Wilson is quoted from a 1958 talk reprinted in his pamphlet "Three Talks to Medical Societies."

Anthony Robbins is quoted from his 2010 primetime NBC television show, *Breakthrough*. While this self-help program lasted only two episodes on the air, it was a thoughtful and constructive standout in a television field crammed with situational shows. *Breakthrough* was the kind of reality programming that one hopes network television could sustain.

The numbers of churches and congregants within the Holmes ministries are from "Taproots of the New: New Thought and the New Age" by Dell deChant, *The Quest* magazine, Winter 1991; "The American New Thought Movement" by Dell deChant from *Introduction to New Alternative Religions in America* edited by Eugene V. Gallagher and W. Michael Ashcraft (Greenwood Press, 2006); and "Religious Science" by Dell deChant from *Religions of the World*, vol. 3, edited by J. Gordon Melton and Martin Baumann (ABC-CLIO, 2002). The number of active churches counted in 2011 within the United Church of Religious Science is my personal estimate based on an assessment of congregations with regularly scheduled services and facility space, as listed in directories published in 2011 issues of *Science of Mind* and *Creative Mind* magazines, the respective organs of the United Church of Religious Science and Religious Science International, which have since merged into Centers for Spiritual Living.

For the 2007 Chicago doctors survey, see "Placebos Are Getting More Effective. Drugmakers Are Desperate to Know Why" by Steve Silberman, *Wired Magazine*, August 24, 2009. D'Eslon is quoted from *Doctors of the Mind: The Story of Psychiatry* by Marie Beynon Ray (Little, Brown, 1942). The protest from Mesmer's patient is from Helmut Hirsch's "Mesmerism and Revolutionary America" (1943). For Harvard's "honest placebo" study see "Placebos Without Deception: A Randomized Controlled Trial in Irritable Bowel Syndrome" by Ted J. Kaptchuk et al., *PLoS One* (www.plosone.com), December 2010. Also see "Fake Pills Can Work, Even If Patients Know It," by Richard Knox, www.npr.org, December 23, 2010; "The Power of Nothing: Could Studying the Placebo Effect Change the Way We Think About Medicine?" by Michael Specter, *The New Yorker*, December 12, 2011; "Putting the Placebo Effect to Work," *Harvard Health Letter*, April 2012; and "The Silent Healer: The Role of Communication in Placebo Effects" by Jozien M. Bensing and William Verheul, *Patient Education and Counseling*, vol. 80, no. 3, 2010. For an example of peer support in Alcoholics Anonymous, see "Secret of AA: After 75 Years, We Don't Know How It Works" by Brendan I. Koerner, *Wired Magazine*, June 23, 2010. John Sarno, M.D., is quoted from his *Mind over Back Pain* (William Morrow, 1982, 1984).

On the quantum measurement problem I am indebted to discussions with Dean Radin; any errors in the section are my own. A distinctly helpful source on the topic is *Quantum Enigma: Physics Encounters Consciousness* by Bruce Rosenblum and Fred Kuttner (Oxford University Press, 2006). On the topic of "information leakage" see "Living in a Quantum World" by Vlatko Vedral, *Scientific American*, July 2011. I also benefited from the paper "Quantum Mechanical Interaction-Free Measurements" by Avshalom C. Elitzur and Lev Vaidman, *Foundations of Physics*, vol. 23, no. 7, 1993.

On neuroplasticity, Jeffrey M. Schwartz, M.D., is quoted from his book *The Mind and the Brain: Neuroplasticity and the Power of Mental Force* coauthored by Sharon Begley (Harper, 2002). Also helpful is Schwartz's book *Brain Lock: Free Yourself from Obsessive-Compulsive Behavior* coauthored with Beverly Beyette (HarperCollins, 1996). Few writers have been as illuminative of the issues and possibilities of neuroplasticity as Norman Doidge, M.D., in his book *The Brain That Changes Itself* (Viking, 2007), to which I owe my note on Santiago Ramón y Cajal.

Dean Radin is quoted ("small but measurable ways") from an e-mail of May 28, 2009. Krishnamurti is quoted from *Think on These Things* (1964).

Acknowledgments

In writing this book I have been blessed to work with Gary Jansen of Crown—an editor, writer, and seeker of uncommon insight, intellect, and integrity. "A true friend," Emmet Fox wrote, "is someone who can help us be our best." Gary has been this, and much more.

Paul M. Barrett has, as always, been a great friend, supporter, and source of guidance and advice.

I am grateful to my agent, Laurie Fox, who provided crucially important encouragement during the formative stages of this book.

My appreciation goes to Molly Stern, the publisher of Crown, for her support of this work.

My interest in these topics never would have taken flight without the influence and friendship of Joel Fotinos, who first introduced me to many of the figures in these pages.

Thanks to Amanda Pisani, under whose editorship at *Science of Mind* magazine I began writing about these topics. Amanda opened the right door at the right moment.

Personal thanks go to Keith McNeil, an indefatigable researcher and historian who provided me with several key historical documents. Keith shared his insights with sensitivity and balance.

I am grateful to those whose ideas, support, and assistance with source materials aided this work: Dell deChant, Gabrielle Moss, Dean Radin, Christy Croft, Ptolemy Tompkins, Mark Gilbert, Theresa Orr, Ronni Thomas, James Porter, Pam Grossman, Emily Grossman (*nam myoho renge kyo*), Sami Laitinen, Nick Viorst, Philip Deslippe, Russ Gerber,

Michael R. Davis, Sally Ulrich, Judith A. Huenneke, Linda Rosenberg, Susan Freeman, and Sally Rhine Feather.

My wife, Allison Orr, provided constant good sense, always reminding me that the point of positive thinking is not just to write about it.

Index

About the Author

Mitch Horowitz is vice president and editor in chief at Tarcher/Penguin, the division of Penguin USA dedicated to metaphysical literature. He is the author of *Occult America* (Bantam), which received the 2010 PEN Oakland/Josephine Miles Award for literary excellence. Horowitz frequently writes about and discusses alternative spirituality in the national media, including *CBS Sunday Morning, Dateline NBC, All Things Considered, The Wall Street Journal, The Washington Post,* and CNN.com. He and his wife raise two sons in New York City. He is online at: www.MitchHorowitz.com.